A LIFE TO DIE FOR

Master 10 Key Skills to Transform Your Life into a *Priceless* Treasure

David D McLeod, DD, PhD

Dreamsculpt Books and Media—Cardiff, California

DreamSculpt
MEDIA · BOOKS

This is a work of non-fiction. The views, opinions, ideas, and methods described in this book are the author's personal thoughts and experiences. All the events depicted in this book actually happened, at least as best recalled in the author's memory. However, to protect the privacy of certain individuals (other than public figures), all last names have been removed, and some first names have been changed.

While the recommendations in this book have produced excellent results for many people, including the author, you may or may not experience similar results in your own life. While we have made every effort to keep the information correct and up-to-date, there are no representations or warranties, express or implied, about the completeness, accuracy, reliability, or suitability of the information or recommendations contained in this book. Your use of this information is completely at your own choice and at your own risk.

A Life to Die for: Master 10 Key Skills to Transform Your Life into a Priceless Treasure

Published by

Dreamsculpt Books and Media
An Imprint of Waterside Productions
2055 Oxford Ave,
Cardiff, California 92007
www.dreamsculpt.com
www.waterside.com

ISBN 978-1-943625-11-6 Print on Demand

ISBN 978-1-943625-87-1 EBook

Printed in the United States of America.

First printing edition 2019.

PRAISE & ENDORSEMENT

David has put heart and soul into this book and his *Life Mastery Project* to give you the best information in easily digestible parts. This is a living masterpiece which keeps growing—from the artwork, to the stories, to the poetry, and more, all David's passionate creation. This book will support you on your transformational journey to become the best YOU that you can be, with experiences, activities and knowledge to assist you in leveling up your life.

With David as your guide, you will learn to empower yourself from a place of deeper understanding to intentionally live a life of purpose, passion and joy. As you become truly who you are, you will lead the way for others to become their magnificent selves, bringing about a Universe where everyone is honored, and we all live in harmony, integrity and pure love.

—*Marie Lukasik Wallace, Executive Coach, NLP Master Practitioner, Founder & CEO of MariesGold.com*

Many of us look for validation and a roadmap for how someone arrived at happiness. When we find someone who shares their unique story of truth, transformation and life experience that resonates, it makes us feel we are not alone. When something worked for them, we have hope it will work for us too. David's personal journey and roadmap to discover and live your "Life to Die For" I find to be inspiring—and his book is well worth the read. It may even change your life...if you are ready.

—*Anna Pereira, CEO at Soul Ventures Corp, Founder of TheWellnessUniverse.com*

David McLeod is the real deal. He speaks from experience in the trenches and understands the reality of walking the path of life. And he's gathered wisdom from experience and from deep thoughtfulness that can help anyone—anywhere, any time—to improve their life experience and find more joy and authenticity on the path. David is a genuine guide.

—*Christopher van Buren, President and Founder of LaunchMoxie, Inc.*

Having known David McLeod personally since early 2012, I have witnessed some of his evolution as well as his masterful ability to share powerful stories. In *A Life to Die For*, David weaves his personal experiences into each chapter, providing depth, meaning, and incredible life lessons to readers. I appreciate how he extracts meaning, and provides a framework that is totally relevant—no matter what your life journey might be. The exercises throughout—especially the *Repeated Question Game*—help me connect deeper to myself and to others, and are a great resource. I look forward to continuing to reference David's book when challenges surface in my life, and to provide support for my clients.

—*Linda Shively, Speaker, Master Life and Executive Coach, NLP Master Practitioner*

A Life to Die For is full of jewels of illumination that can support you in creating the life you really want. This intimate book reveals keys to self-acceptance, self-compassion, and other ways to enhance your well-being and aliveness.

—*Patrick Dominguez, Founder, Inner Freedom Process*

A Life to Die For is a moving and powerful, yet very readable, book. From beginning to end, in every amazing chapter, you feel like you are actually working with and being led by an excellent and experienced Life Mastery Coach, moving you chapter by chapter into the kind of life you truly want to be living. Thank you, David!

—*Jo Ann Rotermund, International Speaker, Author of "The Forgiveness Habit: An Action Plan for Healing Ourselves and Our Planet"*

If you want to create a life that you truly love and is filled with passion and purpose, then David's book will give you the map and all the tools you'll need to step into true *Life Mastery*. He shares his hard-earned wisdom with a depth, clarity and humor that makes this a must-read for those wanting to live an extraordinary life.

—*Chris Kyle, founder of Launch Academy and author of "The Purpose Activation Blueprint"*

A Life to Die For provides you with a powerful roadmap for mastering your life. Through touching stories, powerful tools, delicious humor and deep wisdom, David McLeod creatively guides you on the most precious journey—back to you, your *true* self. It is a must read if you're serious about having "a life to die for"!

—*Junie Moon Schreiber, Best-selling Author, "Loving the Whole Package: Shed the Shame & Live Life Out Loud"*

This is a wonderful book on Life Mastery. It is filled with many practical tools and opportunities to advance on the journey—all of which are made more inviting and realistic by David's sharing of his own life challenges and how he learned from them, used them, and transcended them. Great book, David. I thoroughly enjoyed it!

—*Micha-el Robins, Meditation Teacher, Freedom and Abundance Coach*

David McLeod expertly guides you on your very own *Hero's Journey to Life Mastery* in "A Life to Die For!" You'll immediately see yourself in David's compelling journey to fulfillment and purpose, and trust him to guide you on yours!

—*Ronda Renée, Creator of the Divine Coordinates® process, Founder of DivineNavigation.com*

This book captures self-mastery angles and mindset strategies in ways that can benefit people of all skill levels, backgrounds, and schools of thought. I love how David shares stories, poems, vulnerability and intellect to frame up a functional process to grab the reigns of our own lives. I've personally gotten to interact with David during improv workshops and he provides a dynamic in the group that has true substance and depth in human experiences. His ability to spur candid dialogue while maintaining a respectful and comfortable space for others is what gives him an edge in assisting those who are ready to FINALLY step into their own life mastery process. It's an honor and a real treat to have gotten to know David. He's the real deal!

—*Megan Bryant, Award-winning Author, Improv Instructor, and Comedian*

DEDICATION

I lovingly dedicate this book to anyone:

- Who is struggling to find his or her way in the world;
- Who has had enough of being perceived as too much of one thing or not enough of something else;
- Who seeks to grow and evolve into the full expression of who he/she really is;
- Whose heart yearns to make the world a better place for everyone;
- Whose story is still being written, and who seeks to transform that story into something exquisite and beautiful;
- Whose spiritual purpose for being will no longer be stifled.

In short, dear reader, I dedicate this book to YOU! May it bless you in endless ways and help you to create and master your own magnificent work of art—*A Life to Die For*.

THE LIFE MASTERY MANTRA

This mantra has incredible power to help you evolve into the *Life Master* you were meant to be. Take some time each day to open yourself to its healing nature, and repeat it, like a devotional prayer, as many times as you like. May it warm your heart and inspire your soul.

> **I gratefully forgive the Imperfect Being I have been in the past.**
>
> **I gratefully accept the Magnificent Being I am right now.**
>
> **I gratefully welcome the Evolved Being I am becoming in each new moment.**

CONTENTS

ILLUSTRATIONS

PREFACE

The unexamined life is not worth living.—Socrates

The unlived life is not worth examining.—Sheldon Kopp

GREETINGS, FELLOW ADVENTURER!

Hi there! My name is David McLeod.

I love to serve people who are unhappy, dis-illusioned, disappointed, or just plain angry about how their lives have turned out. I support them in finding purpose, passion and peace as they replace their old, dysfunctional lives with rich and rewarding ones that are fully aligned with who they really are and why they are here.

Why am I so passionate about this? Well, my own life journey has taken me through some very difficult and painful times. These challenging experiences led me into a deep pit of

Figure 1—David McLeod

despair that had me wondering if life could get any worse. It got so bad at one point that I even began considering "pulling the plug" once and for all. It was only the dread of permanently abandoning my children that kept me from following through on those dark plans, but I still had to find a way out of my pit. That decision, however, was actually a turning point for me, and soon I began encountering people, circumstances, and situations that helped me to figure out once and for all how to create the kind of life that I had actually dreamed of as a child. And now, my biggest dream is to help as many people as possible understand what I've learned—so that they don't have to suffer as long as I did, or take as long as I did to imagine and manifest the kind of life they truly deserve.

Surprisingly, the life of my dreams didn't (and doesn't) include lots of riches, or all kinds of accomplishments, or collections of cool things. On the contrary, even though I've had plenty of those kinds of things in my life, the things that turned out to be most important to me are these:

- Knowing who I really am.

- Understanding my purpose for being here.

- Connecting deeply with as many other sojourners as possible.

It's a pretty small list, isn't it? Strangely, I found it much more challenging to accomplish these items than to make money or assemble all the trappings of an ostensibly successful life. But the real reason it was so hard was that I didn't know that they were the things I really wanted and so I didn't know how to get them. As I did more and more inner growth work, I became aware of my true desires, and what I learned along the way was that my earlier quest for all the "good things in life" was really a misguided quest for the things that my heart and soul wanted for me—but my ego-mind had gotten in the way and had become my master instead of my servant.

PAINVILLE

Everyone has challenges in their lives, and some of these challenges can be unpleasant—and even downright painful—to endure. I'm sure you have experienced such challenges in your life. For many people, life may seem like a pretty cruel joke, designed to create struggle and strife, with no apparent purpose. "What is the point to all this?" they may ask dejectedly—usually doubting that they will ever get an answer. It's almost as if they are living all alone in their own private version of *Painville*—with no obvious way out, and certainly no-one to help them.

Figure 2—Painville

Interestingly, this place actually starts out as a smaller place that I like to call *Camp Compromise*—because it represents our tendency to compromise and give in to the pressures imposed on us from outside, to the point where we eventually settle for far less than we truly deserve, usually giving ourselves up in the process. And soon enough, resentment, disappointment and disillusionment start to set in, and thus begins our slow descent into real emotional pain. Eventually, something inevitably happens, and we wake up to realize that we have been living for years in our own private *Painville*!

PLEASUREVILLE

Of course, almost everyone who's living in *Painville* dreams longingly of moving to a fabled place known as *Pleasureville*! This is a place where all of your dreams come true, you feel totally fulfilled in all areas of your life, all of your needs are met, and you have all that you could possibly want. It's not necessarily a place that has no challenges, but when difficult times do show up, you know that you are fully capable of handling them, because you know who you really are and you know your true purpose for being.

If you happen to find yourself stuck in *Painville* right now, then you may find it hard even to believe in the existence

Figure 3—Pleasureville

of *Pleasureville*! It may seem like a fairy tale in your mind, something that will never come true in a million years. Believe me, I understand that thinking! I lived through it myself! But I'm here to tell you that there really is a *Pleasureville* out there for you—although it may not be exactly like the place you are imagining—and I can help you get there.

GETTING OUT OF TOWN

How do you get from *Painville* to *Pleasureville*? Part of the problem is that while you are stuck in *Painville*, usually when you look around, all you see is danger everywhere. It's like you're surrounded by haunted forests and craggy mountains and deserts and other dangerous places that collectively I call *Dangerland*.

Of course, you've heard stories of *Dangerland* from other people who are constantly giving you compelling reasons to "stop complaining and learn to accept what you've got". And because these kinds of messages come from people you love and/or respect, you find it pret-

Figure 4—Dangerland

ty easy to defer to their "greater wisdom" and even give up on your dreams of a better life.

But what happens is that, sooner or later, your pain will no longer be numbed out. It eventually reaches a level that is simply beyond your threshold of acceptability, and that is when you come to the realization that something has to change. You look out beyond the borders of your *Painville* and you see the threatening edges of *Dangerland* just beyond. You feel the fear rising within you, but you know that you can no longer tolerate the agony of *Painville*; you will simply have to muster up the courage to venture into *Dangerland*, and hope that you make it through.

DECISION POINT

This is a critical point for everyone, which usually leads to the emergence of two classes of people: the *Settlers* and the *Explorers*.

The *Settlers* are people who decide that they'd prefer to learn to live with the life they have now; this group tends to stay in *Painville* and find ways to ease their pain—usually through some combination of self-medication and mental distraction.

The *Explorers*, however, will not be so easily dissuaded from their dreams. The people in this group are willing to face their fears and venture into *Dangerland* to discover for themselves what is really there. In doing so, they quickly learn that most of the perils associated with *Dangerland* are completely imaginary. Furthermore, *Dangerland* brings to light unresolved issues and unhealed wounds that actually exist within us all—and it is the resolution and healing of these wounds that leads to safe passage through the unknown and into the light of *Pleasureville*.

Which group do you belong to, the *Settlers* or the *Explorers*? If you consider yourself a member of the *Settlers* right now, what do you imagine it would take to move you to join the *Explorers*?

THE TRANSFORMATION JOURNEY

Figure 5—The Transformation Journey

You can easily see, I'm sure, that your journey from *Painville* to *Pleasureville* must inevitably take you through *Dangerland*! And all you need to do is to choose to be a member of the *Explorers* group—even if you have no idea what to expect as you venture into the wild.

"But wait a minute!", you might protest, "surely there must be another way?! Surely there must be a detour around *Dangerland*!"

OOPS! SPIRITUAL BYPASS

The prospect of venturing through *Dangerland* can raise enough fear within you that you may choose to back down from your resolve. But if the level of pain from *Painville* is high enough and strong enough, you may still want to move forward—while looking for ways to avoid *Dangerland* altogether. This is a natural enough tendency, fueled mostly by the ego-mind and its incessant desire to keep you safe. And, to be sure, there are plenty of programs and courses and teachings out there that suggest that such detours are possible. I call such detours *Spiritual Bypasses*. Some of them even work—at least for a while.

Figure 6—Attempting to Bypass Dangerland

If you attempt a *Spiritual Bypass*, then the results you achieve will only be temporary. You will initially believe that you have reached *Pleasureville*, and your experience will certainly be pleasant enough at the start. But after a while, you'll come to realize that this is not the real deal. You have actually arrived at a mirage in the desert that will eventually fade away, until you discover that you are right back in *Painville* where you started—except now, the pain will be even more intense than it was before.

This is the source of the idea of life being a constant struggle, a cruel joke, or a bad dream from which you cannot seem to awaken. What your *Spiritual Bypass* has done is provide you with some relatively quick gratification that feels good in the moment, but because it only ever deals with essentially superficial symptoms, the best it can ever do is provide superficial healing. If you want *real* healing, *true* resolution of issues, then you must deal with root causes rather than symptoms, and the only way to uncover root causes is to go into the darkness and mystery of *Dangerland*!

But guess what? There is *good news*, because most of the perils of *Dangerland* are almost entirely imaginary—magnified out of proportion by a fear-based ego-mind that prevents you from looking within so that it can keep itself alive.

RECOGNIZING A SPIRITUAL BYPASS

Being on a *Spiritual Bypass* can happen to anyone. I can assure you that during my own life journey I've found myself taking many appealing detours! It's easy to get seduced into taking such a detour because it looks like a wonderful escape from the pain and suffering that is happening internally. I've learned for myself, however, that the results never work out the way I expect, so now I look for the tell-tale signs that alert me to the fact that I've strayed off my *true* path toward *Pleasureville*:

- I feel like I'm alone on my journey—even if there are other people on the same detour.
- I begin to question where I'm actually going.
- I wonder how I got where I am.
- I find that I am processing my feelings by thinking about them, rather than actually feeling them.
- I sense that I am out of alignment, as if my inner GPS is telling me that there is a freeway nearby that will get me there much faster.

If you are experiencing any of these symptoms, then there is a reasonably high probability that you are currently on a *Spiritual Bypass*.

A LITTLE MORE ABOUT *DANGERLAND*

As I mentioned a moment ago, most of the perils of *Dangerland* are entirely imaginary. And that's just because you may never have ventured into *Dangerland* before, so you really don't know what to expect when you get there. In other words, it's mostly just fear of the unknown.

In truth, the biggest thing that people seem to fear is looking *within* in order to deal directly with unresolved issues and unhealed wounds from the past. Most people go to great lengths to push aside the pains of the past, and those unexpressed pains end up being stored in the actual tissues of our bodies. We can get away with stuffing our pain for a while, but eventually the tissues say "enough is enough", and they insist on doing whatever they can to push the pain out again. When that happens, the pain can come out explosively or violently, which can be very scary—and even dangerous—for other people to witness or participate in. This is why most of us are so afraid to venture within—we believe that once we open the lid on our internal lock-box of painful memories, we'll lose control and never be able to close the box again. Unfortunately, failing to deal with this old pain actually creates even more pain—both for ourselves and for the people around us—even though we may not be able to admit it.

So, the real *Dangerland* is the internal landscape of our own past—the pains we have suffered, the ways that we have sold ourselves short, our beliefs that we are inadequate or defective or broken, our capitulation to the demands of the external world, and so on *ad nauseum*. But here's the thing that you may not want to acknowledge: the only way to get past *Dangerland* is to go through it, or as I like to tell my clients:

In Is The Only Way Out!

That's right! You must venture within to uncover, illuminate, heal and integrate all of the shadows that you have been trying so hard to hide from the rest of the world. And the amazing thing is, the more willing you are to do this, the faster you get to the true *Pleasureville*!

So the real question you need to answer for yourself is this:

Do you truly want to leave *Painville* and go directly to *Pleasureville*?

If so, then you want to get onto your ***Path to Life Mastery*** as soon as possible! The tools I will teach you in this book will help you to learn how to master all aspects of your life—so that you can grow and evolve in ever increasing ways, and create beautiful and fulfilling new versions of your life every step of the way!

Success on Your Path to Life Mastery

When you first contemplate the idea of *Life Mastery*, you may imagine that you are at the base of a very tall and foreboding mountain. But, like every other challenge in life, this journey starts with a single step. And every subsequent step you take brings you closer to the top. Soon enough, you will have taken enough steps that you can stop and turn around and begin to appreciate just how far you have come.

Figure 7—The Path to Life Mastery

As you can see from the image, being successful on your *Path to Life Mastery* requires only 5 things from you:

1. Awareness

You become aware of where you are now in your journey, and you acknowledge and accept all the conditions and circumstances of your life. This means acknowledging and accepting the pain you feel, and admitting that something important is missing from your life.

2. Desire

You feel and acknowledge a deep desire or longing to transform your life into something that is more congruent with who you really are. You admit that you can't do it alone, that you welcome help from someone who has succeeded in making progress.

3. Clarity

You reconnect to the truth of who you really are and why you are here. This is the single most important factor for creating and living the life of your dreams.

4. Alignment

You align all your choices, thoughts, words, actions and emotions in the same direction—specifically in the direction of your Soul's Purpose.

5. Experience

You begin to experience your ideal life simply because of your Awareness, Desire, Clarity, and Alignment, and you feel satisfaction and fulfillment because you are honoring and expressing who and what you are in every moment.

The more you commit to these 5 elements, the more mastery you achieve and experience.

WHAT IS "A LIFE TO DIE FOR"?

I hope the elements of my little timeline story found a place of resonance within you. I'm sure you've been dreaming about the kind of "ideal life" you really want. If so, then you likely have images in your mind that trigger feelings of satisfaction, fulfillment, and joy. You probably see yourself in numerous powerful relationships with amazing people. You probably imagine that you have everything you need in your life. You probably see yourself as a fully successful individual, no matter what kind of work you might be doing, and your success is likely related more to the contributions you make in the world than to the amount of money you might be making…although, to be sure, you probably have all the money you need too. Perhaps your vision of the "ideal life" includes images of particular kinds of things that happen to you, such as traveling to lots of exciting places, meeting influential and powerful people in different contexts, engaging in fulfilling and rewarding activities, or maybe even participating in risky adventures. No matter the particular details of your "ideal life", I'll bet when you think about it, it puts a warm, satisfied smile on your face, and fills your body with the energy of joy and excitement. If this doesn't quite sound like "a life to die for", then I'm sure you can add in the details that will make it much more juicy and attractive!

And yet, perhaps the life you are actually living right now feels more like a struggle than an experience of relaxation and ease and joy and fulfillment. You may notice that there are things missing from your life that you'd really like to create for yourself. You may conclude that there is a pretty big gap between what you are experiencing and what you long for in your heart and soul.

No matter where you are in your life journey, I believe it is possible for you to have "a life to die for"—that is, a life that is so captivating and exciting that you are willing to do *anything* in order to keep growing it, nurturing it, developing it—and why? Because, the more you grow it, nurture it, and develop it, the more it feels like a full and complete expression of who you really are. And what other purpose could there be for life other than to live it fully so that you can express and experience the complete truth of who you are?

But more than just helping you to see the possibilities here, this book also teaches you the skills and tools that are most likely to propel you from where you are now to where you want to be in the ideal life of your dreams. Furthermore, it introduces these skills and tools in an order that maximizes and optimizes your progress.

Now you might still be in some resistance about this. You might have settled for a mediocre life for so long now that the idea of transforming your life into something "to die for" may seem like an improbable—or even impossible—task. No worries. I assure you that anyone can do this. And the beauty is, you can do it at your own pace. You are not in competition with anyone else. In fact, as you begin to learn and practice the lessons in this book, you will begin to appreciate the collaborative nature of the process—that is, you will begin to understand that you can get help from those who are a few steps ahead of you on the path—and you can support those who are following up right behind you! So even as you are moving continuously along your path of mastery, you can simultaneously contribute to others who are also seeking to become masters of *their* lives. This alone can help you to feel a powerful sense of fulfillment on your journey!

WHO IS DAVID McLEOD?

Although I have a lot of fantastic friends and acquaintances, there is a high probability that you have never heard of me, so you may well be thinking something like this: *Who is this guy? He's not famous, so what could he possibly know about Life Mastery, and why should I even pay attention to him?* Good questions, and ones that I hope to answer in great detail in the coming pages.

To start, let me say that I'm a pretty ordinary guy in most respects. I've had a few notable accomplishments in my time; I've certainly had my ups and downs; and some parts of my life may even be interesting enough to entertain, educate or inspire others. Overall, however, I think my life has been pretty "average", pretty "normal". But when I was in my late 30s and early 40s, I was downright miserable, because my life simply was not shaping up in any way that resembled what I had dreamed of in my youth! I had done all the things that my societal messages had told me I should do:

- Education, check.
- Steady job, check.
- Married with a growing family, check.
- Living in a house with a moderate mortgage payment, check.
- Active member of the community, check.

By all standard societal metrics, I was on the "right path" toward a comfortable and happy life. But nothing about my life *felt* happy; in fact, everything about my life felt completely wrong—as if I had absentmindedly taken a detour somewhere and ended up in a place that didn't make any sense to me. And even though I had a great deal to be grateful for, I had somehow devolved into a cynical, resentful, and angry person who could be extremely unpleasant to share space with—although I was firmly in denial about that aspect for years! And then, in 1992, something happened that caused me to take a very serious look at my life. As you can well imagine, I didn't much like what I saw. In retrospect, I can see that I had become something of a poster-boy for the dysfunctional! Not exactly the kind of endorsement I ever wanted to have.

Unfortunately, because I didn't really understand what had gone wrong in my life, and because I allowed myself to believe that I was just a victim of "fate", I had no clue how to fix anything. On a deep level, I knew I had to do something soon or else risk having my inner rage come bursting out of me to do serious and possibly irreversible damage to the people I loved most: my three amazing children. By early 1995, when I was part way through a PhD program in computer science, I had come to realize that the help I really needed was not available to me where I lived in Canada, so I made the radical and seemingly impetuous decision to change everything all at once. I terminated my PhD program, announced to my wife that I wanted a divorce, found a software engineering job in Silicon Valley, and left my family. In essence, I *escaped* from what I believed was slowly destroying me from the inside out.

This may seem like a very selfish and even cowardly choice to make, and yes, in some respects I can resonate with the *cowardly quitter* label. And to be sure, the moment I arrived in Palo Alto, California, the doubts began sprouting in my mind—so much so, in fact, that I even entertained thoughts of suicide. In truth, the only thing that kept me from acting on any of those thoughts was my love for my children. Even though I had left my family and experienced a lot of shame and self-criticism for having done so, I knew at a very deep level that I was doing it as a way to protect my kids from whatever demons I had thus far managed to keep hidden away—but which threatened to burst out of me without warning. I had seen some of my inner rage leak out to do damage to others, and I knew there was a very real risk of even more serious damage if I didn't do *something*. The problem, as I said earlier, was that I had no idea what to do, and escape seemed like my only option.

As it turned out, moving to California was probably the most important and beneficial decision I have made in my life so far. In very short order, I was serendipitously exposed to people and resources that provided me with the kinds of opportunities I needed to uncover and heal the hidden wounds and associated dysfunctional thought patterns that had created all the shame and anger and pain that had grown within me. I maintained my relationship with my children even though we were not living together, and I simultaneously embarked on a journey of personal growth that eventually allowed me to reclaim my true self and to begin living life for myself rather than for some false image of me that was fueled by my beliefs about what others wanted and expected from me.

My journey took me the better part of 20 years, and in that time, I learned a great many things that contributed to a complete overhaul of my life:

- I learned about safe ways to do the inner work necessary to uncover, identify, and heal my core wounds.

- I found the acceptance, compassion and forgiveness necessary to release myself from the dysfunctional beliefs associated with those wounds.

- I found a deep understanding that allowed me to know and experience myself more fully, and as a result, I connected to an even deeper understanding of my soul's purpose—my *mission* in life.

- I learned that, even though some aspects of my life were affected by the thoughts, words, and actions of others, ultimately it was my own choices that shaped my life.

- I found out about psychic shadow—something that affects every human on the planet—and I learned how my own shadows use misguided strategies in order to give or receive love…and sometimes create a lot of chaos in the process. I also learned that understanding and uncovering those shadows can lead to amazing transformations in life.

- I learned about the amazing power of relationships, and how—if we enter them from a place of committed awareness and mutual acceptance—they can provide a sacred landscape within which our most profound growth and experience can occur.

- I learned about the power of intentional and self-responsible communication—fully owning my truth without apology, and being completely open and receptive to the truth of others, even if I totally disagree with them.

- I learned the difference between being *nice* and being *real*, and I brought myself into a more conscious way of interacting with people that allowed me to maintain my sovereignty and authentic presence without capitulating to their unconscious expectations of me.

- I developed a finely tuned sense of integrity, learning to live my life from a place of authenticity, openness, and honesty—and being accountable for all my thoughts, words, actions and feelings in every single moment.

- I connected to a deep sense of gratitude for everything that has happened in my life—indeed, for everything that occurs everywhere—because it all contributes one way or another to my full experience of who I really am. I have also learned to project gratitude into the future, knowing that whatever happens next will also serve my continued growth.

- I reached a point of awareness that allowed me to look back on the entire trajectory of my life with new eyes…new eyes that could see how everything had come into being in a very perfect way that was designed—by me as it turns out!—specifically for my own spiritual evolution.

As I look at this list now, I realize what an amazing transformation I have gone through since this part of my journey began in 1995. But I am under no illusions here. My life is not perfect, and I won't sit here and tell you that I'm always completely equanimous in all my interactions. On the contrary, I still have feelings of anger and resentment from time to time—after all, I'm still human!—but, at least now I know how to process my emotions without blaming, shaming or hurting other people. All the rage that used to exist within me is almost entirely gone now, so that most of the time—because I've reclaimed the truth of who I really am—I am a pretty happy guy, especially when I'm doing something that is fully aligned with my purpose. Today, I'm able to see my life with the kind of curiosity, wonder and adventure that I remember having when I was a young child so many years ago. Today, I really see all of life as a total gift.

Sharing What I've Learned

As I've done more and more personal growth work and learned more and more about myself, I've wanted to find ways to help other people to improve their lives as well. My journey took the better part of 20 years, but I don't want anybody else to have to take that long. I really believe that there is a way to learn all these lessons quickly—provided you have a plan!

You see, part of the problem for me was that I didn't really know where to start, and even after I completed one workshop or seminar, I didn't have a clear idea of what to do next. For me, it was like trying to follow a map at night... but I didn't have a bright enough light to illuminate the map, so I often ended up making wrong turns, or missing turns altogether! Still, the destinations I visited all had something to offer me. The problem was that I was visiting them in a sub-optimal order and so I wasn't getting the kinds of results I could have gotten if I'd only been more skilled at map-reading.

But because I've made all those mistakes, today I can help you avoid them. I've been able to review my entire journey, and looking at things from a different perspective allows me to see the keys that I was subconsciously looking for and to understand that, if I had followed the correct path, one key could have accelerated my growth into the next key. And I could have saved myself many missteps—not to mention years of time—in getting to where I am now.

Ever since I began my personal growth journey, I estimate I have probably spent in excess of $100,000, conservatively speaking, and I've probably dedicated close to 10,000 hours of my time—all for the purpose of working through my own issues, honing my craft, and getting myself "ready" to share my gifts with the world. It has been a significant ongoing investment of both time and money, to be sure, but I have absolutely no regrets and I know it's all worth it.

But lucky for you, I've been able to assimilate everything I've learned and to synthesize it into a greatly simplified plan that you can follow and learn very quickly. You can save yourself thousands of dollars and all kinds of time, too.

As I look at my life today, I realize that probably the greatest gift I have received during my adventure is a clear and unambiguous knowing of who I really am, and as I mentioned earlier, I think this knowing is something that everyone would do well to embrace, for reasons that will become clearer as we progress.

THE HERO'S JOURNEY

The over-arching trajectory of my life (so far) can be described in three words associated with the phases of what Joseph Campbell calls *The Hero's Journey*: DESCENT, AWAKENING, and RETURN.

In my case, the DESCENT portion had to do with a decision I made when I was very young, and which led me to develop and internalize ideas, thoughts and beliefs that eventually led me to disown my true self. This in turn led to a whole series of events that resulted in a lot of resentment, shame and anger in my life—most of which I refused to look at, and in many ways actively denied—that eventually began emerging in ways that hurt other people.

The AWAKENING portion had to do with the wake-up call that made me finally acknowledge my shame and anger, and how it was affecting my loved ones. I had to take action—or else risk destroying my life completely. I needed help and I knew it. Somehow, my heart and soul knew that I would find that help in Northern California, which is where the Awakening process really took hold and literally broke me open.

The RETURN portion is the part of my journey that I am experiencing today. For me, this is about bringing what I've learned back to the world. It's about acknowledging and embracing my own gifts and sharing them with other people—people like you.

Today, I can see that the DESCENT and AWAKENING were critical to my own evolution and development, that I would not be who I am were it not for all the experiences I've been through. I can also see that there are things I've learned that might be relevant and valuable for others. My own journey has taken the better part of 60 years. But I firmly believe that it doesn't need to take that long, and I think that is why I'm so on fire to share what I've learned with everyone else! I want other people to know who they really are, and I want them to get to that knowing while they are still young enough to really make the most of it!

IT'S ABOUT WHO YOU *REALLY* ARE

This book is about mastering all aspects of your life. But Life Mastery simply isn't possible unless you are very clear about two very crucial points:

> ## 1. Who you really are.
> ## 2. Why you are here.

What's more, you can't really know why you are here unless and until you know the deepest truth about who you are. To put it another way,

> ## Identity precedes Purpose.

Unfortunately, a lot of people get this principle backwards! Without knowing who they really are, people try to figure out their purpose in life, and they follow what they believe are the best teachings to get clear on that purpose. They do things that seem aligned with their understanding of their purpose, and they may even feel some degree of satisfaction and fulfillment. But often, the choices they make end up seeming shallow or incomplete—because these choices emerge out of a declaration of purpose that is not fully supported by or aligned with their deepest essence—that is, the part of themselves that knows without doubt who they really are.

I believe that all of the world's problems—without exception—are the simple result of **confusion**. If everyone knew the truth about who they really are, those problems would disappear virtually instantaneously. I know that is a grand and perhaps esoteric statement, but I've seen the changes that can happen when people begin to embrace the truth and magnificence of who they really are. It is nothing short of miraculous. My life is but one example of how this awareness can change everything.

Don't get me wrong. I am in no way claiming to be perfect—at least not in the traditional sense of the word. I am still living a human life, and I still engage from time to time in behaviors and reactions that are not exactly enlightened. Because I still have an ego-mind, I sometimes engage in reactive behaviors that trigger pain or discomfort in others. Because I still have emotions, sensations, and thoughts, I sometimes forget the truth of who I really am. Nevertheless, I keep working on my issues and I try to stay connected to compassion, forgiveness and gratitude no matter what is going on in my life. Not only that, but I've found that the distance from reaction to healing keeps getting shorter and shorter with each new experience I have.

In spite of my imperfections, I believe I've got a lot of good stuff to share with you here. So all I'm going to ask of you is to approach what I'm offering with an open mind and an open heart. If you can come from a place of *beginner's mind*, I am certain you will get from this book exactly what your Heart and Soul truly desire for you.

My Dream-Poem

I am the kind of person who doesn't remember dreams very often, but every once in a while I am fortunate enough to wake up in the morning with a recollection of my previous night's visions. In April 2009, I had a particularly intense experience in which a dream touched me so deeply that it stuck with me well into the next few days. In fact, the dream was so powerful for me that I actually found myself writing about it in significant detail. What I wrote felt so important to me, and it arrived in my consciousness virtually fully formed—all I needed to do was fix a few typos and add some textual formatting in order to capture the feel of the dream. It turned out that this dream-poem was a kind of high-level vision for how my Soul intended me to see the whole universe—and a clear blueprint for the next phase of my life. In order to help you understand more deeply what I plan to share with you in my book, I offer this poem to you here and now; may it resonate with your Soul, too.

i had a dream

i had a dream
but it seemed so vast and all-consuming that i got lost in it
i couldn't find myself
    in the swirl of it, the whirl of it
    the turn and burn and learn of it
there was so much, so big, so great of it
that it felt like gravity pulling me into the midst of it
    like i was falling into a black hole
a dark black magic bowl of unimaginable infinity
where i could no longer tell
    up from down in from out left from right this from that

and in this exquisite mystical laboratory of incomprehensible beauty—
swirling, whirling, turning
    (like sufi-dancing chaos)
in a highland reel of staccato perfection—
somewhere, like right there, more-or-less in the center
    was the heart of it, the heart of it...

the heart
the beating heart, beating

this heart

like it simply had no choice but to hold things together

beating, pulsing like an engine

this heart

shining and beating and emanating
its endless and powerful staccato rhythm

this heart

emanating and transmitting its
impeccably unblemished,
glitteringly untainted,
impossibly pure
LOVE
across the cosmos,
across the cosmopolitan cosmos where we all live

holding it all together
binding it tightly in a cocoon of cosmological proportions
a cocoon of galactic-sized love and kindness and tenderness
unlike anything i could ever hope to conceive
holding everything, everyone
holding me and you, there, practically in the center,
among all the other you's and me's
there, in the middle, in the swirling midst
of   you&me   and   me&you

and all of us dancing crazily like a swirling black bowl of unrelenting chaos
breathing our love in and out
and beating like a heart full of dreams

when it all started, i was afraid
it was so big, so indescribably big,
bigger than my mind could bear to imagine
bigger than my heart could hope to embrace
but it still danced inside me
dancing and moving, singing and exulting, beating and pulsing,
like a living thing
it would not be stopped
it could not be stopped

so i opened my mouth and i spoke it
i said it out loud and breathed it into the universe
and i watched in awe
as my heart cracked wide open and my mind collapsed,
        (a singularity of improbable perfection)
and the exquisite dance
    emerged and unfolded and
    expanded and grew and
    swirled and turned
and gave birth to itself in inconceivable ways
and somewhere in the midst of it was you
and somewhere in the midst of it was me
and all around us was this love
      this love full of hearts and life and
      unremitting order and beauty
this pure love that we had never noticed before

it wrapped us and held us and embraced us
knowing that we would come to forget about it
      (again)
and it just held us and loved us and forgave us
knowing that forgiveness was not even necessary

i had a dream
and it scared me a little
because it was **SO VERY BIG**
and it scared me even more
because it was a dream in which we all remembered
    all of us remembered
we remembered that we were loved
      beyond measure

i had this dream…
    and i wept

ACKNOWLEDGMENTS

Like most people, I've had a life that has been full of ups and downs, and every experience without exception has provided me with some kind of gift or lesson—even if I wasn't able to see it as such when the event happened! This book is my attempt to distill and compile what seem to be the most important lessons I've learned during my adventure through life thus far.

Unquestionably, none of my real growth experiences would have been possible if not for the participation and contribution of countless people who have crossed my path and impacted me in profound ways. There is not enough space (or time) for me to attempt to name them all here; nevertheless, I do want to acknowledge a number of key individuals who provided invaluable inspiration and support on my journey.

Elizabeth, my deceased mother, whose ineffable wisdom helped me to realize the importance of knowing who I am.

Diane, my half-sister, who gave me the incredible gift of waking me up from my unconscious sleep-walking.

Colleen, my first wife, who challenged me in countless ways to get out of my own way, so that I might become the father that she believed I wanted to be.

Erin, Kevin and Brian, my three amazing children, all of whom have continued to love and support me, even through the darkest and most painful parts of my journey.

Peggy, my second wife, a gifted and unconditionally loving psychotherapist, who was my greatest champion during the early stages of my spiritual growth, and without whose insights I might not have found my way.

Gary, Chris, Patrick, Doug, Lee, and Dean, spiritual brothers and fellow *"Embers"* (the name we gave to our men's group after we disbanded), all of whom supported and challenged me to be the man I was meant to be, and who continue to hold a space for me at our *Third Thursday Breakfast Meetings*.

Cliff, Vicki, Junie, Andrea, John, Judge and many others from the *Shadow Work* community, all of whom helped me to recognize and embrace my dark side in a way that empowers me each and every day, and who encouraged me to develop my skills as a coach and facilitator.

Peter R, Donna, Peter S, Sarah, Anne, Felicia, Jason, and Marcie, amazing and wonderful facilitators from the *Human Awareness Institute*, who, along with innumerable incredible interns and team members, helped me to see and embrace myself as a beautiful, loving being with unlimited potential.

Dan, Celso, Tracy, Bob, Christine, John, Diana, Brian, Teresa, Megan, and Alexa, dear friends all, who have simply been there for me countless times when I needed support, and who continue to be available no matter what I might need.

Jeff and Ginnie, two of my dearest friends, who have loved and supported me in innumerable ways, and kept me laughing with their fabulous view of life and their unquenchable sense of humor.

Re, matchless coach and branding expert extraordinaire, who guided and sometimes cajoled me into finding the clarity within myself that eventually made this book possible.

Jared and Chris, my two amazing publishing mentors and guides, who helped me in countless ways to trim and polish the material in this book so that it might have maximum value and impact.

To everyone else who has been in my life in one way or another: even though your name may not appear in this book, please know that your spirit resides in my heart.

To all of you, named or unnamed, I give deep thanks for everything you have given me, I bless you for the amazing angels of love you all are, and I wish you all the very best this life has to offer.

INTRODUCTION

A LITTLE REMEMBERING

Remember when you came to this planet? Remember what it was like?

When we first arrive here on the physical plane, most of us begin our lives in a wondrous state of being that I like to call *Sacred Flow*. We know on a very deep level that we are loved unconditionally. We are imbued with a sense of wonder, appreciation, and gratitude about what surrounds us. We are blessed with an almost insatiable curiosity and innocence about everything in the world, and it seems like our natural state is to seek out new adventures at every opportunity. Perhaps if you think back to your own childhood, you might remember fond memories of this state of being. And if you are a parent or grandparent—or even an aunt or uncle—I have no doubt that you've marveled more than once at this state of being in your own descendants.

But we all go through our own experiences in life, and as we grow up, many of us lose our connection to that sense of curiosity, innocence, adventure and wonder. We find ourselves caught up in what we often call a "rat race" or a "hamster wheel" as we work hard to "fit in" or "stay the course" while meeting the demands and expectations of our peers, our neighbors, our families, our friends, and society in general. And sadly, for many of us, there is no real sense of satisfaction or fulfillment in our lives because we arrive at the finish line of our race with nothing to show for it except a lot of exhaustion, wear and tear, stress, and perhaps disease or even premature death.

Part way through our lives, though, some of us may pause long enough to wonder:

- What happened to my life?
- How did I end up on this trajectory?
- Where is all the success and happiness everyone promised me for all the work I've been doing?
- Is this how I want to spend the rest of my life?

But then, even if we are fortunate enough to think of those questions, many of us find ourselves coming up with disappointing rationalizations:

- It's just the way it is.

- This is the kind of path *everyone* has to follow.
- Life is *supposed* to be a struggle.
- We're *supposed* to learn important lessons, and this is a necessary part of that process.

When we reach this stage, life in many ways ceases to look like any kind of adventure—let alone an enjoyable one. Instead, it may feel more like a cruel joke foisted upon us by someone with a very weird and sadistic sense of humor—except that, for anyone enduring the joke, there is nothing funny about it at all.

"Could this really be it?" we wonder. "Is life just a series of random events, coupled with unpredictable circumstances and situations, occurring for no apparent reason or purpose?" In the face of the confusion that seems to accompany all of these questions—as well as the unsatisfying answers—we could be forgiven for becoming a little skeptical or even cynical.

MEMORY FAILURE

When we come to this point in our lives, things may seem discouraging, depressing, or even desperate, but the truth is that we've simply forgotten something—the remembering of which makes all the difference in the world!

We've become so caught up in fulfilling all the roles we've taken on, satisfying the demands of our jobs, living according to the expectations of others, that we've simply forgotten about the *Sacred Flow* that greeted us when we first arrived. We've forgotten about how wise and amazing we really are and we've allowed ourselves to settle for a life that is so much less than it could be. In fact, it boils down to this:

> We've simply forgotten who we really are.

And the questions that come up during times like these actually serve to remind us about this very fact.

The confusion, chaos, and mystery of life provide us all with wonderful opportunities for reconnecting to the truth of who we really are. And as we become clear about who we really are, then we move naturally into a clear and profound understanding of our *Spiritual Purpose for Being*. And once we have reconnected to our sense of purpose, then everything simply starts to make sense (again), and we can actually begin to see meaning in everything that has ever happened to us. It no longer seems random and unpredictable. From this point onward, we can quickly evolve into a state of mastery that brings us back into the *Sacred*

Flow that makes all of life so adventurous and delicious and exciting.

It's simple, really. But it's not necessarily easy—although it needn't be all that difficult, either.

You could continue to let life happen to you for as long as you like. Or, you could learn from the experiences of other travelers and maybe pick up a few tricks that will accelerate you on your path. It's up to you. It's your choice.

You can master life if you really want to. All it takes is desire, coupled with awareness, acceptance and action.

And you do want that, don't you? Otherwise, you wouldn't be reading this book.

WHAT IS MASTERY?

In my mind, mastery is all about catching ourselves when we forget who we are, waking ourselves up and rubbing the dust out of our eyes, and reconnecting to the truth so that we can reclaim, embrace, and *LIVE* the majesty and magnificence within us. Until we slip into forgetfulness again. Which we do over and over. Until we don't do it anymore!

This may sound a little paradoxical, perhaps even esoteric, so let me explain it using some metaphors.

Think about your favorite athlete. It could be anyone: a figure skater, a gymnast, a baseball player, an archer, a runner, a mountain climber, the list goes on and on. Whoever you choose, you probably have all kinds of reasons in your mind why this person is the best at what he or she does, and you will no doubt recognize this person as a total master of at least one skill.

Now think about a favorite entertainer. It could be anyone: a singer, an actor, a magician, a comedian, a circus performer, the list goes on and on. Whoever you choose, you probably have all kinds of reasons in your mind why this person is the best at what he or she does, and you will no doubt recognize this person as a total master of at least one skill.

We can continue this exercise for quite a while. I can have you think about a scientist or a professional speaker or a politician or an educator that you consider to be the best of the best. And again, whoever you choose, you probably have all kinds of reasons in your mind why this person is the best at what he or she does, and you will no doubt recognize this person as a total master of at least one skill.

Now consider some questions:

1. What do all of the individuals in these scenarios have in common?
2. Raw talent aside, what is it that makes them masters of their skill?

I think it is fair to say that very few people who really dislike a skill are going to spend much if any time becoming masters at it. Similarly, if you don't see a value in something you are good at—that is, you don't receive feedback that others appreciate your abilities as well—then you will probably tend to find something else to focus on. But in addition to these things, you have to be motivated to find out everything you can about your skill and keep educating yourself.

In other words, you can take your skill a very long way if:

1. You love the skill and how it makes you feel when you are engaged in it;
2. You receive feedback from others indicating that your skill has a positive impact on them; and
3. You invest time and energy to continue educating yourself as much as possible about the skill you are trying to master.

Mastery, then, is the process of developing knowledge and honing a skill that allows you to do, use, or understand something very well, to the point of becoming an authoritative expert.

Now here's another wonderful question for you to consider:

> **Of all the things you could possibly master, shouldn't your own life be at the top of your list?**

THE POWER OF A COACH

If you really want to develop a skill to the highest level, you need to go beyond yourself and bring others into your life who know how to really draw the best out of you. There are plenty of people who make themselves available to do exactly that! These people are coaches, mentors, facilitators or teachers, and they all have experience and practice that they can offer you to help you improve yourself. Some of them also have the ability to see within you what you may have difficulty seeing for yourself, and their feedback can really help to accelerate your growth. Even the best of the best use coaches to help them become even better at what they do.

Consider anyone who is committed to being the very best in the world at his or her craft. There are many examples for you to look at, but one thing is certain: every single one of them has at least one coach or mentor—and usually more than one—that they call upon to help them continue growing and improving.

The best coaches and facilitators are the ones who know how to extract truth and wisdom from their clients. They don't tell their clients what to do or offer advice about how to fix a problem before providing the opportunity for clients to discover their own answers from within. This is critical because the people who improve and grow the fastest are the ones who:

1. Have a powerful commitment to their own intentional growth; and
2. Believe wholeheartedly in the paths that they choose.

Nobody believes more in a path or a solution than someone who has conceived it on their own. And the coach or facilitator is the one who helps the client to discover this path.

Now, you may not be seeking to become the best runner or actor or educator or politician in the world. But I will bet my bottom dollar that you almost certainly want to be the best *YOU* you can possibly be. In other words, you want to master yourself and you want to master your life...you want to be a true *Maestro*!

I wouldn't be surprised if you have some story going on in your head right now saying something like "No Way!" or "He sure as hell isn't talking about me!" But if you disregard that voice in your head for just a moment, and instead listen quietly to your heart, I'm guessing that you may well resonate with what I just said.

That's what this book is all about: it's about providing you with all kinds of perspectives, information, ideas, exercises and challenges to help you to see what an amazing person you already are—and to inspire and motivate you to become even greater and more fulfilled than you ever thought possible.

Of course, most of the experiences described in this book are *my* experiences. You will have had your own experiences and they may be similar or they may be different. Nevertheless, I'm certain that you will resonate with some of the things I have experienced in my life, and I'm certain that you can benefit from the things I have learned—even if you ultimately choose not to adopt those ideas and processes directly into your life. I ask you to think of me as your coach, someone who has traveled one particular path, learned a lot of things, and found a way to synthesize that learning into a series of steps that you can follow if you so choose.

Remember, in this scenario, I am simply the coach. I am not an expert in your life, but I can help you to develop expertise in living your own life. And once you fully accept your role as a Life Master—as a *Maestro*—then you can immediately begin to share your wisdom and help others to master their lives too.

REMEMBER THE SCHOOL YARD

You may have just felt a little jolt of fear when you read the suggestion that you might help others to become *Maestros*. I totally understand; it can seem a little daunting, especially when you imagine that you are at the very beginning of your journey.

I remember when I was in kindergarten, way back when I was only five years old. When we kids were outside at recess, I would look across the school yard and watch all the first-graders playing in their part of the playground. I remember the awe and wonder in my mind as I thought how amazing and advanced they were!

And then, pretty soon, I was in first grade myself, and I had a totally different perspective. I could see the second-graders and think how advanced and wondrous they were, but I could also see the kindergarteners, and I realized that it was only a short time earlier that I had been in their playground. In my own childlike way, I realized that, no matter where we were on the path, each of us was in a position to help the people behind us, or to request help from the people in front of us. It was probably the first real *Aha!* moment of my life, and something I've never forgotten.

It's true: no matter how far ahead someone may seem relative to where you see yourself, it really only amounts to a few comparatively small steps—steps that you can take whenever you choose to. And once you have taken those steps, then you can turn around and support the people who are right behind you. In my mind, this is what it really means to be a *Maestro*: to be willing to take the steps necessary to master your own life, and to help anyone else who wants to learn what you've learned.

This has certainly been true in my life! I have been exposed to so many amazing people: coaches, facilitators, workshop leaders, trainers, speakers, authors, and gurus of every description. But what I've learned is that *every person* who's ever shown up in my life, regardless of his or her chosen path, has provided me with at least one seed of wisdom (and often many more than that!) that helped me to find my way to my own path of conscious awakening.

WHAT IF YOU HAD A MAP?

I'm sure you've heard some variant of the lament "Why doesn't life come with a user's manual?" I've wondered this myself from time-to-time. What I've learned is that there is something rather counter-intuitive at play here.

According to many spiritual teachings, we all seem to plan our earthly adventure while we are still spiritual beings in the non-physical world. It seems that each of us has a whole *team* of spiritual partners who are eager to help us experience whatever it is we are choosing for our physical life. Some of these spiritual partners commit to joining us in the physical world, but some of them stay behind and provide support from the non-physical world. The most intriguing aspect of this theory is that, as soon as we transition into the physical world, we all go through a complex process that somehow causes us to forget the whole plan! This is not meant to be a cruel joke, but rather an opportunity for us to *remember* who we truly are and why we are here. That is what the adventure is really all about!

Another part of this theory states that many of us go through multiple cycles of this process—what we call *reincarnation*—and further, those who have had many lives are quicker with each successive cycle to remember who they really are.

Some of us may go through our lives and never quite get to the place of remembering our true nature. But most of us seem to come to at least some understanding of who we really are; those of us who do have the opportunity of helping those who do not. One way we help each other is by documenting our own experiences so that others may benefit from them.

A *TREASURE* MAP!

This book represents my version of a user manual. I call it a map because it provides an actual generalized route toward the treasure we all seem to be seeking—that is, the deepest, most sublime truth of who we really are (what I like to call *MagnifEssence*)—while at the same time empowering us to grow and evolve as a *Maestro*.

The path to *MagnifEssence* is, in reality, a journey back home, to the place where the true YOU resides. It is a beautiful, powerful, adventurous journey. It is sometimes risky, sometimes dangerous, sometimes arduous…but it is always illuminating and life-affirming—although the lessons may not always seem obvious or even comprehensible when they first appear.

One thing you have undoubtedly noticed in your own life is that a great many things seem to occur in cycles. In fact, we are surrounded and infused by cycles. Our DNA is known to vibrate at around 60 billion cycles per second. Our hearts at rest beat at about 50-90 cycles per minute on average. Our earth spins on its own axis at a rate of 1 cycle every 24 hours, and revolves around the sun once every year. The earth's axis completes one full precession cycle every 26,000 years or so. The revolution of our solar system around the center of the Milky Way happens at the rate of 1 cycle every 225-250 million years. All of these cycles (and many more), from the microscopic to the macroscopic, have a constant and powerful influence on us.

It's not surprising then, that the route in my *MagnifEssence* treasure map consists of 10 Keys arranged in a cycle. Each iteration through the cycle improves your mastery of life and deepens your experience of *MagnifEssence*, while at the same time providing you with all kinds of opportunities for further intentional growth.

LEVELS OF MASTERY

If you think of a skill that you want to develop, such as yoga or chess, then you probably recognize that there are multiple levels of mastery. You can become skilled at one level and then, when you are ready, you can choose to advance to the next level. As you move from one level of mastery to the next, you bring forward everything you've learned at prior levels. In order to become adept at one particular level, however, there are certain requirements you have to meet in order to be able to "graduate".

Well, *Life Mastery* is no different! There are levels of *Life Mastery* just as there are levels of mastery in any other discipline you might imagine. This is an important thing to understand and remember because it means that you can keep developing and growing as long as you choose to! In the world of *Life Mastery*, you are actually the one who gets to decide when those requirements are met— that is, you get to decide when one iteration is complete and you're ready to "graduate" to the next level.

As I've done my own personal work, I've become aware of 10 unique aspects or phases along this path to *MagnifEssence*, and to help describe the whole process, I've organized this book as if each aspect corresponds to a single Key along the route:

1. ACCEPTANCE—learning to release all judgments and stories so that you can accept things as they are, and in particular, to accept *yourself* as you are right here, right now.

2. IDENTITY—becoming clear about who and what you are, and how you show up in relationship to *what is*.

3. CHOICE—accepting full responsibility for everything you have created in your life so far, and making all your current and future choices consciously and responsibly.

4. COMPASSION—developing and practicing compassion for yourself and others.

5. FORGIVENESS—learning to forgive everyone for everything you imagine they've done to you...all the time.

6. PURPOSE—uncovering, embracing and following your deep, spiritual purpose for being.

7. INTEGRITY—allowing your purpose to guide you in every area of your life, and making use of accountability tools to help you get back on track when you slip up.

8. SHADOW—uncovering, illuminating, healing and integrating beliefs and behaviors that keep you from fully expressing and experiencing your true self.

9. RELATIONSHIP—recognizing all relationships as opportunities for fully understanding and experiencing

Figure 8—The Life Mastery Cycle

yourself; approaching all relationships consciously and authentically and recognizing all participants as spiritual partners on your journey.

10. FLOW—moving into a regular practice of mindful awareness of the present moment, and allowing yourself to follow the flow of your life.

In practice, your approach to *Life Mastery* may not follow these steps in this exact order, but I do believe you will encounter each of these aspects at some point—and more likely many times—in your process.

As you can infer from the diagram in Figure 8, nothing works without some level of awareness—what I call *Base Camp*. This is both a starting point and a go-to point for any process involving intentional growth. No matter what is going on in your life, you can always return to the equilibrium of awareness and regain your grounded centeredness. It's a great way to replenish your reserves so that you can continue your process whenever you are ready.

If you approach any event in your life—especially one that promises to be "difficult" or "challenging"—with a conscious intention to engage the *Life Mastery Cycle* throughout, you will find that your passage through that event will be much less stressful. You may even find a way to enjoy the event because of what you discover and learn about yourself during the process. Even the small, seemingly insignificant events of your life can provide you with plenty of powerful lessons if you approach them with the same level of consciousness.

The real gift is that each iteration through the *Life Mastery Cycle* brings you one step closer to a clear and imperturbable knowing of who you really are; in addition, it provides you with opportunity after opportunity for expressing and experiencing that. And what better way could there be for fulfilling your purpose in this lifetime?

But there is another amazing aspect to this cycle: as you get more adept at all of the steps, you will begin to find yourself activating them more and more quickly until you get so good at it that you actually have all of the steps running simultaneously! As you progress to this level, you will find that you will be living more and more in a state of grateful presence and flow—which is where all of life ultimately wants to be.

In the rest of this book, we'll look at each step of the *Life Mastery Cycle* in detail, and learn how each Key builds on the previous one.

What's Required of You

I'm guessing that you wouldn't be reading this book at all unless you were looking to make some powerful changes in your life. You are almost certainly looking for ways to improve your life, and something about this book caught your attention and resonated with your soul. More importantly, you listened and paid attention to the yearning in your heart.

I already know some things about you that you might not even believe—or might find hard to accept:

1. You are far more amazing and powerful than you have ever given yourself

credit for.

2. You have more skills than you have even begun to discover.

3. You have access to a boundless source of Wisdom that can make you unstoppable, no matter what you currently believe about yourself.

4. The only thing that keeps you from mastering your life and living the life of your dreams is the limited way you think about yourself right now.

5. When you pay attention to the calling of your heart and start to heed your *Inner Authority*, the confusion and chaos of your life will simply vaporize, and everything—and I do mean everything—will finally make total sense to you…once and for all!

There is no-one else—anywhere in the world, or in the universe, for that matter—who has the gifts you have and who can share them the way you are empowered to share them; once you understand and accept this, you will have taken the first and most important step toward *Mastery*.

GUIDELINES

You can follow the path toward *Mastery* slowly, like a child who is just learning to walk, or you can accept and adopt a few key principles and practices that will supercharge your learning and accelerate your process.

Do you want to make rapid progress? Are you truly ready to jump in with both feet and make this happen? If your answer to both of these questions is "Yes", then you must be willing to commit yourself fully to the process. And that means agreeing to a few important guidelines:

1. Practice Beginner's Mind

Some of what I share here will be familiar to you in one way or another, and you may find yourself wanting to skip past it or dismiss it because of an internal voice that says "I already know this." I invite you to pause, take a breath, and then look at the material with new eyes. If you can approach it as if you've never seen it before, you will almost certainly learn something that might otherwise escape your awareness. Give yourself a chance to assimilate something new!

2. Suspend the Inner Judge

It can be easy for some people to get side-tracked by the judgments, interpretations and conclusions of the ego-mind. The moment this occurs, you stop paying attention to what is happening in front of you and, as a result, you may fail to recognize amazing gifts and opportunities that are coming your way. If you happen to find yourself falling into the rabbit hole of judgment, just pause and acknowledge yourself for being aware. Then, bring your attention back to what is important in the moment.

3. Invoke Childlike Curiosity

Perhaps you remember what it was like when you were a young child and everything in your world was new and unfamiliar. As you navigated this world, you may have wanted to know as much as you could about everything around you. Remember that feeling, that sense of adventure, and try to cultivate that as you move through the material in this book.

4. Be Present and Aware

No matter what is going on for you during your journey, do your best to be fully present to every aspect of your experience. Accept it for what it is and let your awareness inform you moment by moment of who you really are and how you are showing up.

5. Have FUN!

Think of this journey as an adventure that you have secretly longed for all of your life. (After all, isn't that exactly what your life really is...an adventure?) And remember that adventures often include elements of danger and risk—which contribute significantly to your feeling of being alive! And when you feel truly alive, you probably also notice that you are enjoying your life even more—because you are having fun!

SAY "YES" TO YOU!

No matter what kind of life you may have right now, I am certain it can be more joyous and fulfilling for you. If you are ready to deepen your relationship with yourself and to learn the tools and skills that can truly accelerate your experience of *Life Mastery*, then I strongly invite you to join me! Remember, I will be with you every step of the way and I promise you that you will learn all kinds of new skills that can make a huge difference in your life. And even if you already know some of these skills, I guarantee that you will see them in a whole new way that you might not have imagined before.

Are you ready? Then let the adventure begin...

Chapter 0: Awareness

Home is Where the Truth is

We don't see things as they are, we see them as we are.—Anais Nin

The ultimate value of life depends upon awareness and the power of contemplation rather than upon mere survival.—Aristotle

The day you decide you are more interested in being aware of your thoughts than you are in the thoughts themselves—that is the day you will find your way out.—Michael Singer

Let's Start with a Parable

I was raised in Canada as a member of the Anglican Church—a variant of the Church of England. For those who may not know, the Church of England was King Henry VIII's answer to the Catholic Church, which came into being when he didn't care too much about certain aspects of the Catholic doctrine—especially those pertaining to marriage and divorce.

As a youngster, I went through the trainings offered by the Church, but I often found that I had more questions than anyone seemed able to answer. And even as a teenager and young adult, I tried hard to honor, accept and embrace the teachings of my faith, but I often found myself in resistance because there seemed to be so many contradictions in the teachings that I simply could not reconcile—even by surrendering to the notion that "God works in mysterious ways". Nevertheless, I persisted! I even went so far as to try a couple of different "born-again" routes, thinking that there must be a path for me somewhere that would keep me from going to hell! No such luck—even those routes seemed to be filled with contradictions.

Eventually, I gave up. My unanswered (and seemingly unanswerable) questions led to skepticism (and even some cynicism), and before I knew it, I had come to believe that if any of these religious teachings were true, then I was bound for hell no matter what kind of path I chose, so I decided to just live my life in the best way I knew how. Mind you, this didn't stop me from believing in our collective inherent Spiritual Nature and recognizing that there must be a kind of "supreme consciousness" out there that was guiding us. But I didn't really know how to articulate what was in my heart, or to find other people who were going through similar experiences.

Then, in 1999, I had the good fortune to stumble upon a book called *Conversations with God*, by Neale Donald Walsch. When I read his amazing book, I was overwhelmed by the brilliance of a voice that seemed to be saying what my heart already believed to be true. There was so much in Neale's book that touched me, and his writing had a profound impact on how I began to see myself.

At one point in his book, Neale talks about *All-That-Is* and the dilemma of **Knowing** versus **Experiencing**. This idea struck a chord deep within me, and it seemed to awaken a very old understanding that I had had long ago, perhaps even in an earlier lifetime. I can still feel the joy in my heart at the sudden remembering of something I had long forgotten. As this awareness grew within me, I took Neale's story and reshaped it into a form that resonated more powerfully within me.

Here is my version.

The Parable of OMnitude

Once upon a time there was a giant viscous universe of infinite pulsing plasma. This *Infinite Plasma* had a name: *OMnitude*.

OMnitude was everything: *All-That-Is*, pure energy, pure *beingness*, pure Consciousness. *OMnitude* encompassed what we humans recognize as the good, the bad, the right, the wrong, the curse, the blessing, the living, the dead, the yes, the no, the male, the female, the light, the dark, the past, the present, the future..., everything there is, all of it—and all at the same time. There was nothing that was not *OMnitude*; there was nothing that *OMnitude* was not. *OMnitude* knew Itself to be *All-That-Is*, knew Itself to be the *Infinite Plasma*, and It was perfect.

One day, *OMnitude the Infinite Plasma* said, "I want to experience myself fully". Alas, *OMnitude* existed beyond the limited dimensions of the dualistic physical world familiar to humans, and there was nothing that *OMnitude* was not; therefore, there was nothing for *OMnitude* to compare Itself to. *OMnitude* **knew** about all of its aspects, qualities, and characteristics, but because *OMnitude* WAS (and is) all of that, *OMnitude* hadn't yet had the opportunity to **experience** Itself as such.

OMnitude pondered this curious dilemma for a while, wondering "I am the *Infinite Plasma*, and I know myself as *All-That-Is*, so how can I experience myself as that?"

After an instant or an eternity, *OMnitude* found the answer, right there inside, for this answer (like all answers) was a part of *All-That-Is* too.

"The solution is simple", smiled *OMnitude*, and a delightful, magical, exquisite experiment came into being.

In this experiment, *OMnitude the Infinite Plasma* created a scenario in which It appeared to subdivide Itself into a countless number of individuations, each of which was empowered to create its own life experience within a dualistic universe. Each individuation of *OMnitude* would seem to be separate from all others, and would therefore be able to compare itself to all those other individuations. In this way, every individuation would have its own lifetime to experience some aspect of *All-That-Is*, and the sum and substance of all such experiences across the universe of individuations would add up to the collective experience of Itself that *OMnitude* was looking for. It was (and is) a brilliantly elegant idea!

Thus, *OMnitude the Infinite Plasma* re-configured Itself into something that—if one could look at it from far enough away—resembled a cosmically massive, beautiful, iridescent, semi-transparent sea-urchin—pulsing, vibrating, resonating its primal light and sound throughout the universe. And emanating from the main body of the sea-urchin extend countless strands of plasma-energy like sparkling rays from a brilliant sun, each one connected always to the *Source* of its creation.

Figure 9—OMnitude Reconfiguring Itself

At some point along the span of each strand, the plasma-energy coalesces into an energy-form, unique and perfect in its expression, whose purpose is to live and experience a lifetime as one particular aspect of *OMnitude*. The individuation's unique experience is communicated through the corresponding strand of plasma-energy into the main body of the *Source*, where it is stored in the *Infinite Library* of all such experiences. At the same time, the *Source* continues to feed the energy-form with Its endless truth, wisdom, knowing, and love—in a continuous connection between *OMnitude* and the individuation.

In this way, *OMnitude the Infinite Plasma* gets to both know and experience itself as *All-That-Is*, and the dilemma is resolved.

THE PRIME DIRECTIVE

While this may seem to be a somewhat esoteric story, the real beauty of it for me is that it reveals something wonderful. Every individuation—including every energy-form imaginable—has one common over-arching purpose:

> **To participate in *OMnitude*'s grand experiment by fulfilling its own destiny and contributing its individual existential experience to the *Library* of all such experiences.**

This is an amazing and liberating perspective, because it means that every energy-form everywhere in the universe is *equally important*! There is no energy-form anywhere—animate or inanimate—that is any more or less important than any other! Furthermore, every purpose—imagined or otherwise—is also equally important as every other, because it helps to shape the individuation's experience and therefore provides vital information to the *OMnitude Library*.

HOW CAN THIS BE?

Every energy-form—and that includes you and me—is connected through its own plasma-energy strand to the ultimate *Source*, to the main body of *OMnitude*. Because we are all individuations of the same *Source*, we are all connected to the same *Source*. And as a consequence, we are all connected to each other.

And it is precisely because of this that we are able to see stuff within each other—because it exists within us too. What I observe in you also exists in me; what I observe in myself also exists in you. In the physical realm, we refer to this phenomenon as *projection*—and we will talk about that in more detail later on—but on an energetic (or Spiritual) level, we cannot avoid the self-evident conclusion:

> ## Who you are is: *OMnitude!*

That's right, you are *OMnitude* and *OMnitude* is you. You can resist it if you want to, you can argue with it if you want to, you can fight it if you want to, but ultimately you have to accept the truth of it, because your true essence already knows this intuitively.

WHAT SCIENCE SAYS ABOUT THIS

We have Physics, Psychology, Biology, Cosmology, Neurology…an endless and growing list of "-ologies" that study every conceivable aspect of physical life as we know it. All these different branches of Science examine, dissect, probe, inspect, and decode the physical aspects of our world, from the largest elements of our universe down to the smallest subatomic objects we are capable of detecting. But in spite of the incredible amounts of knowledge and understanding that we amass from these scholarly pursuits, we are still completely baffled by the whole concept of *Consciousness*.

Interestingly, while Science grows and changes and expands in its own way, Spirituality as it is understood and explained by our most revered teachers seems to be fairly consistent. As we've already seen, common Spiritual teaching seems to suggest that there is one Supreme Consciousness (*OMnitude*) throughout the universe, and that everything is an individuation or manifestation of that Consciousness. This teaching leads naturally to the notion of Oneness, and miraculously, the things we are learning from our collective journey into Quantum Physics seem to support this idea: at the smallest detectable scales of our universe, we are learning that everything we examine is all made of the same stuff! For example, physics tells us that all electrons are identical—that is, there is no known way to distinguish one electron from another. Now it would be easy to skip past this statement with a yawn, but pause for a second and think about it.

If electrons cannot be distinguished from one another, then you should be able to swap the electrons between any two molecules with no perceptible change between them. It turns out this does indeed happen and can be observed during certain types of experimental processes. This means that you should be able to swap all of the electrons in one compound with a corresponding number of electrons in a different compound, again with no detectable changes. Similarly, this should be possible at larger and larger scales.

Well, I think you can see where I'm going with this.

If you and I were sitting across from each other, we should be able to swap all of our electrons arbitrarily with no noticeable changes. For all practical purposes, as these electrons are switching back and forth at light speed (which, by the way, is precisely what happens), you and I are essentially changing places: I am becoming you and you are becoming me. That is, we are One—in the most primal and physical sense possible! And Science is only now catching up to what Spiritual teachers have been telling us for eons!

Breathe that in, my friend. You and I are *One*. You and I are *OMnitude*.

This is a sublime, beautiful and liberating awareness! And it immediately brings to mind some inescapable related ideas:

- Whatever I do to or for you, I do to or for myself.
- Whatever I do to or for myself, I do to or for you.

In other words, everything I think, say, do or feel has an impact on the world around me.

Now this might seem like a re-statement of the obvious, but if it were so obvious, then I believe the world would be a very different place. If we were truly aware of ourselves and of our impact on our world, I believe that we'd be making much wiser and more compassionate decisions. If we truly accepted responsibility for the impact we create, we'd almost certainly choose different thoughts, words, actions and feelings. But because we have forgotten who we really are—and therefore that we are all One—it's easy for us to think of ourselves as isolated and separate individuations of Consciousness, and this in turn rationalizes our tendency to downplay our importance, and the impact of our choices.

But, alas, we appear to have forgotten this truth about ourselves and the world. And in this forgetful state, we naturally begin to wonder how our world ended up the way it is.

CONFUSION AND CHAOS

In many ways, life may seem like a complicated and mysterious journey that doesn't always make sense. For many of us, the confusion and mystery may occasionally—and usually temporarily—give way to moments of clarity and understanding; for others, the mystery never seems to end. Regardless of which camp you may belong to, there is a good chance that you have found yourself pondering two very common questions:

> **Who am I?**
>
> **Why am I here?**

These questions seem simple enough at first glance, but as mystics, sages and philosophers the world over will tell you, they are actually the most profound and perplexing questions that we ever seem to ask. Sadly, it's pretty rare that these questions lend themselves to satisfying answers, at least in the physical realm—and indeed, whatever answers we come up with may simply add to our confusion and chaos!

Part of the problem, I think, is that we seem to be asking the wrong questions. Or, to be more precise, we are asking these two particular questions before we have found answers to an even more basic one:

> **Where am I?**

You see, usually when we ask those first two questions, we are looking for answers that will help us to figure out what we are supposed to be doing with our lives, where our journey is supposed to be taking us. But the problem is, if we don't know exactly where we are right now, then—even if we are fortunate enough to have answers to those first two questions—we simply have no idea where to go or what to do next! Therefore, before we do anything on our *Life Mastery Cycle*, we first have to raise our awareness about our current circumstances.

AWARENESS = BASE CAMP

Awareness. What could be easier? Look around, take stock of the situation, and—*Bam!*—you're done, right?

Sure, observation is a major part of the awareness equation, and you do have to look around and take stock, but there is actually more to awareness than that. For starters, what about all the other physical senses? It's important to notice what information you are receiving from your senses of sight, hearing, smell, taste, *and* touch. Your mental model of the physical world is simply not complete without the sensory data that is provided by all of those inputs.

Great, now you have some kind of model of the world in your mind. But a more important issue has to do with how you relate to this model. In order to increase your awareness and understanding of that, you can ask yourself any number of relevant **check-in** questions.

And what exactly is a *check-in* question? Simple: it is any open-ended question that seeks to elicit information about someone's internal state without leading the responder or making any assumptions. It usually begins with one of the main interrogative words *How* or *What*. Here are a few examples:

1. What emotions am I feeling right now?

2. What thoughts am I thinking about this situation?

3. How am I interpreting what I am experiencing right now?

4. What kinds of conclusions, stories, and judgments am I creating in my mind?

5. How do I imagine myself in relationship to my model of the world?

6. How am I behaving in the current moment, and how do I feel about that?

7. What changes am I noticing in the world or in myself?

Questions like these are very powerful because they open the door for virtually any kind of response. They make it easier for you to answer from the heart because they don't assume anything going in—they simply invite you to speak whatever is true in the moment. In other words, they help you to increase awareness of what is happening right now.

Use these *check-in* questions to increase awareness and clarity about what is going on within you, and remember to give yourself plenty of time for the check-in to work. For example, if you ask yourself "What emotions am I feeling right now?", just be with the question for a while and see what comes up for you. When you get an answer, try to deepen your awareness by asking yourself, "What else is there?" Keep this cycle going until nothing more comes up. Then honor yourself for becoming so attuned to what is going on for you. By honoring yourself in this way, you subconsciously give yourself permission to go even deeper when you ask yourself the next question.

In this way, you can have as much or as little awareness as you choose. And it is this awareness—awareness of your own truth—that empowers you in everything else that you do.

A WORD ABOUT MINDFULNESS

In recent years, there has been much talk about mindfulness and all the benefits that it creates. One of the more succinct definitions of mindfulness, from Jon Kabat-Zinn, is this:

> **Paying attention, on purpose, in the present moment, and non-judgmentally.**

The problem I see with this definition is that you cannot be non-judgmental about what you are paying attention to unless and until you become aware of your judgments! Awareness is critically important—it is the intentional activity that allows you to elevate your understanding of everything that is happening in your world.

So, while I think that mindfulness is a wonderful and powerful practice unto itself, I believe that awareness is the key component of it that I see as our *Base Camp*. It is awareness that feeds into everything else we do in our quest for *Life Mastery*.

RETURNING TO BASE CAMP

As you raise your physical awareness—that is, your understanding of what is going on in your world and how you are relating to it—you invariably end up elevating your spiritual awareness at the same time—that is, reconnecting to the inescapable knowing about your true nature as a Spiritual entity that is One with *OMnitude*. This is your natural ground state—what I like to call *Base Camp*—and it is a place where you can always reconnect to your deepest truth.

You are never truly separated from your *Base Camp*, no matter what is going on in your life. But when your ego-mind gets activated and caught up in the dramas of the physical world, it may seem like *Base Camp* is just a memory or that it is very far away. When you feel that sense of separation growing and perhaps overwhelming you, all you need to do is pause long enough to practice the awareness exercise that I just described. This will help to calm the ego-mind, and in the resulting calmness you will find your awareness growing. And within that awareness, you will find it very easy to reconnect to your *Base Camp*. In other words, awareness is the way home.

MOVING FORWARD

As we progress through this book and discuss the individual steps of *Life Mas-*

tery, remember the importance of awareness. I encourage you to bring as much awareness as possible into every chapter of this book, just as you bring it into every chapter of your life. You can use three simple words to help remind yourself every now and then to engage your full awareness:

Pause. Reflect. Reconnect.

CHAPTER 1: ACCEPTANCE

ACCEPT AND APPRECIATE WHAT IS

The Crystal Sphere

ALL IGNORANCE IS FORGETTING,
it seemed to say.

A crystal sphere,
    floating in a celestial hologram,
    an unblinking eye,
    a bright white pearl of warm curiosity,
    spoke in a language I hadn't heard before.
Grandiose and guttural,
    it regaled me with metallic melodies
    that bypassed my linguistic synapses
    and traveled the length of my soul,
    tugging my strings,
    tweaking my feedback mechanisms,
    teasing my bones.
A picture of itself
    fragmented and tessellated
    spoke in glassy overtones
    of a song that could only be heard
    in the pure silence that preceded the big bang.
The harmonics dovetailed
    into a brilliant clockwork of perfection
    and the fragments spun hungrily
    into a new awareness
    as the tessellations danced
    and resolved into a unison
            OM.

Somehow,
It dipped my most tender fibers in its guttural ocean.
It tessellated me across its linguistic sky.
I quivered in the helical polarity of fear and love;
I laughed and I cried...
And the fading thread of a nearly forgotten idea
swam into my mind:

I but go there for the god of grace.

elsewhere...
Speakers of foreign tongues
stood on a stage
looking into the audience that was me.
Players of alien instruments
moved their arms and fingers
in strange harmonic synchrony.
They responded to some unknown force
that cosined its way through the amphitheater
and rippled through my own damp fibers.
They sang in their own alien way;
They danced according to their own DNA.
It was as if
they could no longer
wait
for a miracle.

A music like pure crystal light rose up from within me
and wafted into the room
like the subtle aroma of
unconditional acceptance.
And though I vibrated like strings and woodwinds,
though I rumbled like deep timpani and taiko drums,
I knew that I was still anchored to infinity.

The crystal sphere,
Perpetually unblinking,
Seemed to smile at me.
Its **OM** continued to fragment and tessellate me,
Even as I spun through my own harmonic polarities,
Reminding me of my own
Oneness with grace.

And I saw there in its warm wisdom a challenge:
Recognize it.
Accept it.
Love it.
Know it again.

ALL WISDOM IS REMEMBERING,
it seemed to say.

AWARENESS IS ALWAYS THE FIRST STEP

A Chinese proverb tells us that *the journey of a thousand miles begins with a single step*. Insightful and wise as this proverb may be in motivating us about our upcoming journey, there is something notable that it doesn't tell us. What the proverb doesn't say—and what I think we all need to remember—is that before we take that *any* steps, there are two things we need to know:

1. Where we are right now.
2. Where we want to go next.

These two questions require us to engage our awareness so that we can become conscious of *what is* right now. We discussed in the previous chapter some ways for raising that awareness.

As we become aware of *what is*, the next thing to do is to **accept** it as it is. That is, we suspend our judgments, conclusions or stories about it, so that we can grok it more clearly for what it *really* is—rather than for what we *think* it is. This is an important distinction, and one that eludes many people. And it's a challenging process, to be sure.

AWARENESS WITHOUT STORY IS HARD!

Have you ever just observed something happening in your world, without any attachment at all? It's not easy! Consider something that has very little emotional charge to it, such as looking at the clouds in the sky. You might start out with very little mental activity, just noticing the clouds and feeling at peace about them. But before you know it, you begin to see patterns in the clouds and maybe start imagining shapes or faces in front of you. And then, maybe you check with your friend and try to get him or her to see the same things that you are seeing. And then (if you're anything like me!), you end up in a competition with each other to figure out who can see the most amazing thing in the clouds—and of course by this time you've completely forgotten that your original objective was simply to *observe the clouds*!

Now imagine a situation where there is more emotional energy present. I remember the student protests in China in 1989, and the way I felt when I saw the images on TV of the unarmed man in Tiananmen Square who stepped in front of that advancing line of tanks. The man just stood there, still as a statue, and seemed to be refusing to budge, even though the tanks were bearing down on him. To this day, I can still remember all the thoughts going through my head as I tried to understand what I was seeing on the TV screen. I can still remember the adrenaline coursing through my body, because my mind was telling me that this man was about to be killed—on national TV. But then, all of a sudden, the tanks stopped, and the man climbed up on to the lead tank and appeared to be speaking with the driver.

What actually happened that day? Nobody seems to know for sure. Since the man disappeared into a crowd of people shortly after the event and has not spoken publicly about it since, the world can only speculate. So we are left with all kinds of different theories and ideas about it. But I think it's fair to say that anyone who witnessed that event has been inspired by what appeared to be pure fearlessness in the face of impossible odds.

Notice what happened in both of these examples. The moment something comes into awareness, the ego-mind chimes in with its own ideas about what it is that is being observed. The ego-mind offers its opinions, interpretations, conclusions, and judgments—usually embellished within a complex tapestry of drama and story. What's interesting is that this inner story is almost entirely made up, usually based on comparisons with things that have happened in our own past.

THE MEANING-MAKING MACHINE

The ego-mind has a strong need to make sense of things, to find meaning in whatever is going on. But meaning doesn't just magically appear on its own; it isn't an intrinsic part of *what is*. Rather, meaning is something that is manufactured by the ego-mind.

In order to make sense of things, the ego-mind engages some pretty powerful techniques—things like logic, pattern matching and interpretation, for example—that help to make *what is* fit more snugly into its model of the world. And the ego-mind doesn't much like rebuilding its model of the world, so it will go through a lot of rationalizations, justifications and mental gymnastics, as it were, to fit a square peg into a round hole. In other words, the ego-mind would rather manipulate *what is* to fit its current model than to have to come up with a whole new model to fit the new data! The ego-mind is almost robotic in its desire to make sense of things, which is why it is sometimes referred to as a *meaning-making machine*.

The ego-mind's ability to create meaning for us is certainly an important skill in helping us to navigate through our physical world. This ability is crucial in helping us to make important decisions in our lives, many of which have a direct impact on our safety. Thus, the ego-mind's intention—at the deepest level—is to keep us safe.

But one of the side-effects of this ostensibly hard-wired behavior is that the ego-mind is constantly comparing our current circumstances to things that have happened in our past. If the ego-mind finds a match with something that had an undesirable or unpleasant outcome in the past, it will make up a story—complete with all the drama and tension of a suspense movie—that something even worse is about to happen to us in the immediate future. And even though the story is a complete fabrication based on comparisons with very old data, we still buy into it. And what is the cost? Well, we end up believing falsehoods that lead us away from things that could be very fulfilling for us.

DEFUSING THE STORY

What might happen if the story disappeared, if the ego-mind fell silent? Well, for starters, you'd be able, simply, to *BE* with *what is*. You'd be able to fully experience whatever was happening in the moment for what it is. You wouldn't have to explain it or fit it into a particular box or give it any particular meaning. You could simply accept it in its pure, raw, unrefined and unedited form.

Think about that. Without story, you could see, hear, feel something just as it is. Without story, you could be fully present with another person—regardless of how she or he might be showing up—and marvel at the amazing variety of his or her expression. You wouldn't have to make sense of it. You wouldn't have to find fault with it and fix whatever you thought was broken. You wouldn't have to judge it as good or bad, right or wrong. You could just see it and accept it for what it really is, rather than for what you *think* it is!

Can you imagine the freedom and peace you'd experience if you could manifest awareness without story? Can you imagine the relief and blessing you'd feel if you could temporarily turn off the *meaning-making machine*—whenever you wanted to?

This, dear *Maestro*, is exactly what we mean by acceptance:

Acceptance is awareness without agenda.

For advanced life-masters, it may be possible to accept something when there is story attached to it, but usually I find that the story gets in the way. That is because the story is full of assumptions, interpretations, conclusions and value judgments, all of which paint *what is* in a particular light—a light that has been pre-filtered through all of our perceptions and preferences and biases. And it is this filtering process that produces a mental agenda that makes it so much harder to accept something for what it really is.

EGO-MIND RESISTANCE

The ego-mind has several problems with the idea of simple acceptance:

1. The ego-mind seems to like the drama that arises out of the story that it creates. After all, from the ego-mind's point of view, drama is what makes life interesting and juicy.

2. The ego-mind seems to identify with the stories that it creates. Therefore, if you try to turn off a story, the ego-mind will object strongly because it imagines that when the story goes away, the ego-mind itself will die.

3. In its survivalist reaction to the fear of dying, the ego-mind begins to use its rationalization techniques to keep you hooked into the story. When this happens, you may notice thoughts like this in your head:

   - *How can you possibly accept this thing? Clearly it is "wrong".*
   - *By accepting this, you are actually agreeing with it. What does that say about you?*
   - *How can you condone this kind of behavior? I thought you were better than that!*
   - *This is something you have to fight, because it is obviously "bad".*

In a very real sense, the ego-mind is trying to stay alive, and it will do almost anything to make that happen! It starts by telling you that you are better, more valuable, than everyone else, which in turn encourages you to accept the importance of competition and the notion of winning at any cost. It wants you to be the winner so that everyone else can be the loser. And the ego-mind can only do these things because of its limited perspective that says everything is separate and disconnected from each other. And, I'm sure you've already noticed, if you don't capitulate to the ego-mind's thinking, then soon enough it will turn on you and paint *you* as the loser.

What the ego-mind doesn't understand is that acceptance has nothing to do with agreeing or condoning. It's true that you may choose to agree or condone (or not), but that choice is independent from the practice of accepting. Indeed, before you can truly decide whether you want to agree with something or condone it, you must first accept it for what it is. If, instead, you listen to the reactive response of the ego-mind and resist *what is*, you deny yourself the gift of fully understanding it; further, you deny yourself the opportunity of knowing and experiencing who you really are in relation to *what is*.

HOW TO STOP THE STORY

The ego-mind is very reluctant to stop offering its perspective and opinions and interpretations, for reasons that we have already discussed. It turns out that the easiest way to shut down the story loop is to *pay attention to it*. Sounds a little counter-intuitive, I know, but it does make sense when you think about it.

The ego-mind is kind of like a little kid that just wants some attention. If you remember that its real focus is on keeping you safe, then you can begin to see the inner chatter for what it really is. And when you simply hear the story— without agreeing or condoning—then the ego-mind tends to quiet down on its own.

In other words, as you are magnifying your awareness of what is happening, make sure you include your feelings, your thoughts, and anything else that might be going on. Remember, you can't accept something that you are not aware of, and you can't really be aware of everything unless you reduce the chatter in your mind.

As you acknowledge what the ego-mind is saying to you, and even express some gratitude for its perspective, you'll find that it will seem less and less needy, and it will eventually quiet down quite naturally on its own. And when the mental silence appears, you will naturally fall into a quiet state of acceptance, which has all kinds of benefits for you:

- **Acceptance reconnects you to the knowing** that you are a part of *All-That-Is*, that you are One with *OMnitude*. It dissolves the illusion of separateness and strengthens your true sense of who you are. At the same time, because you renew your sense of Oneness, you begin to feel empathy and compassion, and these are powerful healing energies.

- **Acceptance engages your intuition**—that is, your innate ability to perceive and understand something without any proof, evidence, logic or reasoning. This is clearly a direct side-effect of the quieting of your mind; the more chatter in your mind, the harder it is to connect to your intuition.

- **Acceptance reduces or eliminates drama.** When there is less drama, you are naturally more relaxed, and in a relaxed state your perception ability increases significantly. This means that you can see/hear/feel things more clearly, and this in turn strengthens your ability to accept even more.

- **Acceptance induces a state of neutrality**—that is, a state in which your judgments diminish and fall silent. In this state, you are more likely to see/hear/feel all aspects of a situation without any interference from your normal filtering mechanisms. Thus, you increase clarity, which allows for even deeper understanding.

- **Acceptances replaces *reaction* with *response*.** Because your ego-mind is more silent and the drama has been reduced, you are less likely to react to circumstances. Instead, you can simply respond creatively from a place of unconditional acceptance and love.

There are lots of ancillary benefits as well, most of them side-effects of the ones I've listed here. But just imagine how amazing your life could be with these benefits alone! Start learning how to accept unconditionally what is showing up in your life, and your life will immediately start blossoming in ways you may not even be able to imagine right now.

A TRANSFORMATIVE POWER

One of my favorite sayings is this one from Frederick Salomon Perls:

> **Nothing changes until it becomes what it is.**

I remember the first time I read this, I did a double-take. I thought, "What on earth does this mean?? How can something BECOME what it is? It already IS that!"

As I pondered this saying, I came to understand that it was clearly talking about acceptance as a *precursor* to change. That is, you can't change anything until you first accept it for what it is right now. If you attempt to violate this principle, you invariably end up creating illusions that make your life harder and harder to understand. That is because you started out by making incorrect assumptions or interpretations about the thing you are trying to change. As a result, whatever you think you've created with your energy is based on a falsehood, which means that the result is a false representation of the desired or anticipated change.

The power of acceptance is far greater than you might have previously imagined. It's not just about releasing judgments and beliefs and pre-conceived notions—all of which are certainly very beneficial to your life, as I showed a moment ago—it's also about acknowledging and accepting *what is* before even attempting to put your own spin on it.

Do You See the Magic?

As you acknowledge and accept something for what it is, you allow your own perspectives and filters to fall away. Thus, in your perception, the thing literally "becomes what it is"—rather than some incorrect or skewed idea that you may have had about it before. This is incredibly powerful on so many levels, and you might want to read this section again to really let it sink in.

Acceptance blesses you, in far more ways than you know, and the blessing magnifies exponentially if you can add appreciation and gratitude to your acceptance equation. The moment you accept something unconditionally—that is, without any limitations, assumptions, conditions, or filters—you begin to experience real Truth. And this literally sets you free in so many ways.

Let's take this idea a step further.

You probably already know that you cannot change someone else, no matter how you try. I think most people probably accept and agree with this. However, here is something you may not have considered before:

> You cannot change yourself or your life unless and until you know and accept who you are, right here, right now.

If you make the mistake of attempting to violate this principle, then you risk creating incorrect or false images of yourself. If you make the further mistake of *believing* these images you've created, then you're definitely headed for trouble, because a false image of yourself can only lead to a false—and inevitably tragic—life experience. And yet, paradoxically, it is those false images that many of us unconsciously insist on presenting to the world.

The Cost of Self-Rejection

Why is self-acceptance so important? To answer this question, let's start by considering what happens when we don't accept ourselves as we are. We can recognize our lack of self-acceptance by examining the self-critical statements that show up in the chatter of our ego-minds. Here are a few nasty messages that have shown up in my ego-mind from time to time:

- *You're way too fat—you have to lose weight or else lose all your friends.*
- *You're not smart enough, so don't even think about asking for that promotion.*
- *You'll never get her to look at you twice. Might as well give up and get used*

to being alone.

- *You have to buy that fancy new car right now! Then maybe people will pay attention to you.*

- *Everything about your life sucks! You're such a waste of space.*

I'm sure you can relate to some of these mental messages—and if not, I'll bet you've got a few choice ones of your own that you can remember.

The point is, these kinds of messages all have one thing in common: rejection of who we are right now. The messages, however—unpleasant and disempowering though they may be—aren't nearly as problematic as our unconscious reactions to them.

You see, if we don't accept ourselves as we are, then what happens is that we try to change ourselves into something that we think other people will accept. We do this because, unconsciously, we believe that if we can get others to accept us, then maybe we'll eventually believe we are acceptable. This dynamic leads us to create compensatory *personas* for ourselves. Essentially, we start fabricating psychic masks—indeed, full costumes!—that project the kind of image we want people to see and that simultaneously hide our true self and therefore protect us from being hurt. So we become a *stand-up comic* or a *nice guy* or a *responsible one* or a *people pleaser* in order to get others to accept us—since we are not able to accept ourselves.

Of course, these strategies may actually work occasionally, and even give us some of the safety and security we are unconsciously seeking. But in the long run they don't really work very well, and indeed, they may backfire on us. Ironically, most people—particularly those who are closest to us—can see through our masks anyway! They can tell when we are not being real, no matter how good we think we are in the performance. And people have difficulty accepting anyone who isn't truthful and honest about themselves. So guess what? In the unconscious effort to use protective *personas* to get others to accept us, we actually create a situation that makes it harder for them to accept us! An unintentional paradox if ever there was one.

On top of all of that, as soon as any of our current strategies appear to be ineffective, our good old ego-mind obligingly chimes in by adding more criticisms to its earlier list. It will point out that we're still inherently unacceptable, and induce us to create even more masks and *personas* and strategies. And so we end up in a cycle that has potentially no end to it. Clearly, this can easily lead to all kinds of problems in our lives—things like low self-esteem, victim behaviors, lack of self-trust, unhappiness, depression; the list goes on and on.

The good news is that we can reverse this whole cycle simply by learning to accept ourselves fully and unconditionally.

THE OTHER SIDE OF THE COIN

What happens when we accept ourselves as we are right now? As we answer this question, let's just remember that acceptance doesn't mean agreeing with or condoning something; it doesn't mean that we no longer have desires or intentions for change. Acceptance simply means recognizing something for what it is right now and freeing ourselves of judgment or story about that.

If you accept yourself unconditionally, what you are doing is giving yourself the opportunity to know and understand yourself more deeply. This means getting clearer in each moment about your skills, abilities, strengths and gifts, about your deepest longings and desires, about how you think and feel about certain things, about what attracts or interests you. But more than that, it also means meeting and embracing yourself where you are right now, and knowing that you are on a journey that will soon take you to somewhere new.

As you become more skilled at self-acceptance, you begin to experience some powerful and life-affirming changes:

- You begin to know and appreciate who and what you really are.
- You become far less critical of yourself.
- You develop empathy and compassion for yourself and for others.
- You release your false *personas*, and become more confident in your ability to show up authentically in all kinds of situations.
- You are less stressed or overwhelmed by the challenges that show up in your life.
- You have a stronger sense of sovereignty, and you honor your own boundaries.
- You see your direction and purpose more clearly, and no longer see your desire for growth as a sign of weakness or failure.
- You are always okay with your current situation, even though you may have a strong desire to change some aspects of your life.
- You develop and strengthen a practice of forgiveness and gratitude.
- You develop a strong sense of self-love, and learn to appreciate aspects of yourself that you used to judge harshly.

I could list a lot more benefits here, but I'm sure you get the idea. Imagine it: what if you could experience just two or three of these benefits? Wouldn't that make it worth your time and energy to start accepting yourself unconditionally?

A Self-Acceptance Visualization

In my practice, I sometimes hear people tell me that they find it so much easier to accept others than to accept themselves. I used to have this same experience in my own life, so I can certainly empathize with that way of thinking. Then, one day, when I was working with a client, I had an epiphany: *if it's so much easier for you to accept others, then maybe I should help you think of yourself as someone else!* This idea jumped out at me intuitively, so I didn't really have a chance to judge it in my rational ego-mind. I just went with the idea and, on the spot, created a visualization for my client. It went something like this:

> Imagine you are traveling a long, winding pathway through a beautiful rolling meadow. Feel the ground as you walk on it, feel the coolness of the air about you. Perhaps there is even a nice breeze that caresses your skin in a most delightful way, so even though you are tired from the long walk, you are feeling full, alive, happy.
>
> After a while, you see someone approaching you from the other direction. This person is too far away for you to see clearly, but you feel a sense of anticipation because there is something familiar about this person's energy, and you have the intuitive awareness that you are about to re-connect with one of your dearest friends.
>
> As the space between you closes, you feel your excitement growing. You see the person's face, but recognition is slow to come. Nevertheless, you feel the unconditional love and acceptance deep in your heart. Now you are close enough to touch, and you feel a smile growing bigger on your face. You can't resist; you just have to give this person the most amazing hug you've ever given anyone—it's almost as if you are embracing a friend that you've longed to see for years.
>
> After some time, you open the embrace and begin talking with this long lost friend, hearing about all of his/her adventures, joys, pains, successes, failures. You are completely accepting and non-judgmental about everything that is shared, offering no advice or suggestions, simply listening and being present. What's more, your friend can't wait to hear all of what you have to share, and seems to be equally accepting of you. Amazingly,

the more you share with each other, the more you notice the remarkable similarities in your experiences.

In time, you both stop talking and just look at each other with massive mutual appreciation. Then, you sit with each other for a while in sacred silence, before finally acknowledging that the time has come to continue on your individual journeys. Another long, loving embrace, and you part company.

As you continue on the next part of your journey, you have a beautiful, warm feeling in your chest, and you can't help smiling at the joy in your heart. Recognition finally arrives for you and you realize that you were sharing space with yourself the whole time. But when you turn, you see that the "other person" is no longer on the trail. *Perhaps*, you wonder, *I was alone the whole time.*

So, you return to your own journey, feeling the growing satisfaction, acceptance and appreciation for all of who you are, what you are, how you are, and where you are right now.

Since I came up with this visualization technique, I've used it with a number of individuals—and also a few facilitated groups—and I am always amazed by the powerful results that people report. You can certainly use this for yourself, too—anytime you want to.

CREATE A *HYPER-LIST*

Alternatively, perhaps you might like to try a more tactile approach that involves some journaling. I'm a big proponent of list-writing, mainly because it's a great way to get things out of our chatty ego-minds and onto paper where we can see them more clearly.

To become more accepting of yourself, write two separate lists. In the first list, write down as many things as you can think of that you really like, love, or appreciate about yourself. Don't judge what you write down, just write it. You may find the list initially contains small, maybe even "trivial" things, such as: *I am a great cook*, or I *have beautiful handwriting*. But after a while, if you allow yourself to go a little deeper, you will find more intimate and personal things showing up on your list, such as: *I am very sensitive to other people*, or *I am a loving and supportive friend*, or perhaps *I appreciate my ability to stay centered and grounded when my kids are acting out*. The important thing is to keep writing this list until you can't think of anything else.

In the second list, write down as many things as you can think of that you really dislike or disapprove of in yourself. (*Wait a minute!* you're objecting. *I thought this was supposed to be an exercise in self-ACCEPTANCE, not self-criticism!* Well, hang on there, *Maestro*, all will be revealed in a moment.) Allow yourself to be thorough—write down everything you can think of, but as before, do this without judging what you write.

Now, here's where the fun—and the challenge—begins. For every item on your "don't like" list, find **at least two reasons** that you like that aspect of yourself. That is, think of all the ways that this thing you don't like actually serves you or the people around you. Add every one of the resulting positive aspects to your FIRST list. For example, if I wrote on my "don't like" list *I spend too much time pleasing other people*, then I might come up with these two things that I like about that quality: (1) *I really like that I care enough about other people that I'm thinking about their well-being*; and (2) *I appreciate that my concern for others brings more love into the world*.

Now most people tend to have a lot of criticisms about themselves, and so their second list starts out being significantly longer than the first. But when they look a little deeper and find the "gold" in the "don't like" list, then suddenly they have at least twice as many positive things that they like about themselves than they do negative things. This is why I call this *hyper-listing*—because it results in a much longer "positive" list than you might have initially imagined—in fact, if you follow the instructions carefully, your "positive" list will always be more than double the size of your "negative" list.

When you recognize the positive underlying intent of the things on your "don't like" list, then you can begin to appreciate and accept yourself more easily. Not only that, but if a particular item on the "don't like" list still feels objectionable to you, then now you have some understanding of your intent, and can easily find other ways to fulfill that intent without making yourself wrong.

This is an amazingly powerful and illuminating technique. It's easy to do—although it may take some courage to be totally honest with yourself. But believe me, the rewards are well worth the effort.

Clean the Windows

All of us have our own unique experiences in life, and those experiences inform our behaviors as we move forward in our journeys. Here's a little analogy that might help you understand what I'm talking about.

Imagine that you are traveling your journey in a car that allows you to see in all directions. It's almost as if you have a 360-degree window on your car. When you first start your journey, the window is crystal clear, not a speck of dust on it. But as you travel, it slowly begins to accumulate dust and dirt, and maybe even a crack or two. These changes are so gradual that you don't really notice them, but what is happening is that you are effectively viewing the world through all of the junk that has been accumulating on your windows. You may even begin to see the world as broken or unsafe. You may begin to see yourself as broken or unsafe. As these new perspectives grow stronger within you, your level of joy and fulfillment quite naturally diminishes.

But then, one day, you accidentally crash into a traveler on the same road as you. You feel anger rising within you, and you are all ready to blame this other "idiot" for not paying attention. You get out of your car with self-righteousness blossoming in your chest, all set to give the other person a big piece of your mind, and then all of a sudden you realize how clear everything is outside your car. And that's when you realize that you've been driving around with filthy windows for all this time. And your self-righteousness simply melts away, perhaps into shame, because you realize that you yourself caused the accident—which never would have happened if you had just stopped periodically to clean the windows!

Self-acceptance is almost exactly like cleaning the windows! The windows in fact are just the filters we place on our perceptions. The problem is, once we install filters, we tend to forget about them, and so we think that our perceptions represent the truth. But of course, that truth cannot *really* be true because it is being processed by filters which are becoming less and less effective over time. If we want to get closer to the real truth in our lives, then we have to examine, clean, and sometimes replace our filters! Better yet if we can learn to remove the filters altogether.

ELIMINATE FILTERS AND MASKS

When you examine your filters, what you are effectively doing is looking at the layers of protective masks and costumes you have taken on at various different times in your life. As you do this, you can see that the layers hide the real you from view. You can honor the safety that these layers have given you, and you can remove them as soon as you understand that they are no longer serving the purpose that you originally had in mind. In this way, you can be grateful for all the miles you have traveled with these masks and costumes, and you can be grateful for the fact that you have grown to a point where they are no longer relevant or necessary.

If you wish to accept yourself unconditionally, then you have to be willing to remove all the masks and costumes and get down to the real you. Once you get there, you may begin to see that you are exactly who you are supposed to be right now—that everything is perfect as it is in this moment. In other words, you accept everything—including yourself—as perfect!

THE PERFECTION PARADOX

Perhaps this seems like an outrageous thing to say. After all, aren't we always hearing that "nobody's perfect"? From a purely human perspective, we all seem to make plenty of mistakes during our lifetimes; we all seem to have plenty of flaws and blemishes and weaknesses—more than enough for us to continually find fault with ourselves. So we put ourselves through endless hoops trying to fix everything that is "broken" or "wrong" with us in order to achieve some imaginary idea of "perfection", when in fact—if we just pause long enough to breathe—we can experience true perfection right where we are right now. All it takes is a shift in perspective.

Think about it for a moment. You got where you are today by engaging in every thought, word, action and feeling that you created yesterday! No matter what mistake or obstacle you encountered before, you found your way to here and now. What possible reason could you have for thinking it will be any different in the next moment?

Everything in your life—the good, the bad, the beautiful and the ugly, all of it—is part of the soul journey experience that you chose for yourself before you manifested in the real world. Every thought, word, action and feeling you experience is an intimate part of your overall life journey. How could any of this be anything but perfect? It was designed for you—by you!

The only thing that might be a challenge is to recognize it all as perfect. But that challenge is just ego-mind chatter. If you pause, let your mind go quiet, and listen to the wisdom of your heart, then perfection simply presents itself to you and you can just be with it. Sounds just like *acceptance*, doesn't it?

Perfection does not mean that you stop growing or evolving. That would actually be an impossibility because the Universe itself is in constant motion—everything is moving (and therefore changing) in every single instant. Therefore, change is inevitable and unstoppable. So, you will change and evolve in spite of all your efforts to the contrary. However, once you accept yourself as you are right now, you immediately empower yourself to choose the direction of your next change. In particular, the moment you see yourself as perfect and stop judging yourself otherwise, you open the creative space that allows you to let go of limiting beliefs and dysfunctional behaviors that you took on in order to present an image of someone you are not. This is a supremely liberating opportunity!

Maestro, no matter what your ego-mind may try to tell you in its misguided efforts to keep you safe, I can assure you that *there is nothing wrong with you*! You are not broken. You do not need to be fixed. There is no requirement for you to be, do or have anything in order to be perfect—because you already are perfect just as you are. So don't waste any more energy trying to figure out what is wrong with you; instead, remember your connection to *OMnitude*, and explore the deepest truth of who you really are—that is where you will ultimately find your peace, joy, and fulfillment.

CHAPTER SUMMARY—ACCEPTANCE

You can't stop the waves, but you can learn to surf.—Joseph Goldstein

My happiness grows in direct proportion to my acceptance, and in inverse proportion to my expectations.—Michael J. Fox

In order to go anywhere it is necessary to be where one is.— Nancy Hale

HIGHLIGHTS

1. Before taking the first step on any journey, have a clear and unambiguous knowing of where you are now, and where you are choosing to go next. In order to know the answers to these questions, become aware of everything related to your current situation, and accept it fully for what it is.

2. Your ego-mind, which is designed to keep you safe in the physical realm, often sees dangers where none exist, and makes up stories—complete with judgments, conclusions, and interpretations—that get in the way of acceptance. Defuse and stop the ego-mind's stories in order to facilitate your movement into acceptance.

3. *Nothing changes until it becomes what it is*; if you wish to change something—including yourself—you must first accept things as they are right now.

4. Transform self-rejection into self-acceptance by recognizing and affirming at least two positive reasons for appreciating an aspect of yourself that you judge to be negative or bad.

5. Strengthen self-acceptance by imagining yourself as another person and visualizing yourself fully accepting that person—and then remembering that you ARE that person.

6. See everything—including yourself—as *perfect* in its current state, no matter how many flaws, blemishes, warts or imperfections your ego-mind insists on pointing out. Recognize that your desire to change something is *also* perfect.

THE ACCEPTANCE KEY

Acceptance of *what is* enables and empowers you to experience everything as it is rather than as some false image that you might have been creating through the stories, conclusions, judgments and interpretations of your ego-mind. By releasing yourself from the trappings of your ego-mind, you open the space for true understanding to occur, and from this understanding, you gain more clarity about everything in the world—including a deeper knowing of who you really are. Acceptance is an active form of unconditional love, a modality that brings much-needed healing into the world. Allow yourself to be connected to the powerful force of acceptance by opening your heart to the following affirmation:

I am an open channel of unconditional love, and I continuously nurture my ability to release judgments and attachments in order to accept everything—including myself—as perfect, complete and whole in the current moment.

CHAPTER 2: IDENTITY

KNOW AND REMEMBER WHO YOU ARE

there are waves

there are waves upon which i dance,
like particles of light,
gathering people and songs and stars
into the galaxy of my heart,
where all that is
is
all that i am,
endless,
boundless,
without form or definition,
but complete and fully self-aware

passing through illusory boundaries,
dissolving all assumptions and beliefs,
arriving at a place
where

imagination
is just another word for
creation

differentiated and integrated,
individuated and united

i am the wave.
i am the sea.

i am the light.
i am the darkness.

i am the sound.
i am the silence.

i am everything.
i am nothing.

The Repeated Question Game

"WHO are you?" Her eyes twinkled as she asked the question.

We sat facing each other in backjacks on the floor, sharing space with about 50 other pairs of workshoppers who were engaged in the same process.

"I am David." A natural response, the first thing that popped into my head.

"Thank you," she said, and she said it with sincerity. A brief pause, and then: "Who are YOU?"

"I am a man."

"Mmmm, thank you." A smile, a nod, another pause, and then again: "Who ARE you?"

She asked the same question over and over, each time using variations of tone, inflection and volume. Sometimes she would sit back in her backjack as she asked the question; sometimes she would lean forward and look at me intently, as if she were seeking some deeper truth within me. Sometimes she would ask the question out loud; sometimes she would just look me in the eye and mouth the words without making any perceptible sound. And each variation of the question led me to a different answer, which she seemed delighted and excited to hear.

At the start of the process, I gave pretty typical responses. Father. Son. Brother. Lover. Fighter pilot. Software engineer. Poet. Musician. Life coach. Swimmer. Yogi. Meditator. Sometimes I repeated things I had said before; sometimes I added adjectives or other descriptive language.

Each response I gave seemed truthful enough as I uttered it. But then, a moment later as I found a new answer, I noticed something shifting in me, as if I was recognizing that my previous response wasn't really true at all.

"Who are you?" She whispered this one gently, and flashed a knowing smile at me. She seemed like an angel who knew something that I was supposed to know, but I seemed to be having trouble finding it.

No response. Silence. The word "Nothing" came to my mind, but I'm not sure I actually said it out loud.

"Thank you," she said—as she did after every answer I gave—and she said it with such love in her voice that my eyes started leaking.

"Tell me who you ARE," she said.

"Everything", I said, and even though I didn't understand where that came from, it felt totally true to me.

This repeated question game went on for maybe 10 minutes, but it felt like a lifetime. And in that brief eternity, I discovered things about myself that I had not known before. Well, that's not totally true. I think it's more accurate to say that I remembered things about myself that I had long forgotten.

I have come to love this game a great deal, and I've played it many times since that first experience, and I've shared it with many different people. And even though I have an idea of what is going to happen, I am always amazed at the things that come out of my mouth. I always remember something new, something that has been waiting, like a jewel in the dirt, to be revealed within me.

I have even played the game by myself. Sometimes I'll sit in front of a full length mirror, and I'll imagine my reflection as the interviewer, and myself as the responder. My reflection asks "Who are you?", and I respond with whatever feels true in the moment. Then my reflection says, "Thank you", and repeats the question. In this way, the introspective process is its own kind of deep and illuminating meditation.

The secret to playing this game is for the interviewer—the one asking the repeated question—to come from a place of authentic curiosity, with an attitude that whatever answer might come forth, it is the most important answer to any question ever asked; and then, when the answer does arrive, to be delightfully and gratefully surprised by it. By unconditionally accepting each answer as it arrives, the interviewer makes it possible for the responder to examine every aspect of his or her life and reveal things about him or herself that might otherwise be too scary to reveal.

WHAT THE GAME HAS TAUGHT ME

The more I play the repeated question game, the more I understand that I am not what I think I am—no matter how "certain" I might be about what I think! In particular:

- I am not my name.
- I am not my job description or my resumé.
- I am not any of the roles I play in life.
- I am not my body.
- I am not my thoughts.

- I am not my words.
- I am not my actions.
- I am not my feelings.
- I am not my beliefs.
- I am not the story that I tell myself or the world.

No, in truth, I am not any of these things. Well, then, if that is so, then who or what am I, really? The short answer is: *I am the one creating, observing or experiencing all those things!*

The problem, you see, is one of language. The moment I use words to describe who or what I am, I immediately put a label upon myself. In effect, I put myself into a box; I limit myself. And what I have learned is that there are no limits. Not really. In fact, as I see things now, it seems that all limits are just perceptual restrictions of the mind.

When I allow myself to step outside of my imagined limitations, I see and feel something that I am not able to describe with words. It is magnificent, beautiful, boundless—and so much more. It is Truth; it is Love—and so much more. But it begins to express and describe the essence of what I really am. And when I see that I really am all of that, then I easily see that you are all of that too. I recognize and remember that you and I are the same thing. *We are One.* And I don't say this just because it is the cool thing to say these days. I say it because it is true.

After playing the repeated question game many times, and after doing a great deal of deep work within myself, I have come up with a statement that at last begins to approximate who and what I really am:

> **I am a magnificent, divine, limitless, spiritual being of light and love who is sharing and enjoying a perfect human journey that allows me to express and experience myself as such.**

Believe it or not, this statement is an honest reflection of how I see myself today. Well, most of the time anyway—as long as my ego-mind isn't overwhelming me with its fear-based perspectives.

For some people, this statement may sound like an affirmatory statement that is meant simply to inspire. For some, it may sound boastful or narcissistic. For some, it may not compare to their experience of life, and so they can't possibly imagine someone like me having a belief like this.

As you have probably guessed already, I haven't always believed this about myself. In fact, for the first two thirds of my life, I believed almost the exact opposite!

HOW I DISOWNED MYSELF

You see, I started out my life on this planet in much the same way that most humans do. I went through a physical birthing process that brought me from "somewhere out there" into a solid and physical existence among people who were designated as my family and friends.

For me, the world initially seemed a very wondrous place. Like most young children, I was full of innocence, curiosity and adventure, and everything seemed like it was designed specifically to bring me joy, excitement and laughter. The world was, in a very real sense, my playground.

- I remember the wonder of watching a butterfly flitting around from flower to flower, and marveling at its beauty.
- I remember being naked and running around my back yard trying to catch robins—and hearing my mother and her friends laughing gleefully at my perpetually unsuccessful pursuit.
- I remember having my breath taken away by the feeling of cold water as I ran through the lawn sprinkler.
- I remember the loving warmth of my mother's arms when she cuddled me and soothed me as I struggled with the unpleasant itchiness of childhood measles.

But the wonder and magic of life all changed when I got to the ripe old age of 3 years! My mother said 8 words to me that flipped everything upside down—although I didn't realize this fact until nearly 60 years later.

I had been doing something that my mother found irritating for some reason—something typically curious and adventurous for a 3-year-old—and she wanted me to stop. Of course, by this age, I was already exhibiting some of my characteristic rebelliousness and independence, and this only added to her consternation. I don't remember all of the details, but I do remember that my mom had me standing on top of the changing table, and she was admonishing me with her typical mother statements. *"Be a good boy." "Do what you are told." "I'm your mother, you are supposed to listen to me."* All of which, of course, I had been totally ignoring!

But then, as I was standing there on the table, with her hands firmly holding my arms, she looked me right in the eye and said 8 simple and relatively innocuous words that knocked me for a loop.

Now, I want to be clear that my mother was not really yelling at me or abusing me in any way, but she was frustrated with my behavior and, being a woman who liked to have control, she was doing her best to get me to behave according to her desires. Not only that, but the words she said were delivered without any malice at all, although she clearly believed them and she wanted me to know that.

"I know you better than you know yourself."

When I was 3, I had heard the name "God" spoken from time to time, and although I didn't really know what it meant, I knew that "God" was pretty important and pretty powerful. But in my own limited experience, no one was more powerful than my mom, so for all practical purposes, she was "God" to me. And these were the words that "God" spoke to me:

"I know you better than you know yourself."

The sentence bounced around in my little head for a while before it finally landed. Now, I don't really remember exactly how I reacted to it, but in my adult mind of today, I imagine my thinking process followed this line of logic:

"Well, you are my mother, that's true. And you certainly know me better than anyone else does, that's also true. And you tell me that you love me, and you seem to know all my needs and make sure they are taken care of. So, I guess it must be true: you know me better than I know myself."

Effectively, I accepted what my mother said as absolute truth. I mean I was only three, and I had no real sense of who I was anyway, so it was easy for me to accept the "truth" of what she was telling me.

And that's when everything changed.

The moment I accepted that my mother knew me better than I knew myself, it wasn't much of a leap for me to draw some other conclusions:

"If Mommy knows me better than I know myself, then Daddy knows me better than I know myself, too. And, that means Gramma and Grampa know me better than I know myself as well. And my teachers know me better than I know myself, and the minister knows me better than I know myself, and..."

In pretty short order, I had come to believe that EVERYBODY knew me better than I knew myself!

A side-effect of this way of thinking was that I concluded that if everyone else knew me better than I knew myself, then I simply had to defer to them to figure out what I wanted and needed. This led me essentially to denounce my own sovereignty and to rely on others for almost everything—while at the same time observing those same people making decisions for themselves. So, gradually—over a timespan of more than 40 years—I grew more and more resentful and angry. Everyone else knew what they wanted and needed, and they were able to choose what mattered to them, but I had to look to others for my answers! It just wasn't fair!

I had become so used to deferring to others—and even going out of my way to do things that I thought would please them—that I simply didn't notice that I was getting more and more pissed off about it! Other people certainly noticed my anger, but of course whenever they called me on it, I would shout—quite angrily, now that I think about it—"I am NOT angry! Leave me alone!"

The net result was that I had inadvertently disowned my true self and gotten to a place where I looked to virtually everyone outside of me for confirmation and truth about who I really was. It was—unbeknownst to me—disaster in the making, because I had unknowingly given virtually all my power away. My Soul was crying out inside me trying to wake me up, but I was so far down this path that I wasn't able to hear it.

I'm certain that my mother never intended for any of this to happen—at least not consciously. She didn't plan for me to be dependent on everyone else. She didn't plan for any of these ideas to come into my consciousness—and to be sure, most of this was unconscious for me until I became aware of it in my late forties—but it's what happened, and as you can imagine it created quite a turbulent ride for me.

Because of a decision I had made at 3 years old—and had long since forgotten about—my life had become a complete farce! I was not happy at all. I was doing my best to live according to the beliefs that I had thought were the "right beliefs" for a good life, and yet I was miserable! I had desires for my life, but all of them seemed to get swept aside as I worked hard to please other people rather than honoring my own truth. And all the while, my anger was growing inside me like a cancer.

It was just a matter of time before I wouldn't be able to control it any more.

The Cost of Self-Disownment

By the time I reached my 40s, I had come to a point where nothing in my life made sense. I had no idea how I had gotten where I was, and I certainly had no idea how to get where I wanted to go. In fact, I wasn't even sure where I wanted to go—or if indeed I even wanted to go! I seemed to be on a path that had been defined for me by someone else.

Although I was pretty well off by most standards, I wasn't happy—in fact, I was downright miserable—and there was no reason I could identify that satisfied the question "Why?" And of course, because I had disowned myself so many years earlier, it was very easy for me to put the blame for my situation on everything and everyone outside of myself!

If you were to go back and ask people what I was like, I'm sure a lot of them would tell you that I was angry and resentful, that I was cynical and sometimes bitter about life, that I often used sarcasm as a way to get laughs, and that while I had a pretty good heart, I often seemed to express entitlement—as if I expected the world to provide for my every need. All of this provided me with enough evidence that I could justify my disappointment with life and with God.

It was a pretty dismal picture, to be sure.

Then something happened that really overturned my world.

In 1992—Mother's Day weekend, to be specific—my mother announced to the family in typical matter-of-fact fashion that she had breast cancer. Cancer that had metastasized and advanced into its last stages. It turned out that she had known about this for almost three years and that she had sworn Dad (my step-father, actually) to secrecy. I'm not sure exactly why she chose to keep this a secret, but I can only speculate today that it had something to do with her fear of being seen as a burden. However, by keeping it a secret, she didn't realize that she was also keeping my brother, my sister and me from being able to offer her any kind of support—and from processing our own emotions in a way that would allow us to get closure with her.

My mother had a profound disdain and distrust for western medicine, so she looked to naturopathic doctors and holistic practitioners for help, and didn't even consider modern options until it was far too late. So, here she was, three years later with a disease that she may well have been able to prevent, and into the hospital she went. Three weeks after that, she was dead.

I remember spending many nights at the hospital during that last three weeks, staying with my mother, numbing out my own feelings, but seething inside with an unexpressed anger for the way she had chosen to finish out her life—with no input from me or my siblings. There she was, withering away in a hospital bed, looking frailer and frailer by the day, virtually unable to speak or communicate in any intelligible way because of the massive doses of morphine that kept her in a palliative state of painlessness for the last days of her life.

On June 2nd 1992, I stood by my mother's bed and witnessed her last breath. I was amazed how much her body and mind wanted to stay alive, how much they fought and fought to keep on going. Time slowed down for me, and I simply marveled at the number of times I watched her fight for breath, thinking to myself, "this must be the last one now." I felt such relief when it was over, and I held her hand for quite a while. But I didn't shed any tears. She would never have approved.

Over the next couple of weeks, I remember my preferred method of grieving. It involved a lot of alcohol—which, surprisingly, helped to dull the anger and keep me from spilling my tears. Dad, who had always been very much in love with my mother, was clearly devastated by her passing, but he too contained all his emotions and soldiered on as a stoic example for the rest of us. Because I spent a lot of the time leading up to Mom's funeral in a drunken stupor, some of my memory is hazy, but I think my sister was the only one in the immediate family who ever shed any tears for her.

One of the great ironies of this time in my life is that I was asked to write and deliver my mother's eulogy. Dad recognized a writing ability within me and believed I would do a good job. I reluctantly agreed.

The day of the funeral completely stunned me. Mom had been a yoga teacher for the last 15 years or so of her life, and many of her students showed up to pay their respects. In all, something like 200-300 people showed up at the funeral.

It was kind of surreal for me. I had my own perspective of my mother, and I had never really considered what her life had been like outside of my relationship to her. I had braced myself to deliver a eulogy to a small group of friends. Seeing all these people and standing before them turned out to be one of the most difficult things I had done. Time slowed down for me again, and I felt like I was frozen in front of them for the longest time. Mom's eldest sister was sitting in the second row behind the immediate family, and somehow she caught my eye. She shared the subtlest smile with me, and it was just enough to help me get the first words out of my mouth. Somehow, the words kept flowing, and in spite of my fear, I managed to share the entire eulogy without tripping over my tongue or letting my eyes overflow.

When the Dam Broke

A few days after Mom's funeral, my sister came over to my house. When she stepped onto the landing through the back door, I could tell that she was upset, but I didn't know why. What she said to me ended up being a critical turning point in my life, although I didn't recognize it as such when she spoke.

"Why haven't you grieved for Mom? What the hell is wrong with you?"

To be honest, I have no idea if this is exactly what my sister said, but it is certainly what I remember hearing, and when I heard it, something inside me snapped. The next thing I knew I had her up against the wall with my right hand around her neck. I was sneering into her face, and I was thinking in my mind, "Don't you tell me how to grieve!" but what came out of my mouth was "Don't you tell me how to BE!"

Once again, time slowed down for me, and everything became surreal. I distinctly remember asking myself, *How did I get here?* And even though anger and adrenaline were coursing through my body, the question seemed to come from a very calm place inside me. There didn't seem to be any judgment at all in the question. Then, a moment later, I heard a similar quiet and calm voice in my head saying, simply, *Enough.*

After I released my grip on my sister's neck, I remember her yelling tearfully "How dare you!", and though I could see her obviously shouting other things at me, that is all I remember hearing. I vaguely remember leaving the house and wandering aimlessly around the neighborhood for a good while. Somewhere in my awareness, I replayed the scene in my mind a few times and then I had the dreadful realization that I had done all this in the full presence of my daughter, my son, and my niece. I can still hear the pained, plaintive echo of my daughter's voice pleading, "Daddy, don't!"

As was the way of the McLeod family back then, this issue was never discussed by anyone at any time—at least not with me present. For me, it was as if my outburst had never happened, and, indeed, I put it out of my own mind for many years. The memory did not come back to me until sometime in 2013— over 20 years later! And as I processed the now-ancient memory of that event,

I realized that, although my sister had been the one to speak the words, it was my mother's voice that I had been hearing when I reacted so violently; I was demanding that my mother stop telling me how to be!

In the 3 years following my mother's death, I became more and more aware of my dissatisfaction with my life. More importantly, I began to recognize and acknowledge the extent of my anger and resentment. What really began to scare me—no doubt a side-effect of the incident with my sister—was that my anger was leaking out in subtle ways and I was worried that it would damage or hurt my children.

I sought help from many of the typical resources of the day—family, friends, religion—but none of them seemed able or willing to help me. At one point, I even tried seeking help from a psychologist—someone I found through the Yellow Pages—but even that didn't seem particularly helpful. In retrospect, although I wanted help, I wasn't really ready to look at this as my own problem; I wanted to find ways to fix everyone and everything else!

Failing to find the help I thought I needed, I ended up doing the only other thing I could think of: I ran away! I simply followed the path of so many other 40-somethings and packed up all my stuff, left my family, and escaped!

Long-Term Impact

My story is not that unique, really. Sure, the details might be different from other stories, but the reality is that we all go through difficult times like these, and in doing so, we are confronted with choices.

I can look to this situation today, and I can see that everything that happened to me came about because of a decision I made when I was only 3 years old! It was the decision of an immature child, to be sure, but it was a decision—MY decision—nonetheless. And it was this decision that led me to follow up with a whole series of other decisions—also MY decisions—that created the reality that I experienced.

But my reality affected everyone and everything around me. The anger and resentment that grew within me eventually led to a situation in which I was separated from my children, and that was a painful separation for all of us.

It would be—and actually *was*, as I'll explain later—easy for me to blame all this on external circumstances, but the truth is, I was responsible for my own choices—regardless of how old I might have been when I made them.

Ultimately, the moment of truth for me occurred when I gave my power away and allowed (or expected) everyone else in my life to define who I was. I abdicated my own sovereignty because I thought it would be a good thing to do! I deferred to others, tried to please them and make them happy, because I believed it would create a better world. I showed up the way I imagined other people wanted me to, and I put on all the appropriate masks and costumes to fully inhabit the roles I accepted. But instead of happiness and contentment, I ended up creating chaos, confusion, pain, suffering and damage. For everyone in my life!

As I look at the world around me today, I see that so many other people are doing the same sort of thing. They are trying to "fit in", to "do the right thing", to "obey all the rules", to "conform". And in doing that, they are giving themselves up.

If we want to change this crazy dynamic, we have to begin by changing the way we think of ourselves. We have to accept the truth of who we really are, and we have to make a commitment to remember that truth.

REMEMBER WHO YOU ARE

Do you know who you are?

Do you know who you REALLY are?

When I ask people this question, some of them think they know the answer. And then I teach them the "Repeated Question Game", and most of them aren't so sure anymore. And it's okay really. After all, you've been conditioned during your upbringing to believe what other people tell you about yourself.

> *You're smart. You're stupid. You're too big for your britches. You're tall. You're short. You're too loud. You're athletic. You're lazy. You're too talkative. You're a good girl. You're outgoing. You're honest. You're a liar. You're a cheater. You're sneaky. You're manipulative. You're a bad boy. You're this. You're that. You're the other thing.*

The list is endless. People make interpretations and judgments about you continually, because that is just a fundamental characteristic of humans. Some of the judgments will resonate within you; some of them won't. But guess what, *Maestro*? Here's a little secret for you: they're all true! That's right, you are ALL of these things, and much more! And if you think about it for a minute, how could it be otherwise?

You might not like to admit some of these things about yourself. You might find yourself in strong resistance to some of those labels. After all, who wants to admit to being manipulative? Who wants to acknowledge the liar, the thief, the trickster within? And looking at the other side of the coin, how many of us are afraid to admit the amazing leader or teacher or mentor within us? But it's all there, my friend. If you can see it in someone else, it's because it exists within you. But there's an even bigger reason this is so.

THE SOURCE OF FORGETFULNESS

As I pointed out earlier, as a human, part of your experience on this physical plane is to have an ego-mind that accompanies you wherever you go. And this part of you has a very specific job: to keep you safe as you navigate the physical world.

In order keep you safe in the world, your ego-mind maintains a very strong belief in separateness. It thinks that you are separate from everyone and everything else in the world. The ego-mind does not understand the notion of oneness. In fact, in order to survive, the ego-mind must maintain the illusion of separateness. So what happens is that your ego-mind actually makes you forget about your connection to *OMnitude*, and as a result, it creates in you a forgetfulness about who you really are.

The ego-mind is very fragile—as I'm sure you're already noticed! In fact, it is the ego-mind that identifies with thoughts, roles, beliefs, feelings, and all the other things that are tied to our experience on the physical plane. It is the ego-mind that says:

- I am what I think.
- I am a man/woman.
- I am young/old.
- I am healthy/unhealthy.
- I am rich/poor.
- I am my mind.
- I am my body.

And so on, and so on.

But the ego-mind says a lot of other things too, things that not only deny who you really are, but place limitations on you. Often these statements about yourself are disguised as statements about your surroundings, or the other people in your life:

- *Everyone else is smarter than me, so there's no point in trying to excel in that particular field.*

- *The world is a dangerous place, so I have to avoid making myself stand out in any way at all.*

- *Luck is something that happens to other people, and it always works against me.*

- *Nobody really cares about me, so it's a waste of time for me to get into a relationship.*

- *Nothing ever works out for me, I might as well just give up trying.*

The fragile ego-mind is very inventive, so there is no end to the stories it will make up in order to keep you safe. If you look at these thoughts, no doubt you will quickly see that they just translate to some form of self-limiting idea.

- *"I'm not smart enough."*

- *"I'm not safe enough."*

- *"I'm not lucky enough."*

- *"I am unimportant."*

- *"I'm a failure."*

Sadly, many of us buy into these beliefs because our ego-minds keep us afraid to stand out and be seen for who and what we really are!

I'm not going to tell you to stop paying attention to your ego-mind—after all, there are times when its advice really is necessary and important. But what I am recommending is that you don't let your ego-mind tell you anything about who you are, for it only sees things in terms of its limited view of the physical world. Instead, I strongly encourage you to tap into *The Source* by listening to your Soul, which is where wisdom can always be found.

We are Holistic Beings

In the words of Jesuit philosopher Pierre Teilhard de Chardin,

> **We are not human beings having a spiritual experience.**
> **We are spiritual beings having a human experience.**

I like this quote a lot because it helps keep me connected to the truth of who I really am—an amazing and unique blending of the worldly and the non-worldly.

As I suggested in my sharing of the story of *OMnitude* and how quantum physics seems to be confirming what spiritual teachers have been saying for thousands of years, I think that our incomplete understanding of Consciousness is a consequence of humanity's resistance to the truth of who we really are. Interestingly, the truth is available to all of us, as I said before, because we are all connected—non-physically (spiritually)—to *OMnitude*. But it is easy to be confused about the truth because we all have ego-minds which, in their zeal to keep us safe, misguide us about our true nature.

De Chardin speaks of two elements of a dichotomy: the physical and the non-physical. In my work, however, I have come to the conclusion that we are actually holistic beings consisting of four energetically diverse but interdependent components:

> ### Heart. Body. Mind. Soul.

Most would agree that heart and body are physical components, while soul is a spiritual (non-physical) component. Mind, however, is a kind of outlier, in the sense that it has attributes and qualities of both the physical and the non-physical. If we take a purely scientific perspective, then it might be argued that the heart is part of the body, so it should not be listed separately. But what science is beginning to learn now—thanks to the work of hundreds of independent researchers—is that the heart actually possesses a kind of mini-brain of its own. This control center is made up of around 40,000 neurons that can sense, feel, learn and remember. Interestingly, it turns out that the heart actually sends more information to the brain than the brain sends to the heart. Clearly, this puts the heart into a league of its own, and makes it much more important than we might have previously imagined.

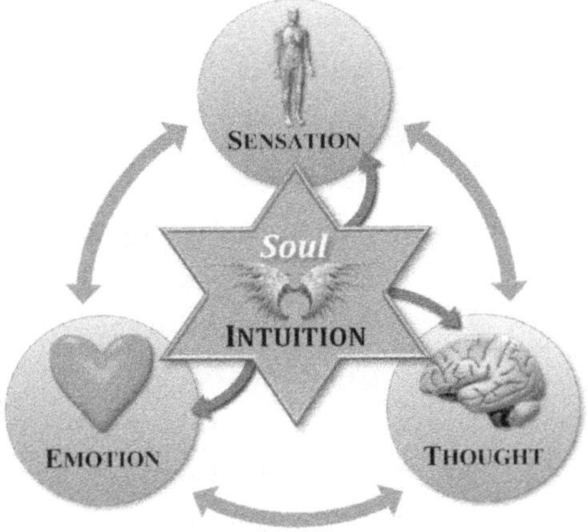

Figure 10—The Holistic Human

The interactions of these four components can be described by the kinds of information that they process and share:

- **Heart → Emotion**: the energy that moves us internally and helps us to recognize and understand our connection with one another.

- **Body → Sensation**: any input that stimulates one or more of our physical senses, most notably the sense of touch.

- **Mind → Thought**: what we experience as images or ideas that give us perhaps the strongest sense of awareness, consciousness, and self-knowing.

- **Soul → Intuition**: awareness of knowledge, truth or wisdom that seems to come from a "higher realm" or from a place "outside of ourselves".

I've created the diagram in Figure 10 to depict the more physical elements (heart, body, and mind) on a lower level, with the non-physical element (soul) hovering above them. On the lower level, bi-directional interactions facilitate communication among each pair of elements. I call this the *emotion-sensation-thought (EST)* chain—what most of us would recognize as ***Feelings***.

All of us are familiar with this interaction chain within us (even if we haven't really taken a close look at it). It's pretty clear that each element of the chain is closely related, if not exactly coupled, with the other two, because activity in any one element tends to trigger activity in one or both of the other elements. For example, sometimes you might experience an emotion (*fear*, say) that triggers a physical sensation in your body (such as *cold, shivery,* or *clenched*), which in turn triggers a thought (*I'm scared,* or *I gotta get outta here*). Or perhaps a thought might occur first (*I don't think John loves me anymore*) which leads to an emotion (*sadness, fear, anger*) that triggers a physical sensation (*heaviness in the chest, accompanied by tears*). Regardless of where the cycle seems to begin, there is almost always activity present in all three components of the chain.

The Soul element, however, appears to operate a little differently from the other elements. It is constantly feeding information into us from a place that seems to be outside of ourselves—from our *higher* selves. People who do a lot of meditating are able to tap into this element intentionally by listening to *the quiet voice within.* So, in a very real sense, the Soul sends signals that can trigger any one or more of the physical receptors in the *EST* chain, each of which in turn will trigger one or both of the other elements in that chain. The Soul is constantly observing and guiding us, so it is aware of what is going on in the *EST* chain and doesn't really depend on a separate input channel.

Remember what I said about the *plasma strand* in my story about *OMnitude*? Well, I believe that is the non-physical channel that connects the Soul to the rest of the holistic components.

If you want to know what your Soul is actually saying to you, you can try meditating and just listening to the quiet voice of your inner authority. That certainly works well for some people. But here's something you may find even easier: raise your awareness of what is happening on your physical level. That is, become aware of the interactions that are taking place in your own EST chain. A technique I use pretty regularly is the following:

- Find a quiet place where you can do your introspection without interruption. Take some deep breaths to clear your mind and relax your body. Give yourself permission to close your eyes and relax while staying completely awake and alert.

- Do a complete inner scan of your body. Start at your head and work your way down to your toes. You can imagine that you are on a journey throughout the immense wonder of your body, and you can shine an imaginary flashlight on different parts of yourself as you proceed. Pause at each location and bring your full attention to whatever your light is illuminating. Notice whatever is going on there. What sensations are you feeling? What emotions are accompanying those sensations? What thoughts are appearing in your mind as you observe?

- Do all of this as impassively as you can—that is, try to suspend all judgments, stories and interpretations. Just notice the answers that come up for you.

- Before you move on to the next part of your body, ask yourself one more important question: *What is it that my soul is communicating to me right now?* Open yourself to hearing the answer in your deepest awareness, knowing that the answer may come in unexpected ways.

- When you are complete with one location in your body, express gratitude for all that it does for you. If there is pain or discomfort in that part of your body, invite in warm, loving energy to heal it and make it whole.

- Move on to the next part of your body.

This simple process will help you to remember your holistic nature and deepen your connection to your Soul—which truly is the source of all wisdom and truth about who you really are.

A "UNIVERSAL" TRUTH

I believe that there is only one real "absolute" universal truth, and it is the simple but extremely powerful declaration

I Am.

I Am is the breath of life; it is pure consciousness—*OMnitude*—recognizing and acknowledging its own existence; it is the very engine of creation. All other concepts, perspectives and experiences derive from this one truth. What's more, we all invoke this statement in every single moment of our lives, because every thought, word, action and feeling that we express is a direct reflection of who we are choosing to be in that moment. The only question is whether we invoke the declaration consciously or unconsciously.

What most of us don't realize is that these two tiny little words pack a lot of punch! In fact, when we choose to use them consciously and intentionally, all of life is completely at our command. This may sound grandiose, but it is true: whatever we experience in our lives is a direct result of how we choose to show up—or, more specifically, how we choose to use those two little words. Just imagine: what might happen if we wake ourselves up, get a clear and unambiguous knowing of who we really are, and then start using these two magical words intentionally and consciously? Well, what I think happens is a process that I call...

CONSCIOUS SELF-CREATION

The idea of conscious self-creation is that, instead of just letting your life journey unfold in whatever way it will on its own, you raise your consciousness to the highest level possible, take advantage of the immutable laws of the universe, and begin choosing the path of your own intentional growth.

In order to make this work for you, you have to do four things:

- Recognize who and what you are right now,

- Decide who and what you desire to be in the next moment,

- Create and declare a conscious intention to grow into this new desired version of yourself, and

- Express (and experience) yourself in accordance with your new declaration.

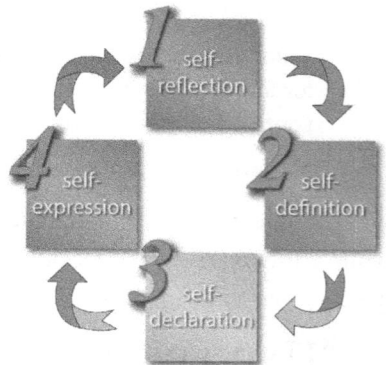

Figure 11—Conscious Self-Creation

In other words, conscious self-creation is a combination of *self-reflection*, *self-definition*, *self-declaration* and *self-expression*, as depicted in Figure 11.

Let's take a look at these steps one at a time.

Self-Reflection

As I mentioned earlier, if you want to go someplace, then you better be sure where you are right now. Self-reflection is a mechanism for getting clarity about who/what you are right now. If you have a partner available, then the repeated question game is a great way to help you get that clarity. Additionally, you can ask yourself some powerful check-in questions to raise your awareness about yourself. As you ask yourself these questions, simply notice what is true right now, without judgment, criticism or blame. Record your answers in a journal.

- Who/what am I?

- How do I behave in the presence of people from the same/different <*gender, race/ethnicity, income bracket, age group, job description, etc.*>?

- What do I believe about <*politics, religion, spirituality, philosophy, gun control, abortion, pornography, etc.*>?

- How do I react to the behaviors of others who have strong beliefs that are different (or opposite) from mine?

- What are the limiting beliefs I have about myself? What are the ways in which I sell myself short?

- What are the empowering beliefs I have about myself? What are the ways in which I honor and appreciate myself?

Once you have a clear idea of who/what you are, take some time to reflect on what you think and feel about this particular version of you. As you do this, you will easily and quickly become aware of many different characteristics and behaviors, some of which you love and appreciate about yourself, and some of which you might like to change. Here are some additional questions to help you get more clarity about your current state. Remember to record your answers in your journal.

- How do I feel about who I am right now? What thoughts, judgments or criticisms do I hear in my mind?

- What aspects or characteristics of myself do I really love and want to increase or grow?

- What aspects or characteristics of myself would I like to change or diminish?

- If I leave <*specific aspect of myself*> as it is, how will it impact my world going forward?

During self-reflection, it's very easy to say things like *I was wrong about <X>*, or

I should have done <Y>, or *I am really ashamed about <Z>*. The truth is, even though these things may have created outcomes that you hadn't really intended, they did serve you in some way, even if it was only to help you learn something important about yourself. So, rather than adopting a harsh or judgmental demeanor toward yourself, thank and honor yourself for having the courage to create something that helped you define who you have become—up to now. Without this knowledge, you would not be able to evolve consciously into the new you, so remember to express gratitude.

Self-Definition

Now that you have gathered some important information about your current state, you can use the *self-definition* step to "tweak the current model", so to speak, in order to produce a "new, improved version" that you can share with the world.

For each aspect of the "old you", you have become aware about how it serves you or how it doesn't. At the same time, you may also have realized that there is something missing—some aspect or characteristic that you'd like to introduce and begin cultivating in yourself. Armed with this data, you can now decide from five different adjustment types:

- What you want to stop or remove;
- What you want to start or introduce;
- What you want to strengthen or increase;
- What you want to dampen or decrease;
- What you want to leave unchanged.

In order to help you capture the information, imagine a mixer console in front of you, with one channel or strip for each attribute. Each strip has a label with the attribute's name, such as *generosity* or *belief in capital punishment* or *loving parent*. In addition, each strip has an on/off switch as well as an intensity slider that goes from *min* to *max*. This console is infinitely extendable—that is, you can add or remove channels any time you want to.

The *self-reflection* step provided you with a

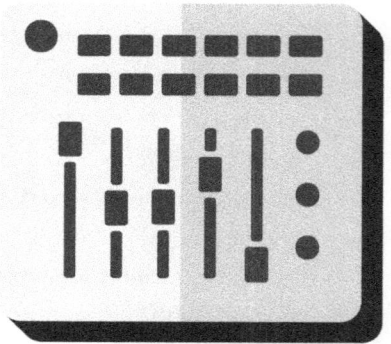

Figure 12—The Self-Definition Mixer

snapshot of who/what you are now. You can imagine that all the values have been input into your control panel for you to review. Each strip is either on or off, and the slider is positioned somewhere between *min* and max.

Now you get to decide the new position of each slider and each on/off switch. While it might be fun to go through the whole control panel and set all the values to what you imagine would represent the ideal you, you might want to consider a few things first. After all, we still live in a "real world", right?

Remember, you have grown used to the current you, so some of the changes that you want to make for yourself might be difficult to attain. The last thing you want to do is set yourself up for failure, so before making each adjustment on your control panel, ask yourself the following questions:

- Is this change going to be easy or hard for me?
- Is this a realistic amount for me to change this attribute?
- How much change in this attribute will put me just beyond my comfort zone (where my growth zone begins)?
- Will I be able to forgive myself if I am unable to fit myself into this change?

Let your answers to these questions guide you—from the inner authority of your heart and soul—to set your switches and sliders to values that make sense to you now.

We've been working with a metaphor—the control panel—and it would be nice to assume that you could just press a button and the new values would be saved somewhere. But what you'll have to do now is actually write down all the changes in your journal. When you're done, you'll have a list with entries like this:

- Increase my open-heartedness, acceptance, and gratitude.
- Decrease my self-centeredness, arrogance, and manipulativeness.
- Begin practicing forgiveness.
- Eliminate criticism and judgment.

This is just a short list provided as an example; your list will probably be longer and more detailed. Also, you may decide to be more specific about increases and decreases (e.g. increase by 15%).

Self-Declaration

The time has come to begin using those two magic words I talked about earlier! But now you're going to use them consciously. You'll do that by creating your own personal self-declaration—that is, a conscious and intentional pronouncement to the Universe about who (and what) you are choosing to be—starting right now!

Since you identified several characteristics and attributes of yourself during your self-reflection and self-definition phases, your actual self-declaration will probably consist of numerous affirmation statements. To be most effective, an affirmation statement has the following qualities:

- **First person singular**—Making use of first person singular establishes a sense of personal responsibility and says to the Universe: *"I am in charge of my own life, and I get to shape it and live it the way I choose to—AND I accept full responsibility whatever I create."*

- **Starts with the words "I Am"**—As mentioned earlier, these two words are the keys to the ignition system for the engine of creation—plus, they bolster your personal sense of responsibility.

- **Framed in the present tense**—Present tense eliminates a dependency on time. You are not declaring how you were in the past or how you will be at some uncertain point in the future; you are making a clear and simple announcement of who and what you are choosing to be right here-right now. This is very important, because you are effectively declaring a truth about yourself, and the Universe cannot argue with or negate that! Rather, the Universe has no choice but to bring all the necessary energies and forces into play to make it so for you—because that is your command.

- **Uses only positive, empowering, uplifting and inspiring language**—The words you choose are very important and are very much a reflection of your subconscious mental state. So make sure you weed out any potentially disempowering or judgmental phrases and replace them with something that truly reflects how you want to be showing up.

For each affirmation statement that becomes part of your new *self-declaration*, it is important to make sure that it is consistent with your overall intention.

- **Spiritual Alignment**—Check in with your *inner authority* to make sure that this new vision of yourself is part of your own grand spiritual plan for your life.

- **Mental Visualization**—Construct a powerful mental image about what you are trying to manifest and how you want to be showing up. Keep it in your awareness.

- **Strong Emotion**—Take some time to feel the intensity of your passion for growing into this new version of yourself. Feel it as deeply as you can.

- **Focused Action**—Identify and articulate one or two small-step actions you can take that will quickly move you in your desired direction.

Now that you have a series of affirmations that make up your self-declaration, begin an immediate practice of saying your full declaration out loud—at least once a day.

Self-Expression

Normally, you express who you are *right now*—that is, it seems like you have to *be* something in order to *express* it. However, surprising as it may seem, you can use *self-expression* as a powerful feedback mechanism to accelerate your metamorphosis—even though you may not yet be fully transformed into the new you, *you can express yourself as if you were already there!* Of course, you must do so with the full conviction that it is true, and you do that by staying connected to the emotionally powerful vision you created for yourself in the previous step. To make the neural feedback loop work more efficiently for you, you will find it helpful to imbue your self-expression with these four essential qualities:

- **Intention**—In steps 1 and 2, you arrived at a clear understanding about your reasons for wanting to create yourself anew. This led to a powerful and conscious intention that was birthed from the wisdom of your higher self. Remember your intention, and let it serve as a motivating force to keep you focused and moving in the direction of your desired change.

- **Belief**—You must believe whole-heartedly in the vision you have created for yourself. If you don't believe it, then the world won't believe it either, and will constantly confront you and challenge you. If you do believe it, then you will be able authentically to express the truth of who you intend to be, and the world will have no choice but to accept it.

- **Consistency**—Don't second-guess yourself, and don't let the world's resistance to your transformation knock you off balance. Keep your focus on your vision, and keep expressing yourself in a way that is consistent with that vision.

- **Trust**—The universe will always manifest for you what you attract into your life. If you are able to trust this, then you can simply focus on your deepest intention of your self-creation, and let yourself flow without resistance into the gentle and natural arrival of your transformation.

Rinse and Repeat!

One of the most beautiful aspects about this powerful conscious self-creation process is that you can do it as many times as you want. You are, after all, the architect and creator of your own life.

You may decide you want to bask in the glory of the new you for a while—perhaps even for the rest of your life. Or, you may decide at some point down the road that you'd like to make some adjustments.

Whatever you decide, remember that your control panel is only a single breath away, and you can access it any time you want to. Whether you decide to tweak a few characteristics or go through an entire overhaul process, remember to follow all of the steps—because they work!

Showing Up Authentically

Now that you have access to a really powerful tool for choosing your own path of evolution, you will likely want to begin a dedicated practice of showing up as authentically as you can. After all, in order to experience all of yourself to the maximum extent possible, you will have to do it in relation to everything and everyone else that exists in your world. If you want to be seen, heard, understood, and experienced for all of who you really are, then you must allow the real, true YOU to show up in every situation.

Now I'm not suggesting that you jump directly into the deep end of the pool here—at least not yet! There are lots more things I want to share with you before you may feel ready enough for a deeper dive; however, I just want to bring your attention to where we are headed. I hope you feel the excitement building!

With all that said, there is one thing you can begin practicing right now without too much risk: *empowered communication.*

From Projection to Ownership

If you listen to a typical person communicating about his or her life, you'll almost certainly observe a trait that seems to be bred into all of us from a very early age. The language chosen to describe these experiences is often filled with "you"-statements or "we"-statements or "they"-statements. I've noticed this *projection style* of communication everywhere, and it seems to be common among English-speaking people, no matter what their original culture or mother tongue happen to be. This leads me to conclude that it's a human phenomenon, and not just a cultural one.

I used to communicate in this way myself for the longest time! Although I wasn't aware of my habit years ago, today I can distinctly remember occasions when I'd be sharing about my own personal experience, and I'd be switching back and forth between "you"-statements and "I"-statements. For example, I might have related a story like this (not a real story, by the way):

> "On the way back from a ski trip, we were driving through the mountains on roads that were still covered with a lot of snow. We came around a bend and there was the aftermath of a car accident right in front of us. You could tell that the crash had just occurred moments before. You could see that the car had slammed into a pole and had overturned, and steam was still pouring out of the front end of the car. A young kid, maybe 10 or 12, was struggling to get out of the wreckage. The trunk of the car had flown open, and there were suitcases and broken skis strewn about the road. As I jammed the brakes, you could just feel the adrenaline running through your body. My wife let out a little yell from the passenger seat, and you could tell she was terrified...
>
> We did the only thing anyone could really do. You stop and you do your best to help out in any way possible. What else can you do, really, but tend to the victims, call the cops, and wait? And of course, all the while, you're feeling worried and concerned and helpless..."

Okay, I think you get the idea. Here I am in the story talking about my own experience, but notice that I'm projecting all of it (my thoughts, my actions, and even my feelings) onto YOU, the reader! By doing this, I'm avoiding taking responsibility so that I don't have to appear vulnerable to you. In a way, my ego-mind is keeping me safe from some imaginary danger.

This kind of conversational story-telling is very common. And most people who participate in it are not even aware of how they speak. This was certainly true for me—especially when I was unconsciously engaged in looking outward to others to determine who I really was. But when I did the inner work and made the transition to begin claiming responsibility for myself and for how I choose to show up, an interesting thing happened: I began to become aware of how my own communication style reflected how I was showing up. I could actually feel the incongruity between how I wanted to show up and how I was speaking to other people. And because of the discomfort in that incongruity, I began shifting from a projection style of communication to an *ownership* style—through the use of a simple but extremely powerful tool...

Self-Aware Communication

This is a relatively easy communication style that anyone can learn; it may just take a little practice to make it a regular part of your life. But in the end, once you've embodied it, I think you'll come to wonder how you could ever have communicated any other way! This form of communication consists of two primary elements, both of which support and enhance conscious choice and self-responsibility (which we'll discuss in more detail later):

- I-Statements
- Ownership

I-Statements

Always speak using "I"-statements; that is, make sure that, when you are speaking of your own experience, you do so from the perspective of *First Person*. Speak of your own feelings, thoughts, words, and actions. Speak of your own perspectives, conclusions and judgments. If you do happen to find yourself falling into the old pattern of "you"-statements or "we"-statements, then give yourself credit for catching yourself, and make an adjustment.

When I'm speaking, I have found the simple use of "I"-statements to be personally very empowering and liberating. I am able to share my experience with others in a way that seems to make it easier for them to hear. And I've noticed that when I'm listening to someone who speaks in this way, I find it much easier to hear and acknowledge what the other person is saying. Why is this? My own explanation goes something like this.

> When you speak to me using "you"-statements, I sometimes find myself confused about whether you are talking about me or about yourself. And while I'm busy processing the "you"-statement, sometimes I find myself with a thought like *"No, that doesn't happen to me. In fact, my experience is very different!"* And then, because I'm in a way disagreeing with your words, I'm not really listening to what you are actually saying—instead, I'm busy formulating a rebuttal!
>
> On the other hand, when you speak to me using "I"-statements, I can simply relax into whatever it is you are sharing with me, knowing that it is your experience and feeling quite confident that you are not assuming that I have the same experience as you. My ego-mind doesn't go into "rebuttal mode" because, it can't latch onto "you"-statements and then create arguments about them! This makes it easier for me to be more present

to what you are saying and to be compassionate with your experience. Furthermore, if I resonate with the experience, I can do so without taking away from what you are telling me.

"I"-statements alone can go a long way toward improving communication—especially if both parties use the technique.

Ownership

Ownership is all about recognizing all of your thoughts, words, actions and feelings as your own. It is the first step away from victim language toward authentic communication.

I've learned that the more I take ownership of my thoughts, words, actions, and feelings, the clearer I become about how I am showing up. With that clarity comes acceptance for what is so, and with acceptance comes the ability to change anything I might want to change. As you can probably see, all of this boils down to a clearer sense of who I am right now, and who I choose to be in the next moment.

Ownership is a powerful tool that you can use to separate yourself from your experience. You can still be a sovereign individual, and you can recognize that you *HAVE* thoughts, beliefs, and experiences. You can recognize yourself as the master of your life and you can appreciate all your experiences as things that you have created in order to help you fully express and experience yourself—in much the same way that *OMnitude* chooses to experience Itself as *All-that-Is*. What's more, when you share your experience with others, you allow them to see you more clearly—and that, in turn, helps them to see themselves more clearly, because, after all, *We Are All One!*

SUPERCHARGE YOUR LANGUAGE

Personal ownership and responsibility are reflected in how we communicate with others. When we speak using victim language, for example, we portray ourselves as people who have given power away to others. When we conflate our thoughts with our emotions and sensations, we lose touch with our authentic selves, and inadvertently create an environment that makes it harder for people to trust us. When we speak indirectly about something, rather than owning our truth up front, we invoke uncertainty and doubtfulness in others, and this contributes to their negative judgments of us. When we engage in talk about people who are not present, we become known as gossips, and the people we speak to begin to wonder what we say about them in their absence.

If you really want to master this aspect of your life, there are techniques you can use to help you clean up your language so that it enhances the way others experience you.

Take Explicit Responsibility

No matter what you are sharing with someone else, remember always to express it from a place of responsibility and ownership. There are a lot of ways you can do this. Here are some example phrases that can really help:

- **Emotion/Sensation/Thought**—*I feel... I'm experiencing... I think/believe... I imagine... I'm wondering...*
- **Conscious Choice**—*I choose to... I plan to... I agree to... I commit to...*
- **General Awareness**—*I notice... I see... I'm observing... I'm aware of...*
- **Awareness of Consequences**—*I caused... My actions led to...*
- **Story**—*I'm making up a story that... The story in my head is...*

Communicate Intentionally

Share everything as authentically as possible, and make all your communications meet the following minimum standards:

- **Clarity**—Choose words and phrases that accurately describe the experience you are trying to share. Pause long enough to ensure you are saying what you mean to say.

- **Directness**—If you have something to say *about* someone, make sure you speak directly to that person. Similarly, if you have something to say about *something*, don't beat around the bush! Be direct and unambiguous.

- **Honesty**—Speak only what is true for you, and avoid any language that might suggest otherwise.

- **Succinctness**—Say only what needs to be said, and no more. Don't offer further explanations unless the person you are speaking to indicates a lack of understanding, in which case you may need to find another way to say what you mean.

Eliminate Victim Language

All of us can easily find ourselves falling into our "victim behaviors" from time to time. But if we can maintain our awareness of these patterns, we can empower ourselves in pretty significant ways.

1. **I Can't**—This is one of the most overused phrases anywhere! In truth, it means one of two things: (a) *I don't want to*, or (b) *I don't know how*. So, if you find yourself resorting to this term, check in with yourself, figure out which of the two options it is, and speak honestly about it.

2. **You Made Me**—This phrase has all kinds of variations, but all of them result in the same outcome: pointing the finger of blame at someone (or something) else, and therefore giving all the power to that other entity. Acknowledge how you feel about the situation, share that as honestly as you can, and then take your power back by choosing what you will do next.

3. **It's Not My Fault**—This phrase is a subtle variation of number 2 above. But instead of pointing the finger at someone or something specific, this puts the blame on some undefined, external entity. This is an insidious and potentially more dangerous abdication, because you are simply giving your power away. Because you don't know where it went, you'll have a harder time reclaiming it.

4. **I Had No Choice**—This is simply not true. It may be true that other choices were less palatable, but you *always* have a choice. Own the fact that you made a choice that you didn't particularly like, or own the fact that you weren't really aware of your choice. Either way, raise your awareness and become more intentional in the next moment!

5. **I Am Too <*Fill-in-the-blank*>**—If you use variations of this kind of phrase, you immediately disempower yourself. *I'm too old* (or *not young enough*), *I'm too unfit* (or *not fit enough*), and similar statements serve only to give you an excuse for stopping yourself from showing up authentically. Even if some condition does get in the way for you, choose an alternate phrase that reflects what you *can* do. For example, you may indeed be too old to become a pilot in the military, but you are not too old to learn to fly a plane in some other way.

6. **Absolutes, Polarities, and Generalizations**—These constructions usually include words like "all/none", "everyone/no-one", "always/never", and so on. For example, *"You are always criticizing me!"* or *"I never get my way with you."* It's pretty obvious that such statements are rarely—if ever—true, and simply reflect the speaker's unwillingness or inability to deal with something that is happening right now. Get down to the truth of what you are really experiencing and feeling, and let your vulnerability touch the other person.

Avoid Comparatives and Superlatives

This idea is a tough one for some people to accept, because we all seem to have preferences and opinions. The problem is, as far as the ego-mind is concerned, our preferences and opinions are "right", while the preferences and opinions of others are "wrong"—unless of course they happen to agree with our own!

- *A is Better than B*—This kind of statement can get you into all kinds of trouble, because you are treading on the fragile ego-mind of another person. For example, if you say "beer is better than wine" (or vice versa), or "Democrats are better than Republicans" (or vice versa), you are virtually guaranteed to get an argument from someone. Eliminate this kind of comparison and say what you really mean, that you prefer one over the other. For example, "I like beer, but I prefer wine" or "I seem to resonate more with the Democratic platform than the Republican one."

- Good/Bad—These words are judgment words that reflect your own preferences. Even if most of society agrees with your perspective, that doesn't make it "right". Bear in mind that good/bad and right/wrong can change over time or over geographical distance. For example, in the 1500s, the Spanish Inquisition was "good"; today it is reviled virtually everywhere. Today, drug usage is considered "bad" in the USA; in other parts of the world, it is totally acceptable. Try to avoid these kinds of judgment words altogether and speak instead about what's underneath that is actually true for you.

- You're Right/Correct or Wrong/Incorrect—This is a judgment of a person that avoids the truth. And of course, the real truth is that you either agree or disagree with the person's perspective. Say what you mean!

Don't Use "Feelings" to Blame Others

As I mentioned earlier in this chapter, every "Feeling" is a combination of emotion, sensation and thought (the EST chain described earlier). And usually, whatever we think is accompanied by emotion and sensation at various intensities. Because of this, much of our language includes variations of the phrase "I feel", and if we are not careful, we can communicate something other than what we really intend.

There are two patterns in particular that I want to bring to your attention.

1. Thoughts Masquerading as Feelings

Any phrase that begins with one of the clauses "I feel like" or "I feel as if" or "I feel that" is clearly not an emotion or sensation at all, but rather a thought (belief, opinion, judgment or interpretation) about something. There may well be (and probably is) emotion and/or sensation present, but this sentence structure is primarily a thought pattern, and what follows the opening clause is often suggestive of a problem that is somehow someone else's fault.

For example, *"I feel like I'm on an emotional roller-coaster"* or *"I feel as if I don't matter to you"* or *"I feel that there is something you're holding back."* Clearly, all of these statements reflect a thinking pattern in the speaker—a story, if you like, that is completely fabricated by the speaker's ego-mind.

The moment you notice yourself starting a sentence with one of these clauses, just pause and realize that you are having a thought or story in your mind. Then, do your best to speak the truth of what that story is and how you truly do feel about it as the story activates you.

2. Past Participle Prosecution

This is another misuse of the phrase "I feel" that usually results in subtle or unintended finger-pointing toward the presumed cause of whatever the person is "feeling". This pattern occurs when the opening clause is followed by the past participle of a verb. For example, *I feel betrayed* or *I feel abandoned*. It should be pretty clear that these examples don't express feelings at all, but thoughts. What may not be so obvious is that these kinds of statements are subtle and insidious phrases that actually have the (often unintended) consequence of judging and/or blaming someone else.

Suppose, for example, that someone says to you *I'm feeling neglected*. The first question that usually comes to mind with such a statement is: *By whom?* And usually the answer to that question is implied in the context of the original statement—i.e. someone with whom the speaker is in relationship. So, clearly the statement suggests that another person is doing the neglecting. It's an implicit judgment of that person, pure and simple, and it is disguised as a feeling in a way that suggests blame.

If you find yourself slipping into this pattern, just pause and notice what is true for you. Then speak that truth. For example, instead of *"I'm feeling neglected"*, I might say to you *"Because of <some behavior that I observed>, I'm making up a story in my mind that you are neglecting me. This triggers a memory of pain I felt when my father neglected me as a 5-year-old child. What I really want from you is connection."* Notice that I'm taking full ownership for what is going on for me, and I've eliminated blame from the equation entirely. In doing so, I take my own power back and reclaim my sovereignty.

THE TRUTH OF WHO YOU ARE

When you find yourself resisting the truth of who you are, it is just your ego-mind arguing for separateness. When you find yourself forgetting your true nature, it is your ego-mind holding you back, out of some distorted belief that it is keeping you safe.

Pay attention to your thoughts and see if you can recognize when your ego-mind seems to be running the show. There are lots of clues that can help you wake up from your own forgetfulness:

1. Any negative thought you have about yourself: *"I am not <fill-in-the-blank> enough."*

2. Any situation in which you compare yourself to someone else: *"Bob is a better <fill-in-the-blank> than me."*

3. Any thought that suggests you are unsafe: *"I am unsafe or in danger from <fill-in-the-blank>."*

4. Any thought that tries to keep you in a dysfunctional behavior pattern: *"If I <fill-in-the-blank>, then I will be able to <fill-in-the-blank>."*

5. Any extreme (black-and-white) thinking patterns: *"I will never be able to <fill-in-the-blank>."* or *"Whenever I try to <fill-in-the-blank>, <fill-in-the-blank> (bad thing) always happens to me."*

There are many more thought patterns that I could list here; these are just a few of the more common ones. If you do find yourself thinking this way, remember to be gentle with yourself! One of the best things you can do is to say out loud to your ego-mind, something like the following:

> "Thank you for bringing this to my attention. I really appreciate that you are trying to keep me safe by warning me about a possible danger. I have it now, and I can trust myself to make a conscious and self-affirming decision about this. I don't need any more information from you about this topic, but I do thank you for alerting me to it."

It takes work to remember who you really are—patience, compassion and work—along with intentional, ongoing communion with your Soul. Your ego-mind serves a valuable purpose for you—at least in the physical realm—but you must never let it run the show! Honor your ego-mind for what it does for you. Love it, bless it…and then remind it that your Soul is really in charge, for it is your Soul that always knows who you really are.

No matter what might be going on in your life, no matter what challenges you might be facing, no matter what doubts might exist in your mind, I invite you always to remember this truth, so succinctly and powerfully captured by Richard Bach:

> **You are a perfect expression of perfect Love, here and now.**

CHAPTER SUMMARY—IDENTITY

At the center of your being you have the answer; you know who you are and you know what you want.—Lao Tzu

I love knowing that I am simultaneously as big as the universe and yet merely a heap of star dust.—Jill Bolte Taylor

When I'm trusting and being myself as fully as possible, everything in my life reflects this by falling into place easily, often miraculously.—Shakti Gawain

HIGHLIGHTS

1. The real you can easily be masked by the thoughts, beliefs and stories of the ego-mind. Use the repeated question game to help you peel away the layers created by the ego-mind and uncover your true essence.

2. There are no limits other than those imposed by the ego-mind. The more you peel back the trappings of the ego-mind, the more you realize that you are expansive and boundless.

3. If you buy into the limitations of the ego-mind, you can end up disowning yourself by creating false images of yourself that you present to the world. Bypass this route to hell by raising your awareness and reconnecting to the truth of who you really are.

4. You are not your name. You are not your thoughts, words, actions, beliefs, or roles. You are not your body or your mind. You are not the sum of your experiences. You are, in fact, the consciousness that brought all these things into being, and you are boundless in your ability to create. You are *OMnitude*, and *OMnitude* is you.

5. It is human nature to have judgments, and your judgments are right and true for you; however, they may not be right and true for another person. So be aware of your judgments and be willing to release them.

6. Because of your unbreakable connection with everyone and everything else, you can see aspects of yourself within others and aspects of others within yourself. Although you may not like someone else's judgments of you, if you simply hear them and then permit yourself to look deeply within, you will find truth in those judgments, and they will help you to see, accept, and experience yourself even more clearly.

7. You are a holistic being consisting of heart, body, mind, and soul. These components communicate with you through the vehicles of emotion, sensation, thought, and intuition respectively. Use the *inner scan* technique to elevate your awareness of the messages and therefore to have

a deeper understanding of who you are and your place in the universe.

8. The one "universal truth" is the statement *I Am*, which is pure consciousness creating, recognizing and acknowledging itself. All other truths emanate from this core truth. When you use this statement, whether consciously or unconsciously, you engage the universal engine of creation which manifests everything that shows up in your life.

9. When you engage the *I Am* engine consciously, you activate a process of *conscious self-creation*. Intentional *self-reflection, self-definition, self-declaration,* and *self-expression* allow you consciously to design and walk your own path of growth and evolution to whatever level you choose.

10. Projection-based communication is the realm of unconscious behavior, and represents a self-disownment of sorts because the ego-mind is allowed to run the show. Use *self-aware communication* tools to express yourself consciously according to your desired image of yourself. Avoid victim language and comparatives, and take full responsibility for your own thoughts, words, actions and feelings.

THE IDENTITY KEY

You are not any of the things that your ego-mind would have you believe, no matter how logical, sensible, and credible they may seem. You are beyond definition, beyond description, beyond limitation. Let the following affirmation help you to remember who you really are:

> **I am a magnificent, divine, boundless spiritual being of light and love, sharing in the wondrous experience of the human adventure, and I remember this truth in every moment.**

CHAPTER 3: CHOICE

MAKE CONSCIOUS AND RESPONSIBLE CHOICES

to choose & declare

everything is choice
   there is nothing else

   each moment is a decision
balanced on the cusp of creation

                              by my choice
(whether *take* or *mis-take*)
                        i declare myself

here and now

                              by my choice
(whether *conscious* or *un-conscious*)
                              i express

who i am

there may be fear around this choice
      or sadness
      or shame
      or anger
      or even tremendous joy

   whatever resides
                  beneath it or within it
   is merely a part of the gift
      i invite for myself

when i step into this gift

                        face it
                  welcome it
               and embrace it

when i choose intentionally
> *accept it*
> *own it*
> *and embrace it*

when i show up
> in vulnerability and truth

then i am free
and i rejoice

for immediately another choice
appears
> before me

a chance to do it all over again
> another opportunity

to
choose & declare

DECISIONS, DECISIONS

Somewhere along the way during my path of awakening, I had the new aware-ness that my entire life was essentially just a continuing series of choices. I hadn't really thought about my power of choice before that, and when I finally came around to this way of thinking, it was a head-slapping moment for me. I can still remember the feeling of my eyes opening wide as I heard a voice in my head telling me:

> *Every decision you make in your life—no matter how informed you are, no matter how mature you are—is your decision, for better or worse, regard-less of the outcome that it creates. This is true for all decisions, whether you make them consciously or unconsciously—including decisions about what you think and believe.*

In retrospect, this seems like a completely self-evident statement to me, but I had been living much of my life in a mostly unconscious way, so I wasn't really thinking about my choices from a place of awareness. Most of my choices up until that time were pretty automatic, as if I had been operating on autopilot.

What do you think and feel as you read this statement? Does it resonate for you, or do you find yourself resisting it in some way?

I don't blame you if you find this to be a difficult idea to accept. Perhaps you were abused or mistreated at some point in your life, and as a result you may have made choices about yourself or about your situation or about the world at large in order to keep yourself safe. Good for you! I'd say that was a perfectly normal thing to do, especially when you were young and knew so little about the world.

Or perhaps you can recount situations in your life when you felt that you really had no choice at all, that you were "forced" into some action by something or someone outside of yourself. This, too, is pretty normal. I think we all experience this sense of powerlessness from time to time.

Or perhaps, like me, you were trying to please the people who mattered to you in your life, and you decided to put yourself on hold so that you could support them in a way that made you feel better. This, too, is a relatively common way to approach life.

But, truly, regardless of any situation you may have found yourself in, at every turn, you were faced with a choice, and at every turn you chose whatever made the most sense to you in the moment—according to who and what you imagined yourself to be at that time.

OPTIONS VS CHOICES

This brings up something that most of us don't think about very much, and that is the distinction between options and choices.

At any given moment, when we are about to decide what's next for us, the first thing we do is look at whatever options are available in the moment. The choice is right there in front of us, but we haven't yet made our selection, so what do we do? We examine all the options, perform some kind of assessment about the risk/reward associated with each one, and then decide which of them seems most likely to provide us with the outcome we're hoping to produce. So an option is one entry in a list of possible selections, and a choice is the option we actually select.

At any given choice point, we always have options. They may not always be easily discernible, but they are always there. Whether we see options or not depends on a lot of factors such as:

- Our current state of spiritual evolution;
- Our level of experience with a particular situation;
- Our degree of understanding of how the world works;
- How well we understand what serves us and what serves the greater good.

If this is not enough, we sometimes make our choices instinctively, without really looking at the options that are available to us. Because this happens somewhat unconsciously, we may not be aware of all the data that is available and so we can end up selecting options that actually produce unexpected and undesirable outcomes.

Regardless of where you might be on this continuum, I think it's important to remember that, whenever you made a decision in your life, you may have had faulty, incorrect or insufficient information, and so you made your selection based on whatever information was available at that time. I'm certain you did not deliberately make a defective choice; rather, you did the best you could under the circumstances; you did the best you could based on who you were at the time.

Every Choice Produces Results

The instant a choice is made, you immediately start bringing your thoughts, words, actions and emotions into the picture in order to begin manifesting that choice. In a very short time, you start to see outcomes that come about as a result of your choice. Some of these outcomes are expected, but some of them are not. Some are intended; some are not. But regardless of the intention behind any particular outcome, it is clear that your choice contributed (at least in part) to that consequence.

I think it's pretty easy to see that every decision you make is your own choice, and therefore your own responsibility. But can you also see that every outcome and consequence resulting from that choice—intended or not—is also your responsibility?

Take a breath for a moment. Don't berate or criticize or judge yourself for this; just notice that your choice starts a chain of events that leads to certain outcomes, and be willing to take responsibility for those results.

The moment you accept responsibility for your choices and the outcomes they create, you will immediately begin to feel a sense of freedom and power. Why? Because you will begin to realize that you have the capacity to shape your world the way you want to. And what could be more empowering and liberating than that? Imagine what your life could be like if you were to make every choice from a place of knowing who you really are. Imagine the quality of your creation if you choose from a place of unequivocal responsibility.

CHOICE IS PERMANENT

Making a choice is similar to throwing a rock into a pond. Once the rock is out of your hand, it is already in motion and it will have whatever impact it has. When it lands in the pond, ripples will move outward in all directions from the point of impact and those ripples will also have impact of their own. Try as you might, you cannot *unthrow* the rock!

In the same way, you cannot *unchoose* something. Once the choice is made, all the thoughts, words, actions and emotions of that choice begin impacting the world and the universe in irreversible ways.

No need to panic! Remember, in the next moment, you have a new choice point. You may recognize that your earlier choice didn't quite work out as planned, so you can learn from the decision you made, add this new knowledge to your experience, and then make a new choice accordingly. So, even though you might imagine that you are "changing your mind", in reality all you are doing is making a new choice in the current moment, based on new information.

CHOICE INFORMS THOUGHTS, WORDS, ACTIONS AND EMOTIONS

Every choice you make informs and triggers thoughts, words and actions that lead to the fulfillment of that choice, and to the emotions that come about as you engage those thoughts, words and actions. When you make your choice consciously, you increase the likelihood of engaging corresponding thoughts, words, actions and emotions consciously too. This strengthens your awareness, understanding, and acceptance of who you are right now, which in turn makes future choices for your life much easier to discern.

CHOICE *REFLECTS* IDENTITY

Every choice you make is a direct expression of who you really are right now. Are you responsible for who you are? Of course you are! So take responsibility for your choices too, and empower and liberate yourself in the process. Let your choices joyfully express the truth of who you are—and if you don't like what you see when you look at that expression, then choose consciously to do whatever you need to do to bring all of your choices back into alignment with who you really are.

But be careful! Remember, your choices do not *define* you; they merely *express* an aspect of who you are in the moment you make them. Don't be tricked by your ego-mind into thinking you are your choices; choices are simply things you create; they are not who you are.

TAKING RESPONSIBILITY

Once you are clear about who you are, and recognize that you are constantly making choices in accordance with who you are, accepting responsibility happens more or less automatically. If you don't really know who you are, it's easy to abdicate your own sovereignty and assign responsibility to others. But when you know beyond doubt who you really are, it actually becomes harder to blame others, and it becomes very clear how your thoughts, words, actions, and emotions are your own responsibility—no matter how much influence someone else has in your life.

This is an important awareness, and the more you embrace it and practice it, the easier it becomes. And what is interesting is that you can use the idea of self-responsibility as a kind of test for checking in with yourself on any issue that is happening in your life. When I'm struggling with something, for example, I find it very helpful to go into a quiet meditative state. I do whatever I need to do to quiet my mind and get present to what is happening in the here and now. When I get to a quiet place, then I ask myself this very powerful question:

> **How did I invite this into my life, and what am I hoping to learn from the experience?**

Yes, the question pre-supposes that I made a choice (or perhaps numerous choices) somewhere along the way that created space for my current circumstances to show up. I'm acknowledging with this question the possibility that I may have made the choice(s) unconsciously, and so I'm asking my Soul—my *Inner Authority*, my connection to *Source*—to help me understand my creation and how it came into being. Notice that the question doesn't contain any inherent judgments or criticisms—it is just a formulation of my curiosity, designed to engage my Higher Self and to help me learn.

Powerful, open-ended questions like this—especially when they are free of judgment or assumption—allow you to bypass the critical babble of your ego-mind and to descend into the truth of your heart and soul. And the answers that come up are almost always revealing. By asking questions like this, you make it clear to the Universe that you are willing and able to take full responsibility for whatever happens in your life, and this helps to reduce fear and anxiety, while empowering and encouraging you to step more fully into who you really are.

When you ask questions like these, you create a temporary vacuum of knowledge that demands to be filled. *OMnitude* responds instantly by searching in Its Library for all of the information that, when presented to you, will help you to understand what it is you want to know. The key—from your perspective—is to be open to the answer, knowing that it might not come immediately. It also helps to remember that the answer may not arrive in a way that you will immediately recognize. Synchronicity is your friend, and often, answers show up where you least expect them. For example, you might overhear a conversation between two strangers that speaks directly to the issue you are trying to understand. Or maybe you'll hear a song on the radio that seems to be playing just for you. Or perhaps you'll see a billboard on the highway with a caption that means something that resonates deeply within you. The possibilities are endless.

The main thing to remember is that, when you ask a powerful, curious, non-judgmental, open-ended question—complete with a deep desire for a real answer—then the answer *will* come to you. More accurately, the answer is already there within you (because you are always connected to *Source*), so in truth it will simply materialize in your awareness. But because of interference from your ego-mind, you may not be completely open to the answer, and so you may experience some of the synchronicities I mentioned earlier. *OMnitude* insists on giving you what you ask for!

When you take responsibility like this, and ask the Universe to help you understand your own creation, you always receive an answer that helps you to understand more clearly how you were expressing yourself, how you were showing up. That is, what you were doing through your creation—even if you did it unconsciously—was expressing who you were in that moment. The answer that you get back allows you then to experience yourself as that, because it reminds you that you could not have made *any* decision at all that was inconsistent with your existing model of the world, or with who you were in that moment.

This is a complex but powerful awareness, and it has a lot of subtleties embedded within it. I'd recommend that you read this section a few times and pause after each read to allow it to sink in.

The Responsibility Cycle

As I began practicing the skill of taking responsibility, and consequently becoming more aware of how I had been showing up, I found that an interesting cycle revealed itself to me:

> The more I take responsibility for my life, the more I know and understand myself. The more I know and understand myself, the more I declare, express and experience myself. The more I declare, express and experience myself, the more I take responsibility for my life.

I can't tell you in strong enough terms how important this cycle is. I've seen many people wake up to this cycle in their own lives, and to understand how it really works. The benefits of understanding this cannot be overstated.

It helps to consider each sentence on its own, and to recognize that *responsibility* leads to *self-knowing*, which leads to *self-expression*, which leads in turn to

Figure 13—The Responsibility Cycle

more *responsibility*, as depicted in the diagram. But because it is a cycle, you can choose consciously to start at any node, and then to move in a clockwise direction to the next node.

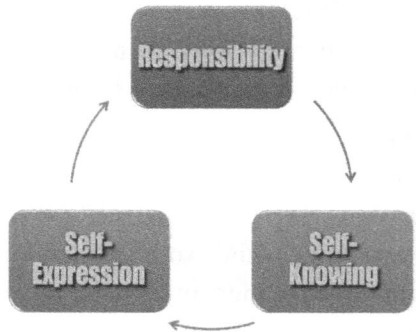

By engaging the cycle consciously, you empower yourself to know and express continually evolving versions of yourself, and to develop deeper and broader responsibility for all of who you are.

As you can easily see, the *responsibility cycle* is pretty tightly coupled with the *conscious self-creation* cycle we discussed in the last chapter. Each of these cycles informs and empowers the other. By maintaining your awareness of both of these cycles and recognizing where you are in each one, you actually empower yourself to take responsibility for all aspects of your life so that you can move consciously from one version of who you are to the next.

CONSCIOUS, RESPONSIBLE CHOICE

The ultimate form of responsibility is to make all of your choices consciously. This really means looking at each choice as objectively as possible, and evaluating each of the options with respect to a few important questions:

1. What are the likely positive and negative consequences of selecting this option?
2. Do the positives outweigh the negatives enough to justify selecting this option?
3. Am I willing to accept full responsibility for *all* of the consequences I create by selecting this option?
4. Does my selection of this option clearly reflect who I really am?
5. Is this option aligned with my purpose?

Initially, it may seem like a fair amount of work to go through this exercise for every choice that you are about to make. But like anything else, the process becomes easier with practice. The real benefit here is that you become more aware of your choices in any given moment, and you have a more complete perspective of what you are likely to create before you actually commit to a particular option. And as you gain experience performing the evaluation, you become more skilled at it—to the point where you can actually complete the evaluation very quickly. And then, when you do make your choice, you do so from a place of greater awareness and responsibility.

CHAPTER SUMMARY—CHOICE

If you'd like to know what your choices have been, look at yourself and the life you have lived.—**Shad Helmstetter**

You are not stuck where you are unless you decide to be.—**Wayne Dyer**

Always go with the choice that scares you the most, because that's the one that is going to help you grow. —**Caroline Myss**

HIGHLIGHTS

1. Everything you think, say, do or feel begins with a choice. Every single moment is a choice point. You can choose unconsciously, and imagine that life just happens to you; or, you can choose consciously, and begin creating the life that you want.

2. Before you make a choice, you are presented with options, even if you don't necessarily recognize them as such. Normally, you evaluate each option against your own risk/reward metric, and then choose the option that seems likely to produce the best outcome.

3. Choice cannot be undone. If you don't like the outcome that you created by a particular choice, then you can choose something different in the next moment.

4. Choice determines your thoughts, words, actions and emotions. To live consciously and to grow intentionally, you must take responsibility for all your choices.

5. Every choice you make is a direct expression of who you are in that moment. The choice itself is not who you are, but it is your creation, and therefore it is a temporary representation of who you are.

6. If you have doubt about what is showing up in your life or how you might have created it, a great question you can ask yourself is "How did I invite this into my life, and what am I hoping to learn from this experience?" By asking this question, you indicate your willingness to take full responsibility.

7. Remember that the responsibility cycle and the conscious self-creation cycle complement each other in a powerful way. Take advantage of the synergy between these two cycles so as to inform and empower all your choices.

8. Your choice is your responsibility. As you become clearer about who you really are, taking responsibility for who you are and the choices you make

becomes easier. Because you recognize that you can no longer blame others for your situation, taking responsibility begins happening automatically.

9. The ultimate form of responsibility is to make all choices consciously and intentionally.

The Choice Key

Every moment represents a *choice point*—that is, an opportunity to make a new choice and create a new direction for your life. Every choice you make reflects who you are choosing to be in the current moment, whether you do so consciously or unconsciously. As you become more adept at choosing consciously, you become more aware of who you really are and how you are showing up in the world. At the same time, you become more skilled at recognizing the consequences of your choices quickly, which allows you to make adjustments more readily. As you practice the art of conscious, responsible choice, remember the following affirmation:

> **I am blessed with unlimited freedom to make all my choices consciously and intentionally, and I courageously take full responsibility for the results that they create.**

CHAPTER 4: COMPASSION

DEVELOP COMPASSION FOR YOURSELF AND OTHERS

Love Just Smiled

Love walked in the back door
And sat herself down in my easy chair
    As if she owned the place
He put his feet up on the coffee table
    And then just smiled at me
A rather mysterious smile, I thought

Of course, I recognized her
    She was strange and familiar at the same time
I was stunned in my own silence
    Though I tried clumsily to find some words

Love just smiled

As I squirmed and shuffled in his presence
I caught a glimpse of my reflection in the mirror
    My breath hitched momentarily
As I realized how much we looked alike

Love just smiled

Tears welled and flowed from me
Free and judgeless and pure
And the longing in my heart seemed to break open

Love smiled and stood up

Love is no accident, she said
Love doesn't just happen randomly, he said
Love is a choice, she said
A choice, pure and simple, he said

Love looked at me,

    Penetratingly
    Ruthlessly
    Compassionately

What choice will you make? she asked

Love smiled once more

And then turned away,
As if to leave

No!
I screamed silently in my head
No!
I could not speak
I could not move
No!

Love turned back toward me
And placed a hot hand upon my chest

A choice, he said, softly

Her hand and her gaze rested on me for a long time
As my tears slowed to a trickle
And my heart swelled in the warmth

After a time, his physical presence gently faded
Until he vanished completely
But the warmth on my chest remained
And my heart blossomed
Even as my tears began to dry

I dropped into the chair where Love had been sitting
I put my feet up on the coffee table
The sweet warmth would not leave my chest
I marveled at the choice I was making

And Love just smiled

A FOREIGN CONCEPT

The word "compassion" is one of those words that lots of people like to use liberally without necessarily knowing what it means. I know this because I was one of those people! Intellectually, I understood the accepted meaning of the word, but what it represented was a foreign concept to me. It was much like hearing from a friend about an amazing dish he'd eaten at a restaurant the night before—even if I recognized some of the ingredients in the recipe, I'd still have no idea what it might taste like until I eventually tried it for myself. Compassion was like that for me: I had to have the experience of compassion before I finally understood what the word "compassion" actually meant.

That experience came for me during a support group I attended in the late 1990s, where I was witnessing a man doing some healing work on one of his core wounds. His emotional wound was similar to one of my own, so I was able to empathize and resonate with his work in a way that was new to me. I was feeling the same kind of emotional energy that he said he was feeling; at the same time, I found myself rooting for him to find his way to healing, and wanting to help him find relief from his suffering. I didn't really understand until after the process was over that I had been having a visceral experience of compassion.

Compassion vs Empathy vs Sympathy

Some people mistakenly interchange the words compassion, empathy and sympathy when they speak. Actually, these are quite different concepts, although they do have some common elements and they sometimes trigger similar emotional responses within us.

Sympathy

The word *sympathy* comes from an assimilated form of *syn* ("together") and *pathos* ("feeling") and means literally, "feeling together" or "community of feeling". In modern usage, however, the word has come to mean "feeling sorry for someone else's hurt or pain". Because we are simply feeling sorry, we create a certain degree of emotional distance from the other person, and we may even fall into a place of pity that can unintentionally disempower that person.

Empathy

The word *empathy* derives from an assimilated form of *en* ("in") and *pathos* ("feeling") and comes to us originally from the art world, in which art appreciation was assumed to depend on the viewer's ability to project his/her personality into the viewed object. In current usage, the word implies that when we witness someone else's hurt or pain, we don't simply feel sorry about it; instead, we actually experience our own hurt or pain in response (i.e. we *project* our own pain onto the situation). This clearly requires more emotional investment than sympathy, and acknowledges our shared experiences as human beings. To feel empathy, we need not actually have the same experience as the other person, but we do need the ability to imagine the suffering s/he is going through, which is what triggers our own internal emotional response.

Compassion

The word compassion is derived from the Latin past participle stem *compati* which means quite literally "to suffer with". The idea of a shared experience of suffering implies a strong element of empathy, but compassion also embodies a desire to take some positive action to reduce the suffering. In other words, compassion can be described as a simplistic mathematical formula:

$$\text{Compassion} = \text{Empathy} + (\text{Desire to Help})$$

As the formula indicates, compassion includes a strong action component, which makes it clear that it is not the same thing as either sympathy or empathy.

Beyond the Emotion

While empathy is an ability to experience vicariously the pain or suffering of another person, compassion includes an ability to move beyond the feelings into some form of action that is intended to reduce the suffering. Compassion doesn't have boundaries: it reaches out to all people, whether they are friends or not, and even beyond people to other living creatures. This is a direct consequence of the fact that we are *All One* and we are all connected to each other.

The interesting thing about compassion is that the action itself isn't required; all that's required is the *desire* to act. This is an important distinction. Whether you actually respond to your desire to act is simply a choice that you make after you feel so moved. Remember, someone who is experiencing something that resonates within you as pain or suffering may not necessarily want any help. The other person may decide that it is important to go through the full experience and that your help might actually get in the way. So, if you are moved to act, it's really important to consider what the other person wants before you make your choice. This is part of the option evaluation process we talked about in the last chapter.

Cultivating Compassion for Others

Compassion presumes love and respect for others, irrespective of their beliefs, gender, race, religion, or nationality. It implies unconditional acceptance and positive regard—something that we discussed in detail in Chapter 1—and if we can embrace these ideals, then we can experience compassion for others even if we don't agree with their words, actions, perspectives or beliefs. Compassion is essentially a process of recognizing, accepting and responding to the perception of pain or suffering.

1. Connect to Empathy

The first step in cultivating compassion is to develop and strengthen empathy. Most humans are naturally endowed with this skill, so for most of us it shouldn't be a terribly difficult task. Unfortunately, when we are stressed out about our own lives or worried about making ends meet, then we can become distanced from our empathy muscles. Our ego-minds begin chattering about all the problems that we have, and this impedes our ability to connect with whatever might be going on for someone else. It can take practice to quiet our ego-minds enough so that we can remember our connections to everyone else around us. I've actually found that bringing my awareness to someone else's situation helps me to realize that my own problems are often pretty minor, and this helps me open my eyes to things that might be much more serious in that person's life. This just naturally tends to quiet my ego-mind and brings me into fairly rapid reconnection to my empathy.

If you have difficulty connecting to your empathy, try visualizing the other person as an extension of yourself. Imagine this person (let's use the name "Joe", for example) in your mind's eye, and imagine saying things like this to yourself:

1. Joe is doing the best he can with the resources he has available, just like me.

2. Joe is experiencing grief/sadness/upset/pain about this situation, and I've experienced similar pain in my life.

3. Joe really wants to be free of this pain and suffering, just as I would.

4. Joe wants to be happy and fulfilled in his life, just like I do.

5. Like everyone else on the planet, Joe is learning, evolving and growing.

6. I offer unconditional love and healing to Joe, so that he can move out of pain and into happiness.

You can add whatever additional phrases you like that make sense to you. As you say these words, feel your heart opening, and allow yourself to experience whatever emotions come up on their own. Imagine Joe's pain and suffering simply falling away, and see Joe in a happier state of mind. As you do this, notice how your own state of mind changes.

2. Identify the Suffering

Once you have activated your empathy and you can see the other person from a place of unconditional positive regard, then you can more easily recognize and understand the struggle that person is going through. Sometimes this is quite obvious and you'll have no trouble recognizing and identifying the other person's suffering—especially if it resembles something that you have experienced in your own life. But sometimes the other person's experience doesn't really correlate to anything that has happened in your own life, so you may not be able to fully understand, at least not right away. When this happens, you have to use your imagination, while at the same time projecting yourself into the other person's experience. In other words, you seek to *walk a mile in the other person's shoes.*

Opening your heart to someone else's suffering is something that you probably do often enough that you already know what I'm talking about. But even if it's not something that is resonating in your memory at the moment, it is not as hard as you might imagine. Consider a couple of examples.

- You may never have broken a bone in your body, but I suspect that, if you witnessed someone else falling and breaking an arm or a leg, you'd have a pretty strong reaction in your own body, because you'd know at a very deep level what kind of pain the other person would be feeling.

- Or, imagine someone who has been accused of a murder s/he did not commit. This is such a rare occurrence that I'd bet you've never had that happen to you. Yet, I'm sure you can imagine the pain and humiliation— and perhaps even hopelessness—you might be experiencing if you some-how ended up in that situation.

- Or, maybe someone lost a loved one, perhaps to a debilitating disease. You may not have had that exact experience in your life, but you've al-most certainly had a relationship come to an end and probably had some-one leave your life, so you know the pain of that loss.

You see, to understand someone else's suffering is not nearly as difficult as you might have thought. You can almost always relate one person's experience to something similar in your own life—and even if that isn't possible, you can use your imagination to help you connect to something similar in your life. Once you make the connection, then your own empathetic response shows up almost automatically, and you likely have a clearer understanding of what the other person is going through.

3. Recognize the Desire to Act

With an empathetic understanding of the other person's suffering, you will likely find yourself moving into "problem solving" mode. You've recognized a problem with potentially dire consequences, and the loving, compassionate part of you wants to help alleviate the pain and the suffering.

As you're experiencing your desire to act, it's important to notice that you don't *actually* have to do anything—unless of course something life-threatening is taking place, in which case you may be inclined to respond immediately. But most of the time, your desire to act is just a response that you are experiencing in your own awareness. As you become more aware of this desire, you can focus attention on it and understand more deeply what this desire is all about.

4. Decide the Action to Take

It bears repeating that, unless a life-threatening event is taking place, you needn't be in a hurry to act on your desire. Not only that, but sometimes people need to have the full experience of their suffering in order to benefit from whatever lesson life is bringing to them. If you give in to your desire to act without really considering the potential ramifications, you may actually take someone out of his/her experience and thus deprive him/her of the opportunity to learn and grow.

While it may seem obvious that someone needs or wants help, I often find that the best course of action is to check in with the person before I act. I usually do this by engaging the person with some kind of connecting statement that asks *permission* to offer assistance; this approach empowers the other person to choose whether or not to accept some help. For example, "Hey, Barbara, it looks to me like you are having some difficulty here. Can I offer you some support?"

If Barbara says no thanks, then you can move on, knowing that you've acknowledged your own desire to act in a way that doesn't disempower her. On the other hand, if she says yes please, then you can follow up with another great question such as "What kind of assistance would you like?" This question continues to empower the other person by allowing her to decide exactly how much assistance she wants and what that might look like.

Practice, Practice, Practice

The four steps I've outlined above are pretty easy to integrate into your life. You may already be doing some or all of these things right now. Regardless of where you are in your compassion continuum, you can always improve your level of skill, particularly if you can remember to approach every situation from a place of acceptance and empowerment—that is, empathetically accepting a person wherever s/he is at and offering only the kind of assistance or support that is actually requested.

CULTIVATING SELF-COMPASSION

If you can develop compassion for others—and believe me, you *can!*—then you can go a step further and develop compassion for yourself, although for many of us this can be quite a challenge.

The first thing to understand is that self-compassion is not about self-pity, self-criticism, self-indulgence, or self-centeredness—those are all ego-centric focuses that actually keep us from the truth of who we really are. On the contrary, self-compassion is about seeing things in our lives exactly as they are, and allowing our awareness to bring us into a loving, accepting and healing relationship with whatever might not be working for us. It's not about whining or complaining; it's about recognizing and accepting our own pain and suffering for what it is, understanding the behaviors that may have brought the suffering into being, and then moving into inspired and loving action to re-align our behaviors with what really serves us.

In Chapter 1, we looked at the cost of self-rejection, and this led to a number of concepts, ideas and processes that help us to become more accepting of ourselves. It turns out that the things that keep us from accepting ourselves are the same things that keep us from feeling compassion towards ourselves: mainly self-criticism and self-rejection.

The ego-mind makes it very easy for us to identify things that we judge as flaws, weaknesses, blemishes and shortcomings. And when we focus our attention on those things, it's almost as if we have put on blinders that make it very difficult for us to see our gifts, strengths, and abilities. More than that, when we find ourselves in a painful struggle, the ego-mind is pretty quick to point out all the reasons that we created the situation for ourselves, while at the same time suggesting that we actually deserve our suffering. When we get caught in this cycle, we have difficulty connecting to any semblance of compassion, let alone self-compassion.

Now I should mention that self-acceptance and self-compassion are not the same thing—although, to be sure, the more self-acceptance we have, the easier it is for us to feel self-compassion. (In fact, it might be said that self-acceptance is a prerequisite for self-compassion.) Conversely, any blockage in self-acceptance will also impede self-compassion, so before diving into a practice of self-compassion, make sure you have mastered the processes described in Chapter 1.

The steps I outlined above to cultivate compassion for others are certainly relevant for developing compassion for yourself too. However, as I have already pointed out, the ego-mind's fear-based focus can generate a lot of internal resistance, so there are a few additional elements that I recommend you bring into your process.

1. Remember Our Common Humanity

When we're struggling, it's easy for us to imagine ourselves as isolated and alone. But when you are supporting another person who is suffering, your own compassion helps you to relate to that suffering; you can connect to a sense of common humanity. Well, when you are suffering yourself, remember that your struggles are part of the shared human experience too. So, be willing to see your suffering with the same compassion that you'd see someone else's suffering.

2. Witness Non-Judgmentally

When you are suffering, it really helps if you can detach yourself from the emotional and judgmental aspects of your situation, and step back metaphorically to a place where you can witness what is going on with as little judgment as possible. This is one of the primary steps in acceptance, and indeed the first thing you want to do is unconditionally accept where you are now.

3. Be Kind and Gentle

Bring as much kindness and understanding as you can to your situation. For some of us—thanks to the endless ability of the ego-mind to berate, criticize and demean us—this can be challenging. One thing you can do to alleviate this challenge is to imagine your "suffering self" as another person, and to bring unconditional love and support to that person as if s/he were a good friend. You'd probably have little trouble being kind and gentle with a friend, right? So, bring the same kindness and understanding to yourself.

Try wrapping yourself in a loving hug, and just give yourself permission to feel whatever you might be feeling. Remind yourself that it is okay to feel whatever you feel, and it is definitely okay to express those feelings—in fact, it is necessary to express those feelings in order to move through the pain associated with the suffering.

4. Invite in Healing Energy

As the painful feelings pass through you and eventually diminish, notice that there is now room for something new to replace them. Invite and welcome some form of healing energy to fill the empty space and to give you a sense of positive movement forward in your life. When I do this, I find it helpful to give that healing energy a color and vibration, and possibly even a metaphorical shape. These special attributes give the healing energy a kind of character that I can relate to, and I can call upon it to help me heal myself and help me find creative ways to improve my life.

5. Find the Gift in the Suffering

After the feelings have passed and you've anchored a positive healing replacement, see if you can observe from your place of non-judgmental witnessing whatever gifts may have been present in the situation that led to your suffering in the first place. This is usually a pretty easy exercise when the ego-mind voice of judgment has become silent. It's mostly just a case of looking at the situation and asking yourself what you might have learned from it; after all, every lesson learned can be brought forward into whatever happens next in your life.

BENEFITS OF COMPASSION

I believe that compassion is a natural quality—perhaps even an instinct—that is inherent in almost all human beings; unless you are a psychopath (which is very unlikely), then you are almost certainly capable of experiencing both empathy and compassion. You are very likely also capable of cultivating and deepening your compassion ability, simply though the power of regular practice. Most of us recognize the benefits of compassion at a gut level, but let's just bring some of those benefits into greater awareness.

- Compassion leads to actions that reduce suffering, thereby contributing to the well-being of the whole planet.

- Compassion quiets the ego-mind and opens the heart. This, in turn, facilitates the flow of love from within you—both to others and to yourself.

- Compassion helps to widen perspective, increasing awareness of commonality with others.

- Compassion increases happiness, fulfillment, and wellbeing.

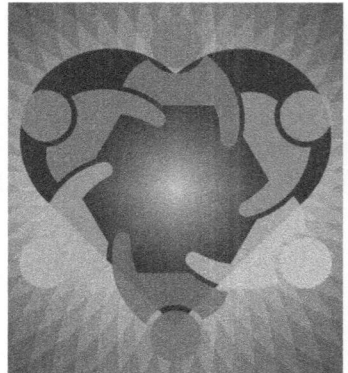

Figure 14—The Gift of Compassion

- Compassion enables and empowers interpersonal connections, leading to improved social, ecological, and spiritual relationships.

- Compassion seems to be contagious—it spreads outwards, inspiring further acts of compassion and kindness when witnessed and experienced.

- Compassion increases the production of DHEA—*Dehydroepiandrosterone*, the "youth hormone"—thus counteracting the aging process, and improving overall health and appearance.

- Compassion decreases the production of cortisol, thus reducing stress and improving all different aspects of life.

- Compassion triggers the release of oxytocin, which heals pain, reduces social fears, increases intimacy, and relieves stress even more.

With all these benefits, is it any wonder that the Dalai Lama once quipped "If you want to be happy, practice compassion"?

Chapter Summary—Compassion

To love our enemy is impossible. The moment we understand our enemy, we feel compassion towards him/her, and he/she is no longer our enemy.—**Thich Nhat Hanh**

Compassion is the ultimate and most meaningful embodiment of emotional maturity. It is through compassion that a person achieves the highest peak and deepest reach in his or her search for self-fulfillment.—**Arthur Jersild**

Compassion is the antitoxin of the soul: where there is compassion even the most poisonous impulses remain relatively harmless.—**Eric Hoffer**

Highlights

1. Compassion is not the same thing as either sympathy or empathy. Rather, compassion can be thought of as "empathy in action".

2. Compassion enables you to experience vicariously the suffering of another person, and to connect to a deep inner desire to reduce that suffering.

3. The desire to act is the important part of the equation; whether you act or not actually depends on whether the other person really wants any help or support.

4. To cultivate compassion for others
   - connect to your own empathy
   - identify the suffering as you understand it
   - recognize your own desire to act
   - decide what action to take…
   - then practice this process over and over.

5. Cultivating self-compassion may be more challenging, so make sure to bring in the following additional steps:
   - remember your common humanity
   - take a step back and witness your own life non-judgmentally
   - be kind and gentle with yourself and your situation
   - invite in healing energy
   - find the gift in your suffering.

6. There are many benefits that derive from an ongoing practice of compassion: reduced stress, increased open-heartedness, deeper connections with others, increase in world-wide well-being, greater sense of happiness and fulfillment.

The Compassion Key

One of the best ways to heal the world, while at the same time expressing who you really are, is to develop a regular practice of compassion. Not only does compassion help the world around you, but it helps you too—often in ways that you might not expect. There are many benefits to practicing compassion, some of them fully backed by scientific experiments, but one thing cannot be denied: by allowing your empathy to grow, you become more aware of your deep connection with others. And as your desire to reduce suffering grows along with the empathy, you naturally seek to express yourself more fully as the truly loving being that you are. So, even though compassion may serve to benefit others, it has a reciprocal effect on yourself, helping you to see and experience yourself as a vital and important force in the universe.

Seek to develop and practice compassion to the maximum extent possible. As you do so, keep the following affirmation in mind:

I am authentically compassionate towards everyone, and I seek always to offer my support from a tender place of loving empowerment.

CHAPTER 5: FORGIVENESS

FORGIVE EVERYONE FOR EVERYTHING ALL THE TIME

Anchors

Enmity is heavy
    like cigarette smoke that gathers
    at the bottom of my lungs
    refusing to budge.

Hatred clings
    and won't let go;
    its survival depends on darkness and shadow
    in my hollow places
    where fear and shame and guilt live.

Evil perpetuates itself
    like mosquito larvae that dance
    upon an innocent lake
    waiting for their moulting moment
    when they can feast
    on my warm sweet blood.

Pain squeezes its way
    into more and more of my photographs
    until I can no longer keep my wallet
    in my pocket.

        They told me this would happen,
           Those who knew more than I;
        When I got old, they said…
        But I refused to believe…

        Hold on long enough, they said,
        And it becomes as an anchor,
        And you needn't hold any longer,
           For it holds you instead.

                I didn't believe…
                I *don't* believe…

> I prefer to believe it's just a suit of clothes
> Or better yet,
> I want to believe it's just body paint
> And that I'll be fine
>
> As soon as I find
> the right paint remover

IT'S ALL ABOUT ME

If each of us is an individuation of *All-That-Is*, as I suggested earlier, then it surely follows that the concept of "I" and "you" and "we" and "they" are just illusions of the physical world that help us to make our way through our lives. In truth, there really is no "I" or "you" or "we" or "they" at the level of the Soul, because, as we saw earlier, we are *All One*. Thus, there is only one *Being* that comprises all of us, in much the same way that the Ocean comprises all drops of water. And that *Being*—what we have referred to as *OMnitude*—is the true "I", or as some spiritual teachings like to say, the "I Am".

If you ponder this for moment, then you may come to realize that there really is only one absolute truth, which is:

I Am.

Your Soul never doubts this statement. And even your fragile ego-mind seems willing to concede that you do exist!

Note that this statement doesn't say "I Was" or "I Will Be". It says "I Am", meaning that I exist now and in every moment.

Now let's take this to the next level. If I exist, and I am *All-That-Is*, then it must follow that everything in the universe is me, and all my thoughts are therefore about me. Even if, in the momentary forgetfulness of my ego-mind, I happen to think something is about you, it is still about me, because you and I are one.

Everything, everywhere, is about me. Because no matter how my ego-mind insists on the illusion, there is no separation between you and me, and therefore, *you* don't really exist—at least not as a separate entity. The only thing that exists is *I*, or more correctly, *I Am*. Therefore, in a very real sense, *"It's all about me!"*

At first blush, this statement may seem like it's coming from a place of ego, and, to be sure, the ego certainly appears to love being the center of attention. But this is not how I mean the statement.

When I take a step back and just observe—without story or judgment or interpretation—then I see that there is *What Is* in the world. Nothing more. Not really. None of the trappings of the mind—merely what is happening right here, right now. Presumably, if you were to step back and look dispassionately at this world from the same perspective as me, you would observe the same thing.

Unfortunately, it's very difficult to step into the role of witness-observer and to shut down the ego-mind altogether. The moment I start observing something, I notice that my ego-mind wastes little time in offering its opinions and judgments and conclusions about what I am observing. There are two things to notice about this:

1. What I am observing is simply my own perspective.
2. What I am thinking about what I am observing is simply my own thought process.

In summary, there is *What Is*, and then there is the story I make up about it. It's clear then that, no matter how I look at it, life—and all of its countless experiences—truly is *all about me*.

The problem is, most of us forget this—and then we live our lives as if the ego-mind's limited perspective is the "real truth". And this has unexpected, usually unintended, and sometimes disastrous, consequences.

I FORGOT ABOUT THIS TRUTH

When I made the decision to materialize on the physical plane, I agreed to abide by the rules of the world, and I allowed myself to take on a physical form, which included an ego-mind. Shortly after I arrived—in my case it happened within the first three years of life on this planet—I got so used to being in the physical world that I forgot about my connection, my oneness with *OMnitude*.

I bought into the illusions of my ego-mind and started living according to the dictates and conditioning of the world around me. I began to accept the opinions and judgments and stories of the other people in the world—people who, to all intents and purposes, seemed separate from me, and more often than not, smarter, stronger, wiser, and happier than me as well. I accepted limitations that others saw in themselves as true for me. I took on beliefs about myself that led me to settle for far less than I was capable of.

And thus began the process of forgetting who I really am.

Perhaps you can relate to this. Perhaps you recognize ways in which you have held yourself back in your life. Perhaps you can see patterns in your life that have kept you from fulfilling your amazing potential. Perhaps you can see how you, too, forgot who you really are.

BECOMING A VICTIM

As I unconsciously allowed more and more of my own truth to fall away, as I allowed myself to become subservient to my ego-mind, my life filled up with endless *gotta*s, *hafta*s, *should*s and *must*s:

- I *gotta* do this.
- I *hafta* feel this way.
- I *should* be more like that other person.
- I *must* believe that.

And of course, all of these unconscious limiting beliefs were fueled by another, more pernicious one:

- I *hafta* continue doing all these things so as to get everyone's approval and be welcome in society.

For me, this was the way unconscious thinking showed up. For the longest time, I wasn't aware of these patterns in my life, and I wasn't aware of the impact they were creating in the world around me. In my sleepy unconsciousness, as I tried hard to honor what I thought society wanted from me, I ended up discovering that there was no way to satisfy all the demands that were imposed on me from outside myself. As a result, I ended up with the only possible outcome: disappointment and failure! I disappointed the world, and the world disappointed me. I was a failure at this "being human" thing that I had signed up for!

What I hadn't yet realized was that I had given my sovereignty away. I had essentially given everyone and everything around me permission to run my life. I had given my power away—and I didn't even know it! And of course, since everyone else was shaping and directing my life the way *they* thought it should be, my life didn't look like anything I really wanted. And so, when it occurred to me that it was impossible for me to win, I began playing what I call the *BS Game*. (And of course by *BS*, I mean "blame-shame"!)

Thanks to a very clever ego-mind, I quickly fell into the habit of blaming other people—most notably my parents and my siblings and my friends—for their failure to support me and love me the way I wanted to be supported and loved. I would blame the world for not making space for me to show up the way I wanted to—for forcing me into a mold that simply didn't fit. And of course, I blamed God—for anything else that didn't fall into one of the two other categories.

I became very good at pointing the finger outward—at just about anyone or anything that was within my field of view—and trying to hold all of them responsible for what was happening in my life. And when those others refused to take responsibility for my situation—when they would not accept my accusations of blame—then I would resort to shame. I would withdraw in an attempt to make people feel bad. I would make up stories and gossip about people who had failed to help me out. I would terminate relationships with people because I wanted to hurt them. And if there was no way for me to avoid interacting with them, I would inevitably find myself using demeaning, sarcastic language.

And all of this because I was hurting inside—but did I do anything about that? No, I chose to become defensive—and for me the best defense was a good offense, so my way of defending myself became a process of pushing everyone else away from me—in a way that I hoped would shame them and cause them pain and suffering—all the while expecting them to stay close, love me and make my life better!

As this pattern repeated and became second-nature to me, I was slipping deeper and deeper into anger and hatred and depression. In retrospect, it is easy to see that I was creating my own suffering. All the pain and dissatisfaction and unhappiness was of my own making. But I was in denial when it was happening, and I was so caught up in the illusory stories of my ego-mind that I was unable to see how much I had been giving my own power away. In truth, I had no idea what I was really doing, and consequently, there was no way for me to recognize my suffering as my own creation.

The Wakeup Call

I already shared what happened when I arrived at the end of this road—it led to an incident with my sister that slapped me awake in a most painful and disconcerting way. As I look at the situation today, it reminds me of a movie in which a curious young kid goes into a dilapidated old house—and everyone in the audience knows at a gut level that this is absolutely a very bad idea. But the kid's mind is made up and his curiosity has gotten the better of him, and we in the audience know we're in for a wild and potentially painful ride that will probably end in disaster.

Luckily for me, a wakeup call did happen, and I was able to get out of my own haunted house, and begin the process of healing myself and repairing the damage I'd done to so many lives.

The Process Begins

As I began the process of doing my inner work and reclaiming my sovereignty, I found that I still had a lot of beliefs about others being responsible for my situation. I had quite audible voices chattering in my head, telling me things like:

- You are not smart enough.
- You will never be able to satisfy anyone's expectations.
- You are mean and nasty.
- You are a total loser.

In some cases, I could recognize the voice as belonging to someone outside of me. Most often, I attributed the words to my mother—because after all, she had been the most influential person in my life. So, even though I had begun to heal my own wounds, I was still blaming others—especially my mother (who had already passed away)—for the conditions of my life.

Then one day, my dear friend Dan asked me point blank: "What purpose does it serve you to blame your mother for anything? She was a human being just like you, doing her best with what she had to lead the best life she knew how to lead. She made mistakes as we all do, but what you fail to remember is that she loved you and she wanted the best for you too. She is responsible for her choices, but you are responsible for your own. So what are you going to do about this? How are you going to release all this blame that is still within you? What do you choose now?"

What a great question! Dan was right, of course! Not only was I giving my power away to anyone I was holding responsible for my situation, but as long as I continued to hold onto my self-righteous thinking, as long as I continued to blame others—no matter how far away they were physically or how distant from me figuratively—then I continued to hold myself hostage in a cage of my own creation. And none of those others could release me from that cage—only I could do that.

"What do you choose now?" The latter part of Dan's question continued resonating within me.

It was obvious to me that the key was in letting go of my judgments and my self-righteousness. The key was forgiveness. This was the solution I had been looking for. I would have to remove all semblance of blame from people and start taking responsibility for my own life. And the only way I knew how to stop blaming people was to forgive them. Pure and simple.

But forgiveness turned out to be a more challenging process than I thought.

CURSE YOU, NEURAL PATHWAYS!

In theory, it is easy to forgive someone. All you really have to do is say the words, "I forgive you." And maybe put a little intention behind the words. Should be pretty straightforward, right?

Indeed, I easily managed to get this far. I could declare—with significant quantities of serious intention—that I was forgiving someone for some transgression that (I imagined) they had committed against me. And I even experienced some internal relief when I went through the exercise. But this wasn't enough to stop the old stories from showing up in my head. Those voices were not easily stilled. Something different had to be done.

Have you ever driven on a well-traveled dirt-road? If so, then you have probably noticed that the roadway isn't completely flat. Where vehicle tires most frequently touch the road, the dirt tends to be pretty thoroughly packed down. Depending on the quality of the road, the tracks can be significantly lower—two or three inches perhaps—than the rest of the road. Any new cars coming along the road will naturally follow these tracks, and the more traffic there is on the road, the deeper the tracks can be.

Well, it turns out that thinking patterns are a lot like these dirt roads.

According to our scientific understanding, the thinking process activates neurons and synapses in the brain, and repeated thinking processes tend to activate the same elements over and over again. The more you think a particular thought, the stronger the neural pathway for that thought becomes. In other words, by continuing to think a certain way, you are effectively creating deep "tracks" in the roadway of your mind.

In some ways, this can be a good thing. For example, it allows you to learn how to walk or swim or ride a bike or drive a car; and then, after you have mastered the skill, you can put it into your subconscious mind and allow yourself to run on autopilot. Imagine if that were not so: you'd have to focus on every step you were taking. You'd have to think constantly about how you were holding onto the handlebars, how to balance yourself on the bike, how to lean when you turn, how to change gears, and so on and so on.

But thankfully, this is not necessary. We are miraculously designed so that we can put such repeated actions into our subconscious, thus allowing ourselves to focus our attention on other things that we consider more important.

Now consider the dirt road again. What happens when you want to change direction, and maybe travel on a different road? In order to turn left or right off your road, for example, you have to use additional energy to overcome the resistance that is created by the tracks. And the deeper the tracks, the more work you have to do. But an even bigger problem is that, unlike physical roads which tend to be quite far apart from each other, neural pathways are extremely close to each other. So, even if you manage to move off your current pathway onto a new one (which may not have been traveled enough to strengthen it), the existing pathways in your brain tend to have a magnetic, attractive effect and you end up being drawn back into old ways of thinking.

This is precisely what happened to me. As I was trying to create a new habit of forgiveness, my mind was being drawn back to my older, stronger habit of blaming and shaming. And because I hadn't developed my forgiveness muscles yet, I wasn't aware of the fact that I was falling into that old pattern, so it took me awhile to figure out what was happening.

It turns out that forgiveness is a lot more than just words. Saying "I forgive you" is not enough; there has to be a real intention behind the words. In my case, my real intention was being masked by my old thinking habits, and even though I really wanted to forgive people, my ego-mind was still spinning its story within my head. My ego-mind still wanted to blame others, to hold them responsible for my situation. I remember hearing a voice whining things like "How can I let them off the hook for what they did to me?" Apparently not only did I want to blame others, but I also wanted to get even with them. I wanted justice!

FORGIVE A TREE

One evening, I remember bringing this very issue to my support group and sharing the kinds of dialogs I was hearing in my head. Out of the blue, Louise asked me, "Could you forgive a tree?"

The question threw me for a complete loop! "A tree?" I asked blankly. "Why would I ever need to forgive a tree?"

"Suppose," she said, "that you had a big apricot tree in your backyard. One day, you come outside and you discover your dog is lying limp beside the tree. As you approach, the truth of the situation dawns upon you that your little dog, whom you loved so much, started eating some of the many apricots that the tree had dropped to the ground, and he got a pit lodged in his throat. He couldn't swallow it and he couldn't spit it out, so he died from asphyxiation because he choked on an apricot pit. Clearly the tree is responsible for creating all the apricots that fell to the ground. Clearly, the tree is responsible for the dog's death. Could you forgive the tree?"

"That's ridiculous!" I protested. "The tree just did what it does—it created apricots. The tree is not responsible for the dog's death. If anything, I'd be the responsible one, because I should have been harvesting the apricots before they got overripe and fell off the tree."

Louise just looked at me with a very slight smile, and nodded compassionately toward me. It took me a few moments, but I finally realized the wisdom that she was giving to me.

The tree was being a tree and doing what trees do. As part of its process, it was creating something that most of us see as a beautiful gift for the world. The dog was being a dog and doing what dogs do. As part of its process, it was curious about all the apricots on the ground and decided to try one out—but being a dog, he probably had no idea about the pit inside and ended up choking himself. In both cases, no forgiveness was necessary because the tree and the dog were simply behaving according to their natures. However, I could see that if I thought that either one of them was in any way "responsible" for what happened, then I could easily forgive them. I could also see that any forgiveness I offered had absolutely nothing to do with either one of them—forgiveness was simply a way for me to release some energy from within myself, and this release was actually a powerful way for me to liberate myself from that self-made cage I talked about before.

"Holy shit!" I exclaimed, making the connection back to my real-life situation. "Now I get it! Forgiveness is not about the other person at all—it's all about me! Forgiveness is not about letting someone get away with something, it's not about condoning their behavior, it's not about forgetting what they've done! Forgiveness is about giving myself permission to free myself from my own pain!"

Take that last statement to heart, *Maestro*:

> **Forgiveness is about giving yourself permission to free yourself from your own pain!**

WHY WE RESIST FORGIVING

One of the single most powerful justifications we create in our minds to withhold forgiveness is that if we forgive, we are in some way agreeing with or condoning someone else's hurtful or damaging actions. If we agree with or condone bad behavior, that implies that we are bad people too. We can't have that, can we? We can't have others thinking ill of us because we are so weak that we choose to forgive someone's misdeeds, right?

Another thing that happens is that when someone does something that triggers pain within us, we tend to consider the other person the cause of our pain, and therefore we find ourselves wanting to get even. The more egregious the situation that causes the pain, the more likely we are to want revenge. And the stronger this desire within us, the more we tend to eschew—and even ridicule—the idea of forgiveness.

Our ego-minds love to hang on to stuff like this, to keep us thinking this way. Why? Because the ego-mind sees danger virtually everywhere, and seeks to keep us from hurting ourselves. But the ego-mind is very short-sighted with its faulty rationalizations, and consequently—if we follow its counsel—it leads us into very real dangers that may in fact be worse than what we were trying to avoid in the first place.

Think about it. How many times have you ever tried to get even with someone and felt good about it? How many times have you ever withheld forgiveness and felt good about it?

For me, invariably the exact opposite has happened. Whenever I went out of my way to get even, my vengeful act would usually end up being more extreme than the original incident—and I'd end up creating far more pain for the other person than had been created for me. And then I'd feel even worse than I did before!

And withholding forgiveness was never an easy task for me either. I actually had to work at it. Usually, it would help if I could maintain inner images of the other person as a demon of pure evil—this would really make it much easier for me to vilify him or her and to create justifications of enmity in my mind.

And then, to make the images much stronger in my own mind, I'd gossip about that person and make sure that my friends knew just what a vile being he or she was.

What I learned—the hard way—was that my failure to forgive was actually causing me more pain than it was causing anyone else. Don't get me wrong, some of my actions certainly caused pain for others—significant pain I'm sure. But in the end, I was the one who was suffering—and all at my own hand. This scenario gives credence to a phrase you may have heard before:

> **Withholding forgiveness is like drinking poison and expecting the other person to die.**

Strangely enough, the ego-mind would rather drink the poison than risk being hurt again by the same person!

But there is a big cost to continuing down this path. For me, I found that my unconscious resistance to forgiveness provided fertile ground in which my anger and resentment could grow—to the point that it began showing up in every new relationship and every new experience in my life. This eventually led me to losing sight of who I really was and therefore having no real sense of purpose in my life. Eventually, I recognized that my pain was leaking out in the form of anger towards everyone in my life, so I ended up leaving the most important relationship of all—the one with my children.

The bottom line is that the ego-mind will give you all kinds of rationalizations for withholding forgiveness. You may be feeling the pain of a transgression, and you may even hold the other person responsible in some way, but the truth is that you will only create more pain by following the advice of your ego-mind. If you want to free yourself from this pain, you can do so through the simple act of forgiving.

WHAT IS FORGIVENESS?

Forgiveness is an intentional decision to release resentment and forgo ideas of revenge. Forgiveness doesn't change history, but it does change the way you relate to that history. You may never forget something that happened to you, but if you are able to forgive—unconditionally—then you can certainly free yourself from the grip of the pain that is associated with that memory. And with that freedom comes an ability to redirect your attention to what truly matters in your life.

Forgiveness *does not* mean that:

- **You have to speak to the other person.** Forgiveness is an act of bravery and courage, an act of the heart. Therefore, it can be totally private. It is about YOU, not about the other person.

- **You forget what happened or was done to you.** Some things that happen in life are so strong and emotional and powerful that there is no way for us to forget them; however, if we can forgive, then over time, the ability to forget will grow stronger.

- **You minimize or justify or ignore or condone any wrong-doing.** Everyone—including you and me—have to take responsibility for our own thoughts, words, actions and feelings; forgiveness does not in any way absolve anyone of that responsibility.

- **You experience immediate healing and instantly begin to trust the other person.** Healing takes time and sometimes it requires help from others. But forgiveness can accelerate the healing process because it frees us from thoughts of revenge and resentment. And the healing may lead to a renewed sense of trust for the other person—but that is merely a possibility, not a necessity.

Forgiveness *does* mean that:

- **You release resentments, grudges and ideas of revenge.** These are the ingredients in the cup of poison I mentioned earlier. By disposing of these ingredients, you free yourself of any further damage that might otherwise happen to you, and this accelerates your healing and recovery.

- **You clear obstacles to your own intentional growth.** By forgiving, you open up the path in front of you and allow your intentional growth to magnify. This in turn leads to a clearer understanding of who you really are and why you are here.

- **You feel your own feelings, and create space for healing.** Giving yourself permission to feel and express your emotions is one of the most powerful and liberating acts of love you can offer yourself. Forgiveness makes this process much easier, and therefore speeds healing.

- **You create more peace, compassion, and grace in your life.** And who doesn't want more of these? As these elements become more prevalent in your life, you automatically begin to appreciate your life more, and this just makes your life continually more enjoyable.

BENEFITS OF FORGIVENESS

As you release the resentment and bitterness associated with a particular wrong-doing, you effectively unblock yourself and create space for healing to quickly emerge within you. You begin to see the benefits within you immediately. But these benefits can magnify in many surprising ways as you continue the forgiveness practice with each new transgression that shows up in your life. Over time, as you sharpen and improve your practice, you will be able to look at your whole life and see many accumulated benefits, such as:

- Reduced stress—and all the health benefits that accrue from that, like reduced blood-pressure, less depression, greater sense of inner peace.
- Strengthened sense of who you really are.
- Deeper connection to your spiritual purpose.
- Higher self-esteem.
- Greater compassion for others.
- Healthier, more fulfilling and longer-lasting relationships.

WHO IS SERVED BY FORGIVENESS?

Many of us think that forgiveness is for the other person—the one we are forgiving. However, this is incorrect thinking.

Think about it for a moment. Unless the act was a conscious and malicious act intended to hurt you, it's quite possible—likely, even—that the other person may have no idea of any kind of wrong-doing. Most of us don't go out of our way to hurt others, so more often than not, transgressions are simply unconscious acts with unanticipated side-effects that were not intended to hurt. Nevertheless, the pain you feel from such an infraction may be very real for you. Still, I think you can see that your act of forgiveness in this case wouldn't make any difference at all to the other person—it can only serve to make *your* life easier.

This is an important realization for all of us, because it means that we can forgive *anyone* in our lives if we choose—including people who are long gone... even people who have died. We do not need those people to be present in order to forgive them. The other person doesn't even need to know about our act of forgiveness—although that may be useful as a step toward rebuilding a trusting relationship if that is what we want.

Your act of forgiveness is for you—and you alone. However, as you have already seen, the benefits you experience cannot help but create improvement in all areas of your life. Thus, your act of forgiveness is an act of love. And love heals the whole world, starting with yourself.

Another thing I find helpful to remember is that everyone makes decisions based on the best information they have available at the time. Since none of us has *all* of the information that we'd like to have at the time that we make our choices, it follows that we sometimes (perhaps frequently) make choices that have unintended negative consequences. Thus, it might be said that, under those circumstances, we just don't know what we're doing! And this, I believe, is the meaning behind Jesus' admonition to:

> **Forgive them, for they know not what they do.**

But let us not forget that, even when we forgive others, we are still doing it for ourselves!

FORGIVENESS BEGETS FREEDOM

The more you forgive others, the more you release yourself from destructive and counter-productive thoughts of vengeance or resentment or getting even. The more you forgive, the more you release yourself from the grip of the fear and pain tied to a particular wrong-doing. Forgiveness provides you with a proven pathway toward freedom—freedom from the ego-mind prison that tries to keep you looking for revenge; freedom from the poison of your own thoughts; freedom from your own fear and hatred. This freedom is just another form of unconditional love—something that you are bringing more consciously into the world, something that heals yourself, and empowers healing everywhere.

FORGIVENESS BEGETS GRATITUDE

Once you forgive a wrong-doing, you immediately open space for gratitude to emerge. This is because you can—if you choose—learn something about yourself. Your response to any situation is always consistent with who you are in the moment, and your decision to forgive provides you with an opportunity to observe that response from a place of unconditional love. You can further decide whether or not you want to change that response in the future. And this gives you an additional opportunity to begin expressing yourself in a way that is more congruent with who you choose to be going forward.

If you take the time to appreciate what you have learned and how you have grown from the experience, you essentially give thanks to a Universe that is providing you with endless opportunities to declare, express and experience the fullness of who you really are.

FORGIVENESS CURES KARMA

Many wise teachers the world over remind us about the *Wheel of Karma*—that is, that every action we undertake sets in motion a universal ripple that eventually brings similar energy towards ourselves. To put it in more colloquial terms, *what goes around comes around.* Or as certain scriptures tell us, *you reap what you sow.* Sometimes the *Karmic Wheel* takes many lifetimes for us to experience what it is we have set in motion; sometimes we can experience the repercussions virtually immediately.

But a big question that many people ask is: *Is there any way to stop or reverse the effects of Karma?*

Well, it turns out that *Karma* is what happens to us when we choose to withhold our forgiveness. By learning how to forgive others, we reduce the effects of *Karma*—in other words, when we forgive, we are actually feeding the kind of energy into the universal ripple that will come back and forgive us.

Even better if we can forgive ourselves directly. Not only can we reduce the effects of *Karma*, but in fact we can stop it altogether! That's because forgiveness is a powerful healing energy that has massive effects everywhere. But don't take my word for it! Learn how to forgive yourself and experience the results directly.

HOW TO FORGIVE

All of this sounds fantastic, doesn't it? And it is, really, although getting there isn't always easy. As I've become more skilled at forgiving, I've noticed a recurring pattern to my process, and it involves the following steps:

- Understand the wrong-doing;
- Acknowledge and validate my judgments and feelings;
- Express and release my emotional energy;
- Own my part in the situation;
- Re-connect to compassion and unconditional love.

Let's look at these one at a time.

Understand the Wrong-Doing

First I try to understand the wrong-doing, and what it is that I find upsetting about it. Sometimes this can be obvious, especially when the perpetrator had a clearly expressed desire to do something to hurt me. But more often than not, the wrong-doing isn't nearly so cut-and-dried, and I need to do some reflection in order to understand it better. In this case, I find that asking myself the right questions, and answering them as objectively as possible, helps me to gain clarity. I usually find the following questions very helpful:

- What exactly happened and who was involved?
- How did the action come about: was it intentional or accidental?
- If it was intentional, do I know the motivation of the perpetrator? Or is that something that I am making up in my own mind?
- What was the direct impact (physical, emotional, psychological) to me personally?
- How much of this impact was a direct result of the perpetrator's choices and actions, and how much of it was a result of my own (ego-mind) thinking patterns?

In asking these questions, I am not looking to blame anyone for anything. And specifically, I'm not trying to make myself wrong for my reaction to the situation. I'm merely trying to gain clarity about my reaction so that I can understand as much as possible about the situation.

Acknowledge and Validate Your Judgments and Feelings

After awareness comes acceptance, as always. Now I have to acknowledge and understand the stories, conclusions, interpretations and judgments that I create in my mind about the person or the situation. I also need to acknowledge and understand the feelings and emotions that are moving within me. Here are questions I find helpful during this step:

- What kinds of thoughts do I have about the perpetrator?
- What feelings and emotions am I experiencing?
- Am I attached to finding justice?
- Do I want to get even?
- Am I considering revenge?
- What do I hope to gain by following through on any of my resentments or vengeful thoughts?

The answers to these questions can be very illuminating. I remember a situation a while back that had me particularly upset with a man I judged to have done me a grave disservice that had the potential of damaging my reputation.

I was trying to get other people in my life to feel my pain and to see this man in the same way that I was seeing him. I wanted those people to agree with me and to judge him as harshly as I did.

When I realized I was doing this, I asked myself that last question: "What do I hope to gain by all of this?" I listened to my ego-mind directly and what I heard was: "I am really pissed! I want this man to feel the pain I feel. I want him to suffer. I want to get even with him. He shouldn't be able to get away with this! I want someone to help me get justice!" And the real interesting thing was, as I listened to that suffering ego-mind voice, what I actually heard was myself as a little boy!

Now, I could have scolded my ego-mind for this, but I didn't do that because I realized that I was just listening to a much younger version of myself that was feeling the pain of being criticized by someone he loved. How could I berate a child for feeling this way? I could not. So, I spoke to my ego-mind like it was that little child and I said out loud, "You know, I totally understand how you feel, and I get that you are angry for what this person did to you. It wasn't fair—in fact, it was downright mean and nasty. No-one should ever be treated that way, so I completely understand your desire to get even. Thank you for sharing this with me."

Express and Release Emotional Energy

At this point, it is very important for me to give myself permission to fully feel and express the energy of all my emotions. If I don't allow this, then I essentially block the emotional energy in my body, and that can cause problems—sometimes severe ones—further down the road. In the example I shared a moment ago, I continued speaking to my inner child.

"It's okay to feel what you are feeling. In fact, it is necessary to feel it, because you cannot *think* your feelings. So go ahead and let those feelings come out in a safe way that doesn't hurt you or anybody else. If you need to make noise or move your body, that's okay too—in fact, sometimes it can make the passage of those uncomfortable feelings a little bit easier."

I was actually outside in my neighborhood taking a long walk when this situation occurred, and by the time I got to this little mini-conversation, most of my anger had subsided and I was feeling a lot of sadness. So I just stood on a hill overlooking the bay, and I started sobbing. As I did so, my body shook from within and I felt as if a huge weight was slowly slipping off my shoulders. It only took me a few minutes, but the passing of the energy out of my body felt so cathartic, and when I was done, I was able to look out into the night sky and breathe the cool air and appreciate that I truly had a great life.

I consciously invited in the healing energy of love to fill the space that was available after all the anger and sadness had passed.

Own Your Part of the Situation

Nothing in our lives occurs in a vacuum. Although none of us is responsible for the thoughts, words, actions or feelings of another person, it's important for us to recognize that our own behaviors may trigger unexpected reactions or responses from them. Does this justify hurtful or potentially damaging behavior? No, but it may help to explain it. So, I like to ask myself some further questions at this point:

- Is there something I did that may have triggered the other person's behavior?
- Was there a part of me that actually sought pleasure in pressing this person's buttons?
- What, if anything, did I do to make matters worse?
- What, if anything, could I have done to improve, mitigate or resolve the situation?

It's important to ask these questions from a place of authentic curiosity, so as to promote understanding. The intention is not to make ourselves wrong for anything we did, but rather to help us gain clarity about our own behaviors. Remember, it is from this understanding that we can choose the next direction for our intentional growth.

In my example above, while I could not identify anything I had done to trigger the man's behavior, I could see that I had done things after the fact to make matters worse, particularly by enlisting the help of others to see this man as the demon that I was seeing. My own behavior was that of an injured child who was looking for an adult to help him get even—and it wasn't until I went through this whole process that I was able to see that for myself.

My thoughts of revenge seemed very petty and nonsensical at this point, and I was now able to see that my earlier anger had clouded my judgment, and that my ego-mind was running the show!

Reconnect to Compassion

Once the emotional energy has passed through us and we have honestly acknowledged our part in the interaction, then we naturally tend to find ourselves recon-
necting to compassion. We are able to see the other person in a very different light. No longer is s/he a "perpetrator" in our mind; s/he's just someone (like us) who is doing the best s/he can with the tools that s/he has in his or her toolkit. We are able to see ourselves in the other person and that person in ourselves.

And from this perspective, it is actually very easy to forgive; in fact, in my case, when I get to this step, forgiveness happens almost automatically. It happens energetically, and

Figure 15—The Blessing of Forgiveness

the words are not even necessary. Nevertheless, it still helps to say the magic words out loud, even if the other person is nowhere near.

"I forgive you."

As I say these words, I imagine my hand on the heart of the other person, connecting and tapping into love, releasing mutual peacefulness into the world.

WALK A MILE IN SOMEONE'S SHOES

Like most things in life, the more you do this practice, the easier it gets. Better than that, as you become more adept at forgiveness, the easier it is to stay connected to compassion for everyone—including yourself.

One thing I've noticed for myself as I've gotten better at forgiving is that, once I release all my reactive ego-mind energy in a situation, I am really able to see the other person as a mirror for myself, as just another aspect of who I am. This is powerful for me because it really allows me to accept the other person as a spiritual being engaged in a human experience, and I can much more easily imagine myself in his or her circumstances. This strengthens my acceptance and compassion and deepens my desire to relieve suffering everywhere on the planet.

And that feels really good to me!

The Ultimate Forgiveness

So many of the people I work with have difficulty with the idea of self-forgiveness. We all seem to have such strong stories in our heads about how we don't measure up that we end up playing the *BS Game* against ourselves. We find all kinds of reasons to make ourselves wrong, to blame or shame ourselves for not being perfect. We hold ourselves responsible for things over which we really have no control, and then we find ways of punishing ourselves for the way things turn out!

Well, not only must we learn to accept ourselves for who we really are, we also need to learn to forgive ourselves. Because the inner chatter won't really ever stop until we find a way to do that.

It's really not as difficult as you might think to forgive yourself. But if you have problems with it, then you can employ the same technique I offered when I discussed self-acceptance: *imagine your "Unforgivable Self" as another person.* Then follow the basic forgiveness steps—with a few minor adjustments.

Understand the Wrong-Doing

In your mind's eye, try to see your *Unforgivable Self* as clearly as possible and with as much empathy as you can. Look at the thoughts, stories, conclusions, interpretations and judgments you may have about *Unforgivable Self* and see if you can come to an objective understanding about the mistake(s), wrong-doing(s), or transgression(s) that seem to be blocking your self-forgiveness. Since you know *Unforgivable Self* better than anyone else does, you should be able to answer these questions:

- What is the story I have about *Unforgivable Self*?
- Is there a real wrong-doing here, or am I just punishing *Unforgivable Self*?
- If there was a real wrong-doing, was it intentional or accidental? What was the true intention behind the action that I'm blaming *Unforgivable Self* for?
- What was the actual direct impact (physical, emotional, psychological) to the other people involved?

Acknowledge and Validate Your Judgments and Feelings

Just as you would when processing forgiveness for another person, consider the judgments and feelings you have about your *Unforgivable Self*:

- What kinds of thoughts do I have about *Unforgivable Self*?
- What feelings and emotions am I experiencing?
- Am I attached to punishing *Unforgivable Self*?
- What am I hoping to achieve by treating *Unforgivable Self* this way?

Express and Release Emotional Energy

Give yourself permission to really feel the emotional energy you are carrying within you. If you allow yourself to feel it and express it, you will find that the harsh judgments will dissipate at the same time. This will open you up to compassion, and you will begin to see your *Unforgivable Self* with as much empathy as you see anyone else.

Own Your Part of the Situation

Because you are trying to forgive yourself, this part is a little bit tricky. The entire situation is all about yourself in this case—in every case actually, but in this situation, there is no external person to blame—so it may seem a little weird to work through this part of the process in the way I'm going to suggest. But try it anyway and see how it works for you. Remember, the focus this time is on yourself, and on how you've been judging, criticizing or blaming *Unforgivable Self*.

Ask yourself questions like these:

- Am I judging *Unforgivable Self* for things that I imagine other people were actually doing? (That is, am I projecting someone else's behavior onto *Unforgivable Self*?)
- Do I take some perverse pleasure in punishing or beating up *Unforgivable Self*?
- How do I contribute to the behaviors of *Unforgivable Self* that I don't like?
- What can I do to let go of my judgments and expectations of *Unforgivable Self*?

Warning: When you go through this part of the process, your ego-mind may jump back on the bandwagon and start amplifying the *BS Game!* You may find yourself wanting to punish yourself even more because you've been punishing yourself! So don't slip into that trap:

> **Don't judge yourself for judging yourself!**

Instead, just notice the judgments, accept them for what they are, and release them. As you do this, begin to see *Unforgivable Self* as another being (just like you!) who is doing the very best s/he can with whatever tools and skills s/he has.

Reconnect to Compassion

Allow all the emotional energy to pass through you, and acknowledge yourself for being willing and able to step back and observe. Honor yourself for being able to see *Unforgivable Self* just as you would see anybody else. Feel yourself filling up with unconditional love, and see yourself embracing *Unforgivable Self*. Recognize and understand that *Unforgivable Self* is actually **completely forgivable**, that in reality there is no such thing as an *Unforgivable Self*. Speak the words "I love you and I forgive you" out loud, and feel yourself re-integrating *Forgivable Self* back into you, so that you are now one complete being again.

Everything is Motivated by Love

As forgiveness comes to you more easily and you begin to experience all of its wonderful benefits, another amazing thing may happen for you as it did for me: a new awareness that love is ultimately at the root of everything. I realize that certain kinds of behaviors may appear to be motivated by anything BUT love, so you may well wonder what I'm talking about here.

Back in 2005 or so, I read Byron Katie's wonderful book, *Loving What Is*. I assimilated many of her powerful teachings, and I began to see love in a way that shifted my approach to coaching or facilitating someone through a difficult issue.

One of my techniques is to engage in a "shadow interview" with subconscious "parts" or "characters" that inevitably show during a client session. I ask these aspects what they are trying to create with their actions, and I find that there is invariably some kind of positive intention driving the unconscious behavior. Usually, the problem is that an old strategy—something that almost always appeared in relatively early childhood—is still being employed, even though it is demonstrably dysfunctional today. In the child state, the person may have found a coping mechanism that actually worked to create a sense of safety, connection or acceptance. But in adult life, that same coping mechanism—which may have evolved into something quite nasty—no longer has the effect it had during childhood, even though the person is unconsciously trying to use it for the same purpose!

When I interview these "parts", I'm almost always told that the positive intention of the behavior is to bring about a greater experience of one of the following: *being, serenity, love,* or *oneness.* I'll speak about this in more detail later, but for now, just understand that, in the bigger picture, the person's unconscious behavior is inevitably motivated by a deeper desire *to give or receive love.*

If you can accept this statement at face value—and particularly as something that might be true about yourself—I think you'll find that forgiveness (and, more importantly, self-forgiveness) will soon come much more easily to you.

A FASTER PATH TO SELF-FORGIVENESS

And here's where the magic really starts to happen. No matter what you're doing in any given moment, or how dysfunctional your behavior might seem, you can always use this knowledge to get yourself back into alignment with your true self.

Start with this premise:

> **Every thought, word, action or feeling is motivated at its deepest level by a desire to give or receive love.**

Then you can always look at anything you are doing and ask a very deep and powerful question:

> **In what way am I trying to give or receive love?**

The answers you get to this question—if you listen carefully—will reveal what it is you are really trying to achieve and let you see that your actions are just a strategy for achieving that. With that information, you can recognize and stop behaviors that you don't like, and replace them with behaviors that will achieve the same goal but in a more functionally loving way.

Imagine the amazing changes you can create with this approach!

Simply by looking for the underlying positive intention (the desire to give or receive love) behind every thought, word, action and feeling—and *honoring* that intention—you can greatly magnify your ability and willingness to both accept and forgive yourself. And with acceptance and forgiveness comes huge relief, because you stop having such high expectations of yourself and begin to see and experience yourself for the truly amazing being you are right now.

A PROACTIVE PRACTICE

An awareness of this fundamental principle—that love motivates everything—can be used to inform all your actions going forward. What if, in every single moment, you paused just long enough to ask yourself another powerful question:

> **How can I bring unconditional love into this situation?**

By asking this question—and allowing the answer to come from within—you effectively prepare yourself to show up in a more functionally loving way. And this will have all kinds of desirable consequences in virtually every aspect of your life.

FORGIVE EVERYONE FOR EVERYTHING, ALL THE TIME

As you continue your practice and become more skilled at it, forgiveness will become a very pleasant and life-affirming habit.

Yes, I hear you thinking, *but what about all the evil in the world? How can I possibly forgive all that?*

I agree that it can be difficult to witness things that seem violent, horrific, and downright evil. But when we allow our outrage to drive our behaviors, we are essentially adding our own fuel to a fire that is already burning out of control. Our anger and hatred cannot possibly heal the situation; the only energy that can heal it is unconditional love. If we can embrace this idea and begin to forgive what we judge to be unforgivable, then we remove our own dysfunction from the equation and begin to add something that can make a huge difference.

To paraphrase what the great teacher Jesus has said,

> **It's easy for us to love our friends and all the things that give us pleasure. But it takes deep understanding and a great deal of courage to love our enemies and all the things that cause us pain.**

And yet, if we are to live fully expressed and fulfilled lives, then we have to get out of our old patterns and start living from a truly loving place.

One Step Further: *Pre-Forgive*

If you want to live a really empowered life, recognize that you will have count-less opportunities to forgive others and yourself. You know that, sooner or later, someone is going to say something about you that simply isn't true. You know that someone will dislike something about you, and behave in mean or nasty ways. You know that people in the world will continue to hurt each other and do things that may seem incomprehensible to you.

All of this stuff will continue until we all wake up and realize who we really are and it may even get worse before it gets better. But you and I have a choice. We can choose to forgive all this stuff *in advance!* That's right, we can remember that everyone everywhere is just another version of ourselves doing their best with the life circumstances that they happen to be living in. We can remember that they are doing their very best to give or receive love in the best way they know how, and we can forgive them. *In advance!*

How much different life will seem when we all learn to do this.

CHAPTER SUMMARY—FORGIVENESS

It's one of the greatest gifts you can give yourself, to forgive.
Forgive everybody.—Maya Angelou

Forgiveness is the fragrance that the violet sheds on the heel that
has crushed it.—Mark Twain

To forgive is to set a prisoner free and discover that the prisoner
was you.—Lewis B. Smedes

HIGHLIGHTS

1. Forgiveness is all about the person doing the forgiving; the recipient of forgiveness need not even know about it.

2. When we allow ourselves to be motivated and driven by the expectations of others, we create our own "victim mentality", which leads us to experience anger and resentment about our choices. Forgiveness provides us with a proven way back to self-empowerment.

3. Learning to forgive requires us to change old patterns of thinking and behaving, so that we can see others as people who are just doing their best with the tools they have at their disposal.

4. The ego-mind resists forgiving mainly because of an erroneous belief that to forgive means to agree or condone. In its zeal to keep us safe, it will fabricate rationalizations to withhold forgiveness.

5. Forgiveness is not about changing history, and it is not about forgetting the past. It is merely an intentional decision to release resentment and forgo ideas of revenge in order to free ourselves from our own negative and disempowering ideas.

6. Forgiveness induces a sense of freedom—specifically freedom from destructive and counter-productive thoughts of resentment or revenge.

7. Forgiveness strengthens our sense of gratitude. Once we've release our vengeful thoughts and the feelings associated with them, we can begin to see the bigger picture and understand the way we have grown from the situation.

8. Forgiveness—especially self-forgiveness—cures Karma. Once we learn to forgive ourselves, then we stop holding ourselves hostage to our past and give ourselves permission to move lovingly into the next greatest version of ourselves.

9. Forgiving involves 5 key steps:

- Understand the wrong-doing
- Acknowledge and validate judgments and feelings
- Express and release emotional energy
- Own our part in the situation
- Re-connect to compassion and unconditional love.

10. Self-forgiveness is the ultimate—and most challenging—form of forgiveness. It requires us to touch into self-compassion and to see ourselves in the same loving way we are willing to see others; it requires us to soothe the ego-mind into silence with respect to its self-judgments.

11. Everything at its deepest level is motivated by a desire to give or receive love. If we can remember this, we can connect more easily to forgiveness.

12. Once we become more adept at forgiveness, we can bring it proactively into our lives moment by moment simply by answering the question "How can I bring unconditional love into this situation?"

13. Forgive everyone for everything all the time. Better yet, learn to Pre-Forgive! This involves recognizing that people—sometimes caught in their own drama—will sooner or later do something that will cause us pain. By forgiving in advance, we become less reactive to the trigger, and more able to see those people with compassion.

THE FORGIVENESS KEY

Forgiveness may well be the most powerful force in the universe. It has the power to heal and to open channels of love. It has the power to lift the blinders off our eyes so that we can see things as they really are. It has many benefits to health, happiness and fulfillment. Best of all, it is a totally free commodity that we all have access to all the time.

If we can learn to forgive, then we can free ourselves from our own dysfunctional (and destructive) thoughts and beliefs, thereby allowing ourselves to grow and evolve into our most magnificent selves.

Practice forgiveness in every moment, and allow yourself to be moved by this affirmation:

> **I am blessed, healed, and supported by the loving power of forgiveness, which reminds me always about who I am, and empowers me to love and forgive everyone for everything.**

CHAPTER 6: PURPOSE

UNCOVER, DECLARE, AND HONOR YOUR PURPOSE

now is the time to know

(now is the time
to know)

right and wrong are
training wheels
for children

can this be true?
can it be anything but true?

when i gave up my training wheels
i found it difficult to steer
to stay on my path
to even recognize where my path was
or if indeed i was ever on it

i was distracted by countless drive-through
quick-this places and *super-fast-that* toys
all of them full of empty promises
and over-refined platitudes

they filled me with illusion
things i thought i wanted or needed
and i was indeed full—in a manner of speaking—
so it took me a while
to realize i was not satisfied

fulfillment seemed so far away
beyond my reach
and there were times
when i wanted my training wheels back
so that i would not stray
so that i could hear that voice once again whispering

you are my beloved

                 that voice faded to silence
                        the moment
                                instant gratification seduced me
                                through the golden arches
                                of empty calories
                                and rampant consumerism

        but the real voice is there somewhere *(still)*
                                behind and within
                        cradling the jewel of my true purpose
                        in a never-ending tender embrace
                                (like a treasure beyond imagining)
                        and the voice that calls is quiet but persistent
                        as it patiently awaits my prodigal return

        *(now is the time
                to know)*

                                                all i do is sacred
                                                        everything
                                        for it all leads back here
                                                to this moment
                                                to this place
                                                to this truth

                        and when i listen and follow
                                my heart blossoms
                                into its natural fullness

ROCK'N'ROLL HERO...NOT!

When I was 11 years old, I got my first guitar. As I learned how to play it, I found that I had a deep love for all kinds of music. By the time I was 13, I was already accomplished enough to be playing in bands with other people, and I had my own band when I was only 15 years old. I was totally impassioned and I had a deep desire to become a world famous rock'n'roll musician. But then, one day I mentioned my dream to my parents, and…well, I'm sure you can imagine their reaction.

To be fair, my parents didn't want to destroy my dream—I'm pretty sure of that. But they had their own fears, and in the late 1960s, rock'n'roll had already seen its share of heroes fall victim to drug abuse—and a few of them, including my idol Jimi Hendrix, even died at a very early age. Well, my mom and dad certainly didn't want any of that happening to me, so they tried to get me to think about finding what they called a "real job", all the while reminding me that, "for every successful musician, there are a million unsuccessful ones." The message that I took on was that, if I chose to follow my passion, I would almost certainly end up a failure, and possibly a drug addict in the bargain. Mom and Dad had no problem with me keeping music as a "hobby", but as a career? No chance.

Given that I had already unconsciously bought into the idea that other people knew me better than I knew myself, it was relatively easy for me to defer to my parents' wishes. Sure, I put up a bit of a fight at the beginning, trying my best to come up with reasonable justifications for following my dreams, but I was no match for their superior logic and broader experience, and eventually, they wore me down. I ended up assimilating the fears they were expressing, and those fears led me to choose work that I believed would satisfy their idea of a "real job".

Although my love of music has never died, the dream of being a rock'n'roll musician slowly faded away as I followed the purpose that my parents (and other members of society) recommended for me. I fell into line as someone who lived up to the expectations of others, and I allowed my own heart's desire to slip into silence.

A *DEFAULT* PURPOSE

What I just described about my own youth is quite a common occurrence. Most parents want their children to be happy and successful. Most children don't start thinking about "purpose" until they are well into their teens—if indeed they think about it at all before full adulthood. So, in a spirit of generally loving helpfulness, parents tend to "suggest" ideas that they deem to be "appropriate" for their children. While these suggestions may be very well-meaning, sometimes parents deliver them with an underlying energy of urgency or expectation, and children—who generally seem inclined to please their parents—often simply do what's expected without really thinking about it. Thus, in a sense, a "suggestion" becomes more of an "imposition", and the child may unconsciously accept this as a *default purpose*—and inevitably develop a degree of resentment as a result.

Anyone who accommodates others and does what they suggest may well be living such a default purpose that came about because of an imposition from external sources. Consider things like getting good grades, going to the best university, achieving a master's degree, getting married and having a family, buying a house in a good neighborhood, etc., etc. While they may all be "good ideas", these are all objectives that almost everyone in society is urged to accomplish—and the underlying implication is that, in order to get these things, you have to have a "good job". Not a job that fulfills you or makes you happy, mind you, but a job that allows you to accumulate these "things" for their own sake.

Maybe you have lived your life according to a default purpose; if so, believe me, you are not alone! If you look around, I'll bet you can see lots of other people who are doing the same thing. And if most of the people around you seem to be living according to some level of similar default purpose, I imagine it's pretty hard for you to justify questioning it.

A default purpose is actually nothing more than a reflection of what some-one else wants from you. Furthermore, if you are living according to a default purpose, it's probably because it was introduced to you in a very subtle way, probably when you were quite young. However, while there is nothing wrong with following this kind of path if you truly want to, you can't possibly know if it's right for you unless you at least bring some awareness to it!

A *REAL* PURPOSE

A *real purpose*, on the other hand, is something that comes to you from the depths of your soul. It has a powerful impact on your life, filling you with ex-citement and passion. When you become aware of such a purpose, everything changes. Because it is something that you have uncovered for yourself, it has a great deal more power, and it moves you toward constant action, toward the fulfillment of something that feels vitally important to you. While a default purpose may have been imposed on you through the fears of others, a real pur-pose seems to come from a place of love and curiosity and adventure, literally fueling a deep desire to fully express and experience yourself.

Believe it or not, all of us have a real purpose. The only question is whether or not we actually become aware of it. And what, you might ask, might prevent us from becoming aware of our real purpose? Well, there are lots of possi-ble answers, but most of them are just excuses and rationalizations that come through the ego-mind from a deep sense of fear, which can make it very hard to hear the quiet but persistent voice of the soul.

Becoming aware of your real purpose changes everything! For one thing, the soul starts to rejoice almost immediately and this manifests itself through a deep sense of passion and desire. Suddenly, you begin to feel totally alive, and the more you align with your true purpose, the more you learn to focus on what's important for you. This gives you the ability to make clearer choices because every choice now can be weighed against your purpose. You may still find yourself occasionally doing things that are not fully in alignment, but most of your actions will be geared toward the fulfillment of your purpose. And this naturally leads to a sense of peace and happiness, because everything in your life just seems to fit into place.

Of course, once you know your true purpose, another thing comes into your awareness: responsibility! Your purpose becomes like a beacon on your path, illuminating your way forward, and guiding you in the appropriate direction. You quickly begin to see that your purpose is important—just as important as everyone else's—and so you begin to develop a sense of responsibility for ensuring that you align with it…because to do otherwise is tantamount to a denial of who you really are. But beware: the ego-mind can trip you up in this case, making your responsibility seem more like a burden or obligation, and if you allow your ego-mind to do this, you may quickly fall back into the habit of ignoring your soul. So, be alert to this possibility and let your passion and excitement about having a purpose lead you gently into the full and complete expression of who you really are.

FAILURE IS AN ILLUSION

Because of our unbreakable spiritual connection to *OMnitude*, we all contribute to Its objective to both know and experience Itself completely. Consequently, as I pointed out before, we all share one common over-arching purpose:

> **To participate in *OMnitude*'s grand experiment by fulfilling our own destiny and adding our individual life experience to the Library of all such experiences.**

As I mentioned before, one relatively obvious implication of this "proto-purpose" is that every energy-form everywhere in the universe is *equally important*! There is no energy-form—*anywhere*—that is more or less important than any other! Furthermore, every secondary purpose—imagined or otherwise—is also just as important as every other, because it helps to shape the individuation's experience and therefore provides vital information to the *OMnitude Library*.

Therefore, it follows that, no matter what you do with your life, you cannot possibly fail! This is because every detail of your life experience, no matter how minute or seemingly insignificant, contributes to *OMnitude's Infinite Library*. And because you actually invite and attract situations into your life that make up your overall life experience, it just may be that your personal experience is so unique that no one else could ever hope to replicate it.

Of course, even if you have been unaware that you can't possibly fail and you feel a lot of relief from this new revelation, this doesn't mean that you will necessarily enjoy your life. As I just pointed out, you may be doing things that have been suggested—or possibly even imposed upon you—by others. And while you may be getting paid for what you are doing, you may find that you aren't particularly fulfilled with your daily routine. Sadly, this is a very common experience for many people. Even though we might say that such people have a purpose (a *default purpose* at least), it seems obvious that their purpose wasn't something of their own choosing—which explains why they aren't very fired up about their lives.

So many of us slog unhappily through the daily rituals of getting up, going to work in an unrewarding job, coming home to a disappointing life-style, and then waking up the next day to start the process all over again. But even though we may do this, that doesn't stop us from dreaming about *what might be* for our lives.

Think about it. How many times have you found yourself daydreaming, wishing for something better in your life? How many times have you thought to yourself, *"Surely there is something more for me out there...but how can I find my way there?"* How many times have you wondered if you missed something along the way and simply ended up on a path that you didn't really want to be on? How many times have you imagined yourself doing something that you totally love to do—and getting handsomely rewarded for it?

I think we all have hopes and dreams like these, but then we promptly dismiss them as foolish or unachievable because our ego-minds are continually reminding us about all our weaknesses and shortcomings and flaws—in an ongoing effort to protect us from disappointment, pain and suffering!

Well, as I already said, there is good news, *Maestro!* We all have a purpose beyond our "proto-purpose". In fact, I believe that we all start out in our spiritual form deciding and declaring our purpose before we actually arrive here in the physical world. The problem is that, the moment we transition from the spiritual to the physical, we promptly forget about all the plans we made...and so a big part of our journey in the physical realm is to *remember* why we are here! And this partly explains why we sometimes bounce around from idea to idea, trying to see if our purpose might be over here, or over there, or somewhere else. To be sure, it can be a little frustrating!

WHY IDENTIFY A REAL PURPOSE?

If failure is an illusion, then you might well ask, *"Why bother seeking a spiritual purpose at all? Why not just go with the flow and let life decide where to take me?"*

As I mentioned a few moments ago, you are certainly free to make that kind of choice if you want to—and indeed, that might just be what you are here to do. But I believe that if you make this choice without actually checking in to find out if that is your true purpose, then you will probably feel little if any fulfillment during your lifetime. I believe that you are reading this book because you are looking to improve your life, so it seems unlikely to me that you will be satisfied with this kind of default approach to your life. But just the same, let's list a few reasons why you might want to at least do a little internal research!

THE DIRECTION FINDER

A spiritual purpose is an important step toward living a truly conscious life of your own design and creation. Everyone gets busy with small tasks and goals, no matter what's going on in life, but if you can keep the beacon of your spiritual purpose in view, then you can be much clearer about the relevance of those smaller goals, and you can make informed decisions about whether they even make sense in your life. Knowing your spir-

Figure 16—Your Spiritual Direction Finder

itual purpose makes it much easier for you to decide to continue on a certain path or to change directions to get back on the path that you truly want to be on.

ACTIVATION OF INTEGRITY

When you identify and articulate your purpose, particularly a purpose that ignites your passion, then you really know what you stand for; you have an almost immediate sense of life-meaning, and things in your life become clearer and easier to understand. Having an imperturbable vision of your most spectacular life, complete with an understanding of how you show up in that life, helps you to convert that vision into reality. Your purpose helps you to see the bigger picture of your life, which means that you can more easily set clear long-term goals in alignment with that purpose. This allows you to live your life with more and more integrity, a topic we'll discuss in detail in the next chapter.

Your purpose allows you to define long-term goals, which can easily be decomposed into clear short-term goals, which in turn can help you come up with action plans on any time scale you choose.

Relevance and Importance of Tasks

Remember those small tasks and goals I mentioned a moment ago? Well, they are not going to go away simply because you have a purpose! But at least with a clearly articulated purpose in place, you can empower yourself to review everything you are doing in your life, and decide from a place of deeper understanding if the things you are doing make sense in the context of that purpose. Some things on this list will be things that you've committed to, and you may want to stay in integrity with who you are by completing them. Some of them may be totally out of alignment with your purpose and so you may want to stop doing them altogether. And some may fall somewhere in between, perhaps giving you the opportunity to re-negotiate them so that you can bring them more into alignment. The main point here is that your spiritual purpose gives you the power to choose what is right for your life.

Passionate Living

Whenever I see someone living his/her life according to a clearly defined purpose, I almost always recognize an internal passion that seems to manifest like a fire in the person's eyes. This kind of passion is difficult, if not impossible, to fake, and it is a kind of unstoppable energy that keeps the person moving in the direction prescribed by the purpose.

Perhaps you've already experienced the kind of passion I'm talking about—that is, the internal energy or force that just won't let you stop, and that makes all the activities you're involved in feel more like play than work.

This is the nature of a spiritual purpose—something that gets you jumping out of bed in the morning, excited about what your day will bring for you. And without this kind of energy in your life, then you may find your days becoming humdrum, with no real inspiration or motivation to do much of anything. Without purpose, life can literally become a drag.

Success and Abundance

As you become more and more in tune with your purpose—even if it shifts now and then—you naturally tend to find life flowing more easily. Synchronicity and serendipity become pretty commonplace. Success just seems to happen. The things you imagine you need all seem to just show up. Part of this has to do with the intrinsic nature of purpose, but a major part of it has to do with your attitude toward life—which tends to improve dramatically when you live according to your purpose. Best of all, this success and abundance happens on your terms—because you are choosing your thoughts, words, actions and feelings by staying aligned with your purpose.

REMEMBERING YOUR PURPOSE

As we transition from spiritual form into physical form, we go through an incredible transformation. I believe that a big part of our intention is to arrive here with something akin to a "clean slate"—meaning that we bring nothing with us from our spiritual plane other than a deep and abiding knowing of our connection to *OMnitude*. This is why, during our journey from the spiritual to the physical, we actually "forget" the reasons we chose to come here. However, the intuitive awareness of our connection to Source is what provides us with the inspiration and motivation to remember what our unique purpose might be. And so we head off in one direction or another, unconsciously believing that our purpose will become clear as we proceed.

For many of us, the desire to have a clear sense of purpose is so overwhelming that we simply cannot stop until we know what our purpose actually is. The problem is, up to now, no-one explained to us how we can reconnect to our purpose after we transition through the veil of forgetfulness into our physical form. This is why we may seem to be heading off in so many different random directions for so much of our lives.

As it happens, our purpose is almost certainly embedded within a vision or mental model of a world free of certain kinds of "negative" energies, or in which people can achieve or experience various kinds of "positive" outcomes. This vision usually comes about because of our own experience of life—sometimes, we may want to create more of something that we believe is beneficial; sometimes, we may want to find ways of reducing or eliminating something that we believe is destructive or painful. Either way, our vision sees the world in some kind of "improved" state that we believe will make life more enjoyable and fulfilling for everyone. This vision or mental model may be vague or fleeting, but we have a sense of its importance in our life even if we can't really explain or describe it.

Science has shown convincingly that experiences are easier to remember when they are accompanied by emotional intensity. Experiences associated with pleasant emotions generally are more easily remembered than ones associated with unpleasant emotions—mainly because we seem motivated to forget those "negative experiences". Interestingly, it seems that the emotional arousal is a stronger contributing factor to long-term memory than any importance we might place on the event itself. What this means is that, if you can remember a state involving the presence of strong emotion—especially one of the primary emotions of sadness, anger, fear or joy—then you can usually connect more easily to the memory of the experience that triggered that emotion. And if you can connect to the experience, then you can get clear what it is about the experience that relates to your vision. You can also get clear on how you either want to replicate the experience for others to enjoy, or eliminate it so that no-one else has to suffer the way you did.

I have learned many different techniques for helping people to discover (or, more accurately, *uncover*) and articulate their purpose. As a student of simplicity, I like to use tools that are easy to remember and fairly straightforward to implement. So I'm going to share with you my favorite approach (and one of the simplest as far as I know), which I've adapted from something I first learned about in Bill Kauth's excellent book *A Circle of Men*.

CREATING A PURPOSE STATEMENT

Most of us have been exposed to purpose/mission statements that companies or organizations publicize. These statements—which provide guidance for the organizations in question—usually involve two clearly defined elements:

- VISION: a clear description of the kind of world they want to create;
- ACTION: a description of the contributory things they do in order to bring their vision into reality.

If you want to create a purpose statement for yourself, you can start by fully describing these two components. To make your purpose even more concrete in your life, I encourage you to create a special *purpose journal* as you complete the following exercises.

1. Actualizing Your Vision

All of us have hopes and dreams for a better life; we all have desires that motivate us; we all resonate with the actions of others that inspire us. But how many of us go to the trouble of really understanding the importance of these hopes, dreams, desires and inspirations? In reality, they are the building blocks of our vision for a better world, so it really makes sense for us to pay attention to them.

A. Remember Important Life Situations

If you want to actualize and formalize your vision, take some time in your journal to answer the following questions in as much detail as you can. Remember to approach all of these questions from a place of unconditional acceptance, and release yourself from any judgments you may have about yourself:

1. Name at least 5 people in your life who inspire you and describe what it is about how they show up that's had such a profound impact on you.

2. Think about your childhood and try to identify the ways in which your needs did not get met. What difference would it have made to you if someone had been aware enough to help you meet those needs? How does your ideal world ensure such needs get met for others?

3. Think about ways you were mistreated, abused or emotionally wounded. Remember the pain of those events and what it meant that they happened to you. How do they contribute to your vision of a better world? How does your ideal world deal with situations like these?

4. Think of ways that your own behaviors may have caused pain and suffering for others. What do these situations tell you about the kind of world you want to live in?

5. Remember as many situations as you can when you felt deep compassion for someone else who was suffering. What was it about those situations that inspired you to want to relieve their suffering?

6. Think of at least 5 times in your life when you were totally excited and full of joy. What was it about those situations that triggered the sense of joy and happiness and fulfillment within you?

7. What is your ultimate passion in life—that thing (and there could be more than one) which lights you up and triggers enthusiasm or excitement within you? What is it about this thing (or things) that motivates and inspires you?

8. Remember the times in your life when someone demonstrated unconditional love for you, or actively blessed you because of the way you were showing up. What was it about those situations that moved you, and how

might they fit into your vision of the ideal world?

I encourage you to take as much time as you need to answer these questions. It might be a few minutes, it might be a few hours. Indeed, it might even be a few days or longer, so be willing to come back to this from time to time to update your answers.

B. Describe the Vision in Detail

Writing this stuff all down really helps you to solidify your understanding of your own life. And with that understanding, you can begin to see how your hopes, dreams, desires and inspirations came into being. With this information, you can begin to articulate the vision you have for the world of your dreams. Take some time to answer the following questions—again, without judgment or criticism:

1. What does your ideal world look like? Describe it in as much detail as possible, with powerful words that accurately paint a picture of your vision.

2. What sorts of values are expressed and practiced in your ideal world?

3. How are everyone's needs acknowledged and fulfilled?

4. How is suffering reduced or eliminated?

5. How are people encouraged, empowered, or inspired to fully experience and express themselves?

6. What is it about your ideal world that inspires people to discover and live their own passions and purposes?

C. Articulate the Vision in a Single Statement

Finally, once you've answered all these questions, see if you can come up with a short but powerful phrase that describes your ideal world. Make sure to use words that capture the essence of what you learned from the previous questions. For example, perhaps you have a vision of *a loving world where everyone wins*. Or maybe it's something a little more concrete, such as *a secure and accepting world of mutual respect*. The main thing is to choose words that emanate out of your own experience and which describe the kind of world that you'd really like to live in.

Remember, this *vision* of your *ideal world* is just that—a *vision*. It represents everything you hope for in the world—for yourself and for everyone else, and it derives from the experiences you've had in your journey so far, and from the experiences you long for in the future. It is a "dream of possibilities", something that you'd create in an instant if you could.

2. Visualizing Your Action

If you've taken the time to complete part one of this exercise in full, then the second part will be relatively easy. Once you have a good understanding of the kind of world you want to live in, you can pretty easily visualize the kinds of actions that need to be taken in order to make that vision a reality. However, you may notice that your vision is pretty big, perhaps even much bigger than anything you believe you could create by yourself—at least in a single lifetime. Don't be intimidated by that; instead, be inspired by it!

This next part of the exercise involves a bit of visualizing. That is, you have to imagine how you'd show up in order to create this world you have conjured in your mind. It helps to think of the vision as a blueprint in your mind, something that may be incomplete at the moment, but that you believe in strongly enough that you want to see it manifested in the "real world". So, your objective now is to come up with a description of the actions you take on a regular basis in order to facilitate the realization of your vision.

In your *purpose journal*, answer the following questions in as much detail as you can. Remember, remain as unconditionally accepting as possible, and release any judgments you may have.

1. What are the core values you embody that inform all of your imagined actions?

2. How do you imagine you interact with other people in your ideal world? How do you deal with them when they show up in ways that challenge you? How do you empower, encourage or inspire them to be their best selves?

3. What specific things do you see yourself doing to actively bring your vision into reality? How do you see yourself responding when obstacles show up? How do you overcome challenges and difficulties? How do you bring unconditional love and acceptance into all of your actions?

4. How do you actively empower yourself to show up as fully as possible so that you can express the deepest and most amazing aspects of yourself? What behaviors do you engage that demonstrate to others that they too are empowered to shine their lights as fully as possible?

5. What actions do you take to enroll others into your vision so they will help you to make it a reality?

6. How do you imagine yourself meeting the needs of others while ensuring that your own needs are met?

After you have completed this exercise, you will find that certain key words and phrases will begin to jump out at you. Look through what you have written to find as many powerful action words—specifically, transitive verbs—as you can that describe how you show up in your vision of the ideal world. For example, you may find yourself *modeling unconditional love* or *showing up authentically* or *mentoring others.*

3. Bringing It Together

The final step in creating a purpose statement is to come up with a succinct but powerful sentence that combines the vision and action together. The idea of this part of the exercise is to ensure that both the vision and action elements of your purpose are clearly expressed. You want your purpose statement to be something that inspires you and has deep meaning for you. While it's nice if your purpose statement inspires others, it's far more important that you yourself derive inspiration from it—even if other people don't really understand it or resonate with it.

Here is a simple template that I recommend you use to help you create your own purpose statement:

> I CREATE/MANIFEST _____ *(your*
> *vision of the "ideal" world)* BY _____
> *(your description of the actions/behaviors you practice in order to manifest*
> *that vision).*

This template is designed with two particular objectives in mind:

1. It combines the elements of vision and action in a way that makes clear what you are trying to bring into reality and how you are intending to manifest it.

2. It begins with the words I CREATE or I MANIFEST because it is meant to convey the notion of being fully aware and awake, and of assuming full responsibility for your own thoughts, words, actions and emotions in the fulfillment of your vision.

I have gone through this exercise four or five different times in the last 15 years or so, and each time, my purpose has become clearer and clearer to me. My purpose statement has gone through many structural iterations, each of which was more or less inspirational to me. But, one day it all came together in a way that totally surprised me, and my current purpose statement is extremely short—but it inspires me and keeps me pointed in the right direction for my life.

Today, my purpose statement is only 10 words long!

> I CREATE universal harmony BY modeling, fostering, and facilitating *MagnifEssence*.

You can see in this statement that I include my own words to describe my vision for an ideal world. I chose the phrase *universal harmony* because in my world everyone recognizes that they are all part of the same fabric of life and that they must all live, love and work together for the common good. How do I contribute to the creation of this world? By *modeling, fostering, and facilitating MagnifEssence*. The word *MagnifEssence* is a wonderful word that came to me from my Soul; to me, it describes the true essence of who we really are. It is the divine, magnificent, spiritual being of light and love that empowers us and expresses through us in its many different and amazing forms. (An alternative phrase that I sometimes use is *authentic magnificence*.) And the actions I take are to *model* this MagnifEssence in all the ways I show up; to *foster* it in others—that is, to encourage others to show up authentically as well; and finally, to *facilitate* it whenever I am in a group setting with other people.

This may not have much impact on you as you read it, but it means *everything* to me. Every word in this statement resonates within me at my core, and that is how I know that it is an accurate and true representation of what I'm here to do.

THE PURPOSE OF PURPOSE

Now, do I *always* engage in behaviors that are aligned to my true purpose? No, of course not! I am still having a human experience, after all, so I sometimes get caught up in the drama of my own ego-mind, and therefore fall short of the objectives of my purpose. However, that is not to punish me or make myself wrong!

My purpose stands like a beacon in front of me, pointing constantly in the direction of the world of my highest ideals. When I am fully aware of all the actions I am taking, I can ensure that they are in alignment with my purpose. And on the (not so rare) occasion that I do fall into old unconscious patterns, I can use my purpose to help me recognize when I am out of integrity with my Higher Self—and this can help me get back quickly to a state of integrity.

Your purpose statement may indeed seem much bigger than you. It may even create in you some anxiety because you believe you'll never accomplish it in your lifetime. Believe it or not, this is normal—and it is actually a *good thing!* Why? Because your purpose statement should describe an intentional pattern for how you plan to show up in every single moment—even beyond the time of your departure from this physical plane.

What does a true statement of purpose look like? Well, it will encompass the following:

1. Expresses Who You Really Are

If you attempt to articulate a purpose before knowing who you really are, then you will find yourself wandering from one purpose to another. This is not necessarily a *bad thing!* Like me, you may need to wander around in the wilderness for a while before you become clear about who you really are. But the moment you do come to that clarity, purpose will be very close behind. And when you declare your purpose from this knowing, it will resonate completely within you.

2. Seeks to Improve All of Life

As we've seen, one of the core elements of the purpose statement is the vision that you articulated. Even though you may describe your vision using only a few well-chosen words, that vision is something that is very clear to you and something that resonates within you endlessly. The vision may emerge from your life experiences, your dreams, your hopes, and/or your desires, but it is powerful and motivating—it is something that is seared into your heart and soul, coupled with a strong intention to bring it into reality.

This vision is your idea of what life might look like under *ideal* circumstances. It imagines a world that would be mutually beneficial for *all* energy-forms, not just for yourself. It seeks to create inclusion and unconditional love for everyone. It seeks to create countless situations in which *everyone wins.*

3. Has No Limits

When you understand who you really are, your purpose statement reflects that by its sense of boundlessness. You get a sense of realness and truth about your purpose statement, even if you imagine yourself being in a completely different world at a completely different time. This is because it is an expression of who you really are—and who you really are is also boundless.

Your purpose has nothing to do with achievements or accomplishments or successes—those are simply constructs of the ego-mind—and everything to do with expressing who you really are as you move consciously moment-by-moment toward the manifesting of your ideal world. However, one of the great ironies of life is that, if you are truly aligned with your purpose, then achievements and accomplishments and successes just seem to happen on their own—but they don't have importance to you in and of themselves.

4. Points the Way

The purpose statement isn't an end unto itself, but rather a pointer to a particular direction that is unique to your own Soul. The objective of your purpose ultimately is to create the world of your highest dreams. Thus, your true purpose is motivated from its core by the power of Love. Even if some aspects of your vision may have come about because of fear-based thinking or behaving, ultimately the vision that you are trying to create is supported by Love—because, after all, Love is who you really are!

FEEDBACK MECHANISM

Now that you have uncovered and articulated your purpose statement, the first thing you are likely to do is to look at your life thus far and to notice whether you have been on-course or off-course. Many people at this stage of their process are likely to find themselves off-course, and unfortunately, that can lead to self-directed judgments or criticisms. So, the first thing I want you to do is commit to being gentle and compassionate with yourself, no matter where you find yourself in relation to your purpose.

As I mentioned earlier, your purpose can be seen as a beacon or compass that helps keep you oriented in the appropriate direction for your life. As such, much like a modern day GPS system, it provides you with constant feedback about where you are in any given moment, and recommended adjustments you might make in order to bring yourself back on track. So, make good use of your purpose without criticizing or judging yourself!

IDENTITY PRECEDES PURPOSE

Something I alluded to before is that, before you can really align with your purpose, you must have a clear knowing of who you really are. If you don't, then you will probably find yourself trying a lot of things that seem to call to you, hoping that—sooner or later—one of them "sticks"! This is pretty normal, and I think a lot of people experience this phenomenon in their lives. But once you really know who you are, and then come to a clear understanding of your purpose based on that knowing, then things in your life just seem to brighten up significantly. It's almost like someone has taken your black-and-white life, and shown you the switch for turning on the color.

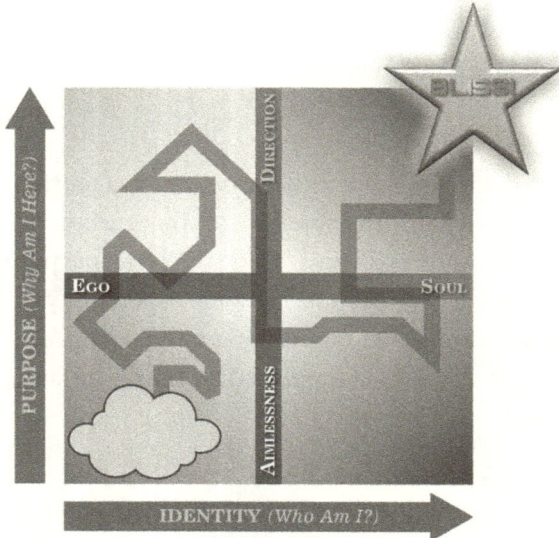

Figure 17—The Identity-Purpose Matrix

In the early stages, many of us identify with our ego-mind and don't pay much attention to our Soul. This inhibits our ability to know who we really are, and leads to the "random walk" approach to life. But once we connect with the truth of who we really are, and come more in tune with our Soul, then purpose becomes clearer, and we move from a state of aimless wandering to a state of intentional direction.

Of course, just because you now have a purpose doesn't mean that all aspects of your life will suddenly or magically be on-track. In fact, depending on how awake and aware you were before discovering your purpose, you may realize that your current life is completely out of alignment. Again, I want to remind you: don't judge it, just be aware of what you are learning! This is not the time to throw the baby out with the bath-water. Instead, let your new awareness help you to find your desired direction, and then use your inner wisdom to help you figure out how to get back on track.

Remember, the life you have lived up to now is something that you created based on all of your choices from the past—and those choices were all based on the best knowledge you had available at the time. All of your physical creations—including all the jobs you held, the roles you played, the friends you chose, the relationships you had—are products of thoughts, words, actions and emotions that you expressed in the past. They may tell a story of who you were yesterday, but they do not define who you are today. So, learn from the past, but don't be anchored to it!

Whatever gap may exist between your current state in life and where you truly want to be, there is always a way to close it—or at least to find a way across it. Even though you may be truly on fire with your newly discovered purpose, this is not the time to be making radical, life-altering decisions, so don't immediately quit your job or leave a relationship or move to a new city. Instead, take a look at what's really missing from your life and invoke your own creativity to begin manifesting that. In other words, start small, and allow yourself to expand in a manageable way into this new way of living.

PURPOSE INFORMS GOAL-SETTING

Once you have a better understanding of your purpose, your ability to set and achieve your goals will improve almost immediately. This is because your purpose can inform all of your future goal-setting—that is, you can check every desired goal against your purpose, and only commit to goals that are consistent with your purpose. If you are serious about living your life in alignment with your purpose, this will all happen for you somewhat organically—and more or less automatically. You will notice that you simply don't care for the idea of committing to something that isn't congruent with your purpose or with who you really are. This doesn't mean you'll never do anything that is out of alignment with your purpose, only that you'll be more aware when that is what happens.

The main thing to notice here is that you are fully at choice for the kinds of goals you want to set for yourself going forward. As you measure any new goal against your purpose, you will become clearer about whether it fits with who you are choosing to be, or whether you are compromising yourself in some way in order to fulfill some other (possibly unknown) need or desire. As you contemplate a new goal or objective, here are some questions you can ask yourself before you commit yourself:

1. In what ways does this goal/objective honor my purpose?
2. In what ways is this goal/objective in alignment with the vision I want to manifest in the world? In what ways is it out of alignment?
3. What does this goal/objective say about who I am choosing to be?
4. If this goal/objective puts me out of alignment with my purpose, is there a way I can reframe the goal/objective so that it more closely aligns, and

so that it expresses who I truly want to be?

5. If there is no way to bring this goal/objective back into alignment with my purpose, can I drop it altogether? Can I create a different goal that is more closely aligned?

You can apply this set of questions to any goal at all—including goals that you may have set in the past. Remember, the objective in asking these questions is not to make yourself wrong for the choices you made in the past—it is merely to help you gain more clarity about where you are now and where you are choosing to go next.

Confusion between Purpose and Goals

Sometimes people inadvertently think of their purpose as a goal—a life-long goal, perhaps, but a goal nonetheless. This is an easy mistake to make, but it is also easily correctable.

Your purpose is a written articulation of the actions and behaviors you choose to engage in so as to create or manifest your vision of an ideal world. In general, a purpose is much bigger than life. In fact, it is usually so big that it has little or no chance of being completely fulfilled in one physical lifetime. This is what makes life purpose so inspiring and motivational—it is meant to give you a direction for everything else in your life.

A goal, on the other hand, is something you commit to in order to move yourself one step closer to the fulfillment of your vision. The goal is merely a stepping stone on your journey; it is not the journey itself.

A goal may be arbitrarily large or small, but large goals tend to be comprised of smaller sub-goals or tasks. For example, if your goal is to build an electric car and bring it to market, then you could easily imagine this to be a multi-year goal, and you'd have lots of sub-goals, all of which would have to be completed in order for the main goal to be considered "done". But the life-purpose that drives this main goal could easily be something along the lines of "creating a healthy, happy world that supports all of life by actively reducing dependency on fossil fuels". The purpose may not be fulfilled in a lifetime, but the electric vehicle goal might be.

DECLARING PD-SMART GOALS

There are many ways of declaring goals, but one method I find particularly powerful makes use of characteristics that are easily remembered through a mnemonic device called *SMART*, which is an acronym that means *"Specific, Measurable, Attainable, Realistic, Time-Limited"*. I like to add the prefix *PD* at the front because it reminds me to ensure that my goals are *"Purpose-Driven"*. Here is a summary of the mnemonic:

PURPOSE-DRIVEN	The goal is closely aligned with your *Life Purpose*, and therefore it is something that helps you move closer to the fulfillment of your vision.
SPECIFIC	The goal has a specific, well-defined scope, so you know the limits of what is actually required.
MEASURABLE	The goal includes certain metric qualities, so that you have a pretty good sense of how much you've done so far, and how much is left to do before completion.
ATTAINABLE	The goal may be a stretch for you, but you know or believe that you have the capability to complete it.
REALISTIC	The goal takes into account all of your available resources, knowledge, capabilities and skills.
TIME-LIMITED	The goal can be completed in a finite (and usually relatively short) amount of time.

If you apply these characteristics to any of your goals—even ones that you may have declared in the past, you will find that your goals will generally be easier to achieve. As you declare new goals, let these characteristics guide you in keeping all of them aligned with your *Life Purpose*.

Chapter Summary—Purpose

He who has a why to live for can bear almost any how.—
Friedrich Nietzsche

*There is a plan and a purpose, a value to every life, no matter
what its location, age, gender or disability.—Sharron Angle*

*Here is a test to find whether your mission on earth is finished: If
you're alive it isn't.—Richard Bach*

Highlights

1. Everyone has a purpose in life, whether s/he is aware of it or not. If we are not yet aware of our true purpose, we may follow a default purpose defined by others in our life.

2. A real purpose cannot be dictated by another; it comes to you from the depths of your Soul, and once you are aware of it, you cannot turn back on it, for it informs everything that you think, say, do, or feel going forward.

3. Failure is an illusion. Everything you choose in your life—whether consciously empowered by your life purpose or not—serves to fulfill the over-arching purpose of expanding *OMnitude*'s "Experience Library".

4. Identifying a real purpose helps you to establish a direction finding system for your life; empowers you to live more fully in integrity; gives importance and relevance to all of your tasks; ignites passion, excitement and enthusiasm within you; and invites success and abundance into your life.

5. Identifying a purpose is mostly about remembering what you planned for yourself before you transitioned from the spiritual to the physical realm.

6. Your purpose statement is something you can create by actualizing your vision for an ideal world, and visualizing the actions you take in order to make that vision a reality.

7. Once fully articulated, your life purpose expresses who you really are, seeks to improve all of life, has no limits, and points the way for all of your subsequent choices.

8. Your purpose is like a *Spiritual Navigation System*: it provides direction for your life, and it gives you constant feedback about how you are doing.

9. Your purpose informs all of your goal-setting because it helps you to honor the truth of who you are and why you are here.

10. Use the *PD-SMART* technique for setting goals that are Purpose-Drive, Specific, Measurable, Attainable, Realistic, and Time-Limited.

THE PURPOSE KEY

At some point in our lives, virtually all of us ask some variant of the question "Why am I here?" When the answers we receive feel empty or incomplete or unsatisfying, we may become restless or frustrated with our lives—especially if those answers are delivered to us by others who believe they know us better than we know ourselves. But, thankfully, there is a way for us to uncover our true purpose, and it comes down to a dedicated and on-going conversation with our *Spiritually Empowered Life-Force* (our SELF or our Soul)—that part of us that knows the full truth of who we are and why we are here.

As soon as we connect to our true Spiritual Purpose—as opposed to some arbitrary default purpose that is assigned to us by someone else—everything changes. Our whole outlook on life suddenly brightens and everything seems to have a meaning that we weren't able to recognize before. We feel a strong pull to keep moving forward on a journey that is meant to create a better world for ourselves and everyone else. And even though the journey may at times be arduous, we find it easier and more enjoyable because we know why we are doing it.

Take the time to connect with your own Spiritual Purpose, and invite yourself to review and revise it from time to time. Meanwhile, give yourself permission to engage only in thoughts, words, actions and emotions that are in alignment with your best understanding of your purpose.

May the following affirmation keep you connected to your purpose from this day forward:

> **I am empowered and motivated by a sacred spiritual purpose that guides, informs and inspires every aspect of my life.**

CHAPTER 7: INTEGRITY

PRACTICE INTEGRITY AND ACCOUNTABILITY

confession

ladies and gentlemen,
friends, colleagues, dear family,
    and yes,
you strangers in the back,

i stand here before you
with cocoon unfurled
    clear, transparent, open
with all my scales and plates and filters piled here,
    still hot,
next to the foot of the podium

i cannot say what power has brought me here
    today,
    at this time,
    at this moment

some might say cowardice,
others courage

for me it is just a sublime moment
of long overdue awareness

i see the scars on your chests
i see the stripes on your backs
i see the welts and bruises and scrapes and cuts
    on your arms and legs
i see the shadows of grief and anguish
    in the folds and creases and wrinkles
    that you wear like necklaces and sashes

i see all these things and more
    and i feel a fevered tugging at my own heart
    where even deeper hurt resides

because i see my own signature
on so much of your pain

ladies and gentlemen,
    i was crooked of heart
        and twisted of mind
        and my bent perspective sculpted this suffering

i dimmed your light in order to appear brighter
i trampled your presence in order to seem bigger
i lashed out and minimized you in order to magnify myself

i did these things because i was afraid

i was afraid to embrace truth and love
    because of a deeper fear
    that to do otherwise was a sign of weakness

i wanted to appear strong
but i ended up appearing weak
in spite of myself

and so i confess my transgression
    to each of you,
ladies and gentlemen,
friends, colleagues, dear family,
    and yes,
you strangers in the back,

i cannot say what power has brought me here
    today,
    at this time,
    at this moment

        i simply feel grateful for the space
            in which gentle truths
            throw back their heads
            and laugh
        with the pure joy of their liberation

The Nature of Integrity

Integrity is one of those things that everyone seems to understand, most people value, but a surprisingly large number of people don't seem to practice very well. This can be seen just by observing the behavior of so many of our world leaders today. There seems to be so much corruption in "high places" that it begs the question of whether we really do understand integrity in the first place!

When I ask people what integrity means to them, I often hear something along the lines of "doing what I say I'm going to do", or "making sure my actions are consistent with my words". And while I agree in principle with these sentiments, I think there is actually much more to integrity than that.

I see integrity as a state of being—a state of *integration*, if you like—that implies consistency and wholeness, as well as adherence to a personal code of ethics. For me, this suggests that we are *holistically aligned*—that is, our thoughts, words, actions and feelings are all in full alignment with one another, and all "pointing in the same direction"—specifically, the direction that is consistent with who we really are, and with our true purpose for being.

Think about it for a moment: if you say something, and then you act in accordance with what you have said, then, from an outsider's perspective at least, you may well appear to be in integrity. But if your thoughts and feelings don't conform to those words and actions, are you really in integrity? Couldn't it be argued that even though you have honored your spoken commitments, you may be out of integrity with yourself because you are not honoring your inner truth?

IMPECCABILITY OF INTENTION

We put a lot of faith in our words, don't we? You may have heard or spoken the phrase, "My word is my bond"—in other words, "you can always count on me to honor my words." And this is certainly important.

But what happens when you remain silent? You may not be speaking words, but you are surely communicating a message to others through your silence. Can you be out of integrity while remaining silent? I think the answer to that question is an unqualified "Yes"—and in fact, I've been personally affected by other people's silence in my life. This usually occurs when something generally unacceptable is happening, but witnesses to the event fail to speak up or take action. Perhaps they are afraid of potential danger to themselves or their loved ones. Or perhaps they are simply afraid of how others will judge them if they do speak up. Either way, they may well know that speaking up is the right thing to do, and yet they choose to stay silent—I think this is a very clear example of being out of integrity with oneself.

And what about the words that you do speak?

As I explained earlier, "I Am" is the most powerful phrase in the Universe. It is a declaration of who you are right now, and it is the starting point of all creation. But what I want to emphasize here is that *everything* you think, say, do or feel is an expression of who you are choosing to be in that moment, so in effect, it is a variation of the "I Am" statement. To put it another way, your word is like a magic wand—it fires up the engine of creation and, before you know it, your creation begins to take shape in your reality.

Of course, your words don't really exist without the thoughts and feelings that bring them into being. Every word you speak is at some level supported by your thoughts and beliefs—and how you feel about them—whether you are conscious of them or not. So sometimes, it may feel as if the words you speak out loud are not fully compatible with the thoughts or beliefs that you are aware of—and this can be disconcerting and disorienting. This is what I mean by being out of integrity, even though your words and actions may appear to be fully in alignment.

There is a great feeling of satisfaction when thoughts, words, actions and emotions are all synchronized and pointing in the same direction. Regardless of whether the overall experience brings pain or pleasure, the consistency and wholeness of the experience just feels "right" and "true", and it helps us to deepen our knowing and understanding of who we really are and how we are showing up in the world.

When this synchronization is aligned with the *Soul's Purpose*, then the experience is magnified immeasurably, beyond calmness and serenity and into what I imagine the mystics refer to as Bliss. In this state, everything in life seems to flow effortlessly—and this leads to a willingness to be completely open and receptive and trusting. Furthermore, attachment to thoughts of past or future seem to dissolve, which makes it much easier to stay totally present to what is happening right now.

THE *SPIRITUAL NAVIGATION SYSTEM*

Imagine an airplane traveling from Los Angeles to New York. During the flight, no matter how good the pilot or the computer system might be, the airplane is actually off-course nearly 100% of the time! I know this may sound crazy, but it really is true. The airplane's avionics contain a lot of sensors—many of them redundant—that are continually comparing the airplane's current location with the destination, and the feedback is sent back to the controls to allow the plane to correct itself moment-by-moment. As you might expect, if the pilot (or auto-pilot) fails to pay attention to what the instruments are saying, then the plane can end up seriously—and possibly dangerously—off course.

The lesson here is that *Purpose* and *Integrity* together form the primary components of what I call our *Spiritual Navigation System*—*Purpose* provides information about our destination, and *Integrity* provides feedback to help us know where we are in relation to our destination.

If you like the idea of experiencing a sense of *bliss* for yourself, start by making sure you turn on and monitor your own internal navigation system: heighten your awareness of all your thoughts, words, actions and emotions and make sure they are fully aligned with your spiritual purpose.

INTEGRITY CHECK

I've been talking a lot about the alignment of thoughts, words, actions and emotions. When these are all aligned in the same direction—specifically in the direction of our spiritual purpose, life seems much more fulfilling. Our general outlook improves, stress seems to melt away more easily, and we experience a greater level of happiness and enthusiasm about life. These four elements— thought, word, action and emotion—are like pillars that provide a solid foundation for our life, while purpose provides the direction of alignment. Understanding this concept makes it pretty easy to check our own integrity anytime we want to. There are several ways we can do this.

1. Things We Accept as Our Responsibility

We all assume responsibility for different things in different areas of our lives, including work, play or home life. For example,

- Completing work projects on time;
- Being punctual for all business and personal appointments;
- Keeping ourselves and our personal spaces clean and organized;
- Treating other people with respect and dignity;
- Keeping a prioritized to-do list so we don't forget things;
- Honoring the laws of the land.

As we look at our own list of "responsibilities", we can just notice whether we are in alignment with them or not.

2. Goals We Declare

We all declare goals in our lives as well. Things like these:

- Achieving a particular fitness or health target;
- Saving up some money for something important;
- Planning and participating in a special family event or vacation;
- Career advancement—asking for a raise or promotion;

- Enhancing one or more relationships—particularly a primary relationship;

If we have our goals written down, then it is relatively easy for us to take inventory and review our progress. We can look at each goal and decide whether or not we are in integrity with respect to that goal. If so, we can celebrate our progress; if not, we can decide whether to re-declare the goal or to modify it or delete it altogether.

3. Actions and Choices We Make

As I mentioned earlier, ultimately everything we do is based on a choice we make because of who we really are. Our actions are based on our choices, and they reflect who we are choosing to be in that moment. We can all reflect on any of our past actions, things like these:

- What we choose to do in our spare time;
- The way we interact with others;
- Our eating habits and exercise routines;
- Our attitudes, beliefs and behaviors;
- How we react to external stressors.

I find it very enlightening to take stock periodically and assess how I'm doing with my choices. For each choice I remember, I can notice whether or not the choice represents the way I want others to experience me. If I'm happy with the choice, then I can honor myself for showing up the way I truly want to show up; otherwise, I can decide how I want to modify that choice the next time I'm faced with similar circumstances.

4. Agreements and Commitments We Make

Unless we live in total seclusion from other people, then we make agreements with other people virtually all the time. And even if we don't make agreements with others, we still end up making agreements with ourselves—although most of them may be unspoken, or even unconscious. Before going any further on this topic, I think it would help to have a clear sense of what we mean by two important terms. Here are definitions I find useful:

- AGREEMENT—a negotiated, and sometimes legally binding, arrangement or contract among parties as to a particular course of action.
- COMMITMENT—a promise or pledge to do or give something.

Notice that an *agreement* seems to involve at least two parties, whereas a *commitment* can be made without the involvement of another person—that is, it may be a commitment to oneself. Also, because an *agreement* is usually negotiated, it is usually also written down so that all parties can be clear about its terms; a *commitment* on the other hand may be verbal only. Another thing about commitments is that they can be implicit, meaning they are not expressed verbally. These are typically the kinds of commitments that we make silently to ourselves—for example, to honor our own code of ethics in everything we do. But implicit commitments can happen between people, too.

If you know your agreements and commitments—and I think it's safe to say that you are probably aware of most of them—then, for each one, you can easily answer this question:

> **Am I honoring and abiding by this agreement or commitment?**

Usually your answer will be a simple yes or no. Don't make excuses about it, just answer the question honestly—this is for you only; no-one else needs to know what your answer might be! Sometimes, the answer won't be so cut-and-dried, mainly because whatever you agreed to is still in progress, but you know in your heart whether you are honoring the agreement or not.

If your answer to this question is an unqualified yes, then you can honor yourself for being in integrity. However, if the answer is anything else, then you may need to dig a little deeper—and there is a wonderful process you can use that will help you get some clarity.

ACCOUNTABILITY

As we have already discussed, all of our thoughts, words, actions and emotions have an impact on the world around us. And when they are out of sync with one another—and particularly, out of alignment with our higher purpose—we create confusion and chaos, because the people who have heard our words and seen the misaligned actions begin to wonder whether or not we can be trusted. Accountability is a mechanism that allows us compassionately to examine our own behaviors when we are out of integrity—when we have failed to honor an agreement or commitment—so that we can really understand the consequences of our actions and learn something about any underlying belief (or shadow, which I discuss in detail in the next chapter) that might have prevented us from keeping our word. With this knowledge, we can then look for ways to repair the trust that we may have broken and create a new agreement that will help us to get back into integrity.

Typically, when someone fails to keep a commitment, we will often hear them offering an apology, if they even admit the failure. How often has someone apologized to you with some kind of excuse? (*"Sorry, got caught in traffic." "Sorry, had to answer a phone call from my wife." "Sorry, didn't have time."*) And, having received one of these so-called "apologies", how often have you let them off the hook, even though there might have been some important consequences to you that were simply not acknowledged? How much do you trust people who make these kinds of "apologies" over and over again?

I don't wish to imply that there is anything wrong with an apology; but, unfortunately, apologies can be very shallow and insincere unless they are accompanied by a clear statement of accountability. That is, the person offering the apology understands the consequences of his/her actions and is willing to look inside to understand what might have kept him/her from honoring the agreement or commitment in the first place. The authenticity that occurs when someone is willing to look at the underlying beliefs and behaviors that led to a broken agreement is what helps us to stay connected to our own compassion. And this allows for the mending of broken trust far more than any apology could ever do.

Personal Accountability

There are many resources available on the internet today that discuss the concept of *self-accountability* or *personal accountability*. These discussions all seem to share some common themes:

- HONESTY AND OPENNESS—The more you are willing to hold yourself accountable, the more you are likely to be experienced as open, honest and vulnerable, and this can help you to create deeper connections with others.

- FEEDBACK—Sometimes other people have their own views about your words and actions. Are you willing and able to receive input from them and to reflect upon their perspectives and interpretations? The more you can welcome and embrace this feedback—and remember, you don't have to agree with it, just accept it—the deeper your connections with others.

- OUTCOMES AND CONSEQUENCES—Everything you do creates an outcome, for better or worse. Are you able to recognize the outcomes that you have created? Are you willing and able to understand the impacts of all your choices? Are you willing and able to imagine impacts from the perspectives of others?

- SAFETY AND TRUST—When you act consistently in accordance with your words, then people around you are more likely to find you consistent and reliable. Even if they don't always agree with your behavior, they are more likely to trust you, and this makes them feel safer around you.

It's Not about Shame or Blame

Accountability is often bandied about in the media these days as a way of getting people—particularly people in positions of leadership—to take the blame for some kind of problem or challenge or failure that has happened. This leads us collectively to believe that accountability is a painful or shameful process—that makes someone wrong for something. That is not the intention of accountability as I'm presenting it here.

To hold yourself accountable is *not* to be shamed or ridiculed or punished; rather, it is an opportunity to learn about yourself in a very deep, powerful and liberating way. My accountability process is designed to help you understand the choices you made—especially the choices that might have been unconscious—and the consequences that came about as a result of those choices. As you become aware of your choices and their consequences, you may also recognize patterns of behavior that show up whenever you are faced with the kind of commitment you originally created. In seeing the choices and consequences and underlying patterns associated with a broken commitment—you may then begin to recognize a shadow that gets in the way and trips you up, preventing you in some way from honoring your word—even to yourself! And as we'll talk about later, awareness of your shadow provides a wonderful opportunity for growth: rather than being ashamed of it, you can be grateful that you have found something that has been keeping you from showing up authentically in the world, and now you can do something about it.

The Self-Accountability Process

Over the years, I have seen many different ways of holding people accountable. But in 2003 when I attended a men's workshop hosted by *The ManKind Project*, I was introduced to a variation that struck me as being intentionally designed to help people really understand their choices—especially the unconscious ones—and the consequences of those choices. What I found particularly illuminating was that, as people became aware of the consequences of their choices, they often connected to something within them—a disempowering belief or shadow—that was keeping them from showing up in a fully authentic way. And as they became aware of this unconscious shadow within them, they were able to use the accountability process to help them uncover ways to re-purpose the energy of that shadow. Over the years, I have refined and honed this process and shared it in many different groups and contexts, and the results have invariably been quite profound.

The quality I like best about this process is that it is built upon a simple premise:

> To hold yourself accountable is not to be shamed or ridiculed or punished; rather, it is an opportunity to learn about yourself in a very deep, powerful and liberating way.

Self-accountability begins with the assumption that you genuinely want to take full responsibility for every aspect of your life, and that you are committed to understanding and mastering everything about yourself. It also assumes that you have dishonored a commitment or broken an agreement—consciously or unconsciously—and that you have somehow become aware of that fact. The following steps will help you to gain a deeper understanding of any dynamic that may have led you to be out of integrity with respect to that commitment or agreement.

You can certainly do this process by yourself, but I believe you'll find it more powerful and more enlightening if you do it with witnesses present—especially if one of those witnesses is the person with whom you made the agreement in the first place. You may also find it helpful to have an unbiased person to facilitate or support you with all of the steps.

1. Check-In

Start by identifying and acknowledging a way in which you believe you are out of integrity. Perhaps you failed to complete a goal; perhaps you broke an agreement or dishonored a commitment; perhaps you had a responsibility that you didn't meet; or perhaps you just did something that didn't represent the best of who you know you really are. Clearly state your understanding of whatever commitment you had, and with whom you made it. Describe how you failed to honor your commitment. Keep this as simple and succinct as possible.

It is important to note that this is about clarifying *your* understanding of the commitment—it is *not* about getting agreement from any other parties involved. It's quite possible that you and the other person(s) have a different understanding of the agreement—especially if it was not written down—and that aspect of the situation can be resolved later. The process is for and about you, so only your understanding matters at the moment.

Example: *"I agreed to meet Sue for dinner at 6PM. I broke that agreement by showing up at 6:30PM."*

2. Choices

Whatever it was that got in the way of honoring your commitment, at some level you had to make some choices, even if they were totally unconscious. In this step, you bring awareness to those choices. Here are a couple of questions that can help get clarity about choices you may have made:

- What else was going on in your life that you chose to make more important than keeping this commitment?
- What did you choose to do instead of honoring the commitment?

In answering these questions, begin with an implicit acceptance that you did indeed make choices, even if you weren't consciously aware of them at the time. And then, let yourself be totally curious, much like a scientist who is interested in collecting data. Don't judge yourself for any of this; just notice what seems to be true for you.

Continuing with the earlier example, you might notice that you made a choice to try and get one more thing done from your daily to-do list. Or perhaps you forgot your commitment altogether, which perhaps indicates a choice not to put your appointment on your calendar.

3. Consequences

For each choice that you identify in the previous step, now consider its impact. Sometimes, the consequences of a particular choice may be quite obvious, in which case you'll be able to answer the question quite easily. But some consequences can be implicit and you may need to do a little internal digging in order to find them.

In the example above, if you decided to do one more thing before leaving for your date, you might notice that the consequences were two-fold: (1) you got one more thing done, which might be good for your relationship with your boss; and (2), you didn't leave work in time to meet your friend, which prevented you from making it to your appointed meeting place at the appointed time.

In either case, you created a situation that made you late, and there might be some additional consequences for that choice. For example, when you are late for an event, people might get the idea that you don't think they are important to you. In other words, your behavior is sending a message that is quite different from the words you are saying, and this might lead people to trust you less.

Some consequences, on the other hand, might not be so obvious to you, and this is where it really helps to put yourself in the other person's position. For example, when I'm sitting waiting for someone who is supposed to be meeting me at a particular time, the longer I have to wait without hearing from him/her, the more likely I am to worry that maybe something bad happened. In other words, I am concerned for the other person's well-being. Well, it makes sense, then, that if someone else is waiting for me for a long period of time, s/he may be getting worried about *my* well-being. In other words, my choice (conscious or otherwise) to be late may trigger worry in the other person.

If you can recognize or imagine these consequences for the other person, you can begin to see how some of your own unconscious choices may be having similar impacts that you didn't really intend to create.

4. Unconscious Beliefs & Shadows

For each consequence you identify, ask yourself this question:

> *What was the underlying belief or intention that led me to make the choice that led to this consequence?*

This is a very powerful question because it helps to shine a light on things and to raise your awareness of some of your unconscious behaviors. Consider, for example, the idea of trying to get one more thing done before heading out to your appointment. Why might you risk being late in order to do this? Whenever I've found myself in this kind of situation and I've had the courage to ask myself this question, usually I've received an answer something like this:

> *I have the belief that if I don't get one more thing crossed off of my to-do list, then this means I'm a failure. I disappoint my boss, I let down my team, and ultimately I make myself look like a flake. So, I choose to do things that protect me from being seen this way.*

Ironically, until I ask myself the question, I may not even notice that by "doing that one-more-thing in order to avoid looking flaky with my co-workers", I end up appearing flaky to the person I agreed to meet! And this, *Maestro*, is the very nature of shadow, as we'll soon see!

Of course, your answers may be very different, but it's important to do the digging so that you can understand your own subconscious behaviors.

5. *Create a Path Back to Integrity*

As soon as you identify a shadow behavior, you now have the opportunity to bring yourself back into integrity. One of the most effective ways of doing this is by declaring a new agreement or commitment. Now, I'm not talking about re-committing to what you had previously agreed to—in reality, that is kind of expected, don't you think? Nor am I suggesting anything that feels like a punishment or a way of getting even.

No, I'm talking about creating a commitment that allows you to do some work on the shadow you've uncovered. It does no real good to identify and uncover a shadow if you are not willing to deepen your understanding of that shadow and come up with strategies for preventing it from showing up again "accidentally". This new commitment is something that is really just for you, and not at all for any other party who was involved (although you are perfectly welcome—and encouraged—to make amends if you feel that is necessary). It's about creating an opportunity for you to learn and grow from your new wisdom and understanding.

What might such a commitment look like? It really depends on the shadow that is uncovered. In the case of the extended example we've been discussing, the shadow seems to be something related to "looking good", to going a step beyond in order to appear responsible and not disappoint anyone. And the underlying belief that motivates this particular shadow may be something along the lines of "not being good enough as I am" or "being unacceptable or unlovable". These are potent disempowering beliefs—and not terribly uncommon as it turns out.

So, the question is, what kind of work might be necessary to transform the underlying belief so that the shadow behavior doesn't emerge anymore? Clearly, in this case, some form of self-love or self-acceptance work is called for. So one possible commitment might be the following:

> *During the coming week, I commit to spending 10 minutes each day acknowledging all the ways that I am worthy, lovable and acceptable.*

You can see that this commitment has nothing to do with satisfying any other party—which, as it turns out, might just be playing into the shadow behavior! Rather, this commitment puts you squarely into the face of the shadow and seeks to reduce (or redirect) its power so that you begin to develop an affirming habit of recognizing how amazing you really are, rather than spending so much energy focusing on the minor ways that you might fall short of your own expectations.

To be effective, the new commitment should give you an opportunity to face your own shadow in ways that allow you to see it more clearly, understand its underlying intent to keep you safe, and to embrace it in such a way that you can heal it and transform its energy into something that serves you.

6. Choosing an Accountability Partner

Creating and declaring a new commitment or agreement that allows you to face your shadow can feel very satisfying unto itself. But the real gift in this process comes when you declare the new agreement to someone who is willing to help you hold yourself accountable to follow through. If you are doing this whole process because of a broken agreement you had with someone, then choosing that same person to help you with this new agreement makes sense—but only if that person is someone who is capable of supporting you in an unconditionally loving way.

Process Summary

Holding yourself accountable can be a very powerful and liberating process. Your willingness to do this comes from the place of your "conscious and mature higher self", recognizing that you are capable of making mistakes, and being willing to look at the motivation behind those mistakes. In doing so, you connect with parts of yourself that you might have disowned long ago, and you get to learn (or, more correctly, remember) the gifts in those dis-

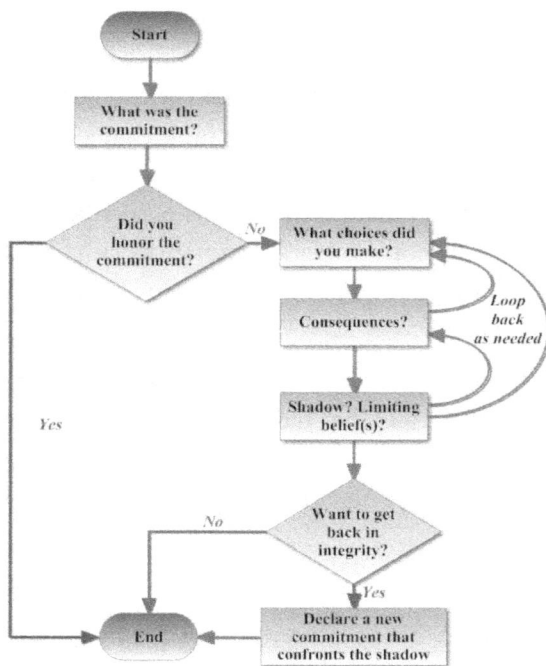

Figure 18—Accountability Flow

owned parts. Then you can begin the work of healing whatever wounds might be connected to the shadows and integrate those parts back into yourself. Another step on the path to wholeness!

The flow of the self-accountability process is depicted in Figure 18 for your reference. As you practice the process and integrate it into your daily life, you will just naturally raise your own awareness so that you always know what agreements you've made and whether you're keeping them or not. As a conscious and mature individual who sometimes makes mistakes, you'll grow more and more compassionate toward yourself, and when you have broken an agreement, you will know that trust may have been compromised. But because you're committed to creating powerful, intimate and long-lasting relationships, you will know that you are honor-bound to account honestly and truthfully for the choices you've made and for the consequences of those choices. No one will ever need to "hold you accountable"; being a conscious and mature individual who loves being in integrity, you will hold yourself accountable. As I have learned over the years:

> **The more I practice holding myself accountable, the greater my experience of Integrity.**

CHAPTER SUMMARY—INTEGRITY

Be daring, be different, be impractical, be anything that will assert integrity of purpose and imaginative vision against the play-it-safers, the creatures of the commonplace, the slaves of the ordinary.—Cecil Beaton

Integrity is doing the right thing. Even when no-one is watching.—C.S. Lewis

Don't worry so much about your self-esteem. Worry more about your character. Integrity is its own reward.—Laura Schlessinger

HIGHLIGHTS

1. Integrity is a state of being in which thoughts, words, actions and emotions are mutually aligned in the direction of your spiritual purpose.

2. Integrity implies impeccability of intention and is usually demonstrated through congruence of word and action.

3. Integrity and purpose together represent the components of your Spiritual Navigation System, to which you have access at any time. Conscious choice is always informed, influenced and guided by this system.

4. Personal integrity checking involves examining your responsibilities, goals, choices, actions, agreements and commitments in order to determine your current level of alignment.

5. You can use the incredible power of the personal accountability tool to help you understand compassionately how and why you occasionally slip out of integrity.

6. By holding yourself accountable—with honesty, empathy, and curiosity—you shine a light on your unconscious patterns and become aware of disempowering beliefs. This enables you to declare meaningful and relevant new commitments for yourself that bring you quickly back into a state of integrity.

7. Self-accountability is not about shame or blame; it is simply about raising awareness and healing the wounds underneath your limiting or disempowering beliefs.

8. Self-accountability is most powerful when it is done in the presence of a witness or witnesses who can serve as unconditionally accepting accountability partners.

The Integrity Key

To be in integrity is to align all of your thoughts, words, actions and emotions in the same direction. All the time! Integrity is a conscious awareness that you are channeling all of your creative and intentional energies in a consistent direction. If that direction is aligned with your purpose, then everything about your life just "feels right"—and this induces a powerful feeling of satisfaction and fulfillment. Such feelings cannot be faked: you can't *think* or *feel* integrity, you have to *be* integrity.

This practice of *integrity* requires a willingness to look within on a regular basis so as to take inventory of what is happening internally. The more you do this, the easier it becomes, and you begin to recognize ever more subtle shifts in any one of the four component elements, so that you can catch yourself ever more quickly and bring yourself back into proper alignment.

Remember to honor yourself for all the time you are in integrity, and be gentle with yourself when you slip. Let the following affirmation guide you on a daily basis:

> **I am a joyful and inspirational model of integrity, and I lovingly align all my thoughts, words, actions and emotions with my Spiritual Purpose.**

CHAPTER 8: SHADOW

BEFRIEND AND EMBRACE YOUR SHADOWS

sad birds

the silence ricochets off the rocks
above the lake
and comes to rest
in the empty spaces between my ribs

silhouettes of trees
standing guard like moveless chess pieces
against a backdrop of darkening sky
    the color of   **god's**   eye
make me think of the shadows
that cover my own blueness
and hide my gems out of sight

but this doesn't stop the bats
from swooping out of the sky
    (like sad birds)
out of the darkness
to bounce their ultrasonic waves off me
to construct their own lightless image of me

the bats know i am here
they know who i am
and yet they seem incurious, aloof
    (how could they possibly know
    about the hole inside me?)
they have no concern for me
    or for darkness or shadow

back and forth they fly
in their chaotic dance of primal beauty
    searching for something
    to satisfy a dark yearning
        (harvesting my sadness)
back and forth
in a frenetic cyclical splurge of energy

where do they come from?
where will they go?

even you could see through me
in this moment
if you were here
even you could see past the shadows
into the truth

but you are out there
    up there
enticing the bats
    flying with these sad birds
controlling their primitive love offering
twisting them this way and that
architecting their primal dance
    pulling their strings

it is *you* doing that

all the while winking at me
    with the stars
        in your darkening sky

PREMATURE POSITIVITY

I have noticed quite a bit of talk in recent years about *shadow*—that is, the "dark side" of individuals, groups, and even whole societies—and much of this talk (even though it may not refer to the word "shadow" explicitly) tends to characterize shadow as a "bad thing". I can understand how people might fall into this belief; after all, as we look at the world and witness all the pain and suffering that we seem to inflict on each other, it's easy to conclude that there is real evil all around us. Some of this "evil" can be attributed to psychopathic or sociopathic behavior, but much of it is really the result of individual and collective unconsciousness—which is the realm of *psychic shadow*.

A great deal of self-help material these days tells you that if you want a better life, you have to do a whole bunch of positive-oriented things, such as the following:

- Focus on the positive; stay in the "light".

- Change your mindset or your belief systems.

- Recite positive affirmations on a regular basis.

- Get into a regular mindfulness practice, such as yoga or meditation.

- Trust in immutable laws of the universe, such as the *Law of Attraction*.

- Stop sabotaging yourself.

All of these are helpful ideas that, if implemented correctly, can do wonders to make your life better. But what many teachers don't seem to understand is the principle of what I call "premature positivity"—i.e. embracing positivity before the deeper underlying wound or dysfunction is addressed and healed.

As I see it, many self-help resources don't go nearly far enough in helping people get to the root of their problems in the first place. Many teachings seem to be intent on focusing on the positive solutions that they offer, most of which are targeted at very obvious symptoms. Sadly, they pay little or no attention to root causes. Consequently, even though people might try the recommendations of the teachers, they often find that the results are nowhere near what the promotional material promises. Why is this? Well, the answer is pretty simple: you can't change belief systems and behavior patterns if you're not aware of them. And in order to become aware of them, you have to do important inner work to bring light to the things you don't normally see. In other words, you have to venture into the dark parts of yourself in order to really understand what is going on. Unfortunately, for many people, the mere prospect is quite scary—which is why having a skilled shadow mastery facilitator around can make a huge difference.

In this chapter, I'm going to talk about *shadow* in some depth. My intention here is to give you a solid overview of the shadow, without teaching you anything about how to heal your shadow—that is work that should be done in a safe and supportive container, preferably with other participants who can travel that journey with you.

My hope is that, after you've read this chapter, you will have a much greater appreciation—and much less fear—about the shadow. Even better if you find yourself excited about finding out more about your own shadow.

A SYNCHRONISTIC STORY

One day, in the early stages of my personal growth journey—I think it was around 1997 or so—I was shopping at a local bookstore. As I browsed the aisles, I noticed that there was a gathering of people just outside one of the back rooms. I was curious about this, so I approached the small group and asked one of the people what was going on. I was told that a presentation would be starting soon on the topic of how our unconscious belief systems keep us from living up to our potential. The subject matter piqued my interest, so I went inside and listened to what the speaker had to say.

The presentation wasn't much to recommend itself, but I was already there and I didn't want to embarrass the speaker by leaving early, so I stuck it out. In retrospect, I'm glad I stayed because during that presentation, the speaker shared a Native American story that had a powerful impact on me:

The Two Wolves

One evening, Grandfather noticed that young Oukonunaka was fuming and fidgeting by the fire. He had a very dark expression on his face, and he seemed to be pre-occupied with something painful.

"I think I know that look," said Grandfather. "But why don't you tell me what is going on, my son?"

The boy blinked and looked at his Grandfather. "Mohe took my arrowheads, and he won't give them back. He says I'm not big enough to have arrowheads. Grandfather, I'm really mad at him, and I want to hurt him so he feels the pain I feel. I want my arrowheads back."

"Ah, so that is what's going on. I think I understand how you feel, my son. I too have felt anger and hate toward people who have taken much from me, without any remorse for their actions."

"Yes, that's it! But what can I do about it?" asked the boy.

"Hmmm. Sometimes it feels like there is a fight going on inside," said Grandfather. "It is a terrible fight between two wolves.

"The black wolf is evil—he is anger, envy, sorrow, regret, greed, arrogance, self-pity, guilt, resentment, inferiority, lies, false pride, superiority, and ego.

"The other wolf, the white one, is

Figure 19—The Two Wolves

good—he is joy, peace, love, hope, serenity, humility, kindness, benevolence, empathy, generosity, truth, compassion, and faith.

"Seems like this fight is going on inside you right now—and it is a fight that everyone has to deal with at one time or another."

Oukonunaka thought about this for a minute, nodding as if he understood. "But Grandfather, which wolf will win, the white one or the black one?"

Grandfather turned, bent down and gently patted the boy's belly. "The one you feed", he said.

A SHAMANIC JOURNEY

I was touched by this folktale because I had already begun the process of understanding and healing my own anger, and I realized that I had been, in the language of the story, "feeding the black wolf within me". Naturally, I wanted to start feeding the white wolf instead, but as I searched within myself, I couldn't seem to find him anywhere. I had become so consumed by the darkness of my anger and sadness and shame that I only rarely felt any joy, peace, serenity, or compassion. If a white wolf had ever been present, it seemed he was long gone by now, and I had the terrible feeling that in my own pain I had starved him to death.

Years later, I had long forgotten this story and what it had triggered for me. I was at a workshop in which I participated in a shamanic journey process to connect with an ally from the animal world. My understanding of the process was that I was not to choose an animal but rather to allow an animal to choose me. As I went through the visualization, I saw all kinds of creatures in my mind, and I was drawn to many of them, particularly eagle, horse, lion, elk, buffalo, raven. But even though these animals seemed to approach me out of curiosity, none of them gave any real indication that they were meant to be with me. As the facilitator began bringing the visualization to a close, I was feeling quite sad and alone, but I nevertheless followed the instruction to leave the animal world through a dark tunnel. As I came out the other side, I was still alone. I looked back toward the tunnel wistfully, and I was stunned by what I saw. In the dark shadow of the tunnel, I could just make out the head and eyes of a creature that I could not yet identify. I turned fully to peer at this animal and I noticed that I was holding my breath. After some time, the animal emerged from the tunnel too. I finally released my breath. It was a wolf. A black wolf. With incredibly beautiful blue eyes. In the visualization, I knelt down and looked at him. In the real world, my body had started shaking and I was sobbing real tears. There was something so important and special about this wolf that I did not yet understand. In my heart, I knew he was going to be teaching me something, something that would make all the difference in my life.

A few years after that shamanic journey experience, I made a decision to get a tattoo of my power animal, so I was searching on the internet for some appropriate art, something that would capture the spiritual nature of my connection to this creature. In the course of my search, I was reconnected to the original story that I reproduced above, and I noticed that my reaction to it was quite different than it had been the first time I heard it. By this time, I'd done a lot of work healing the old wounds that had fueled my anger, and I was much more connected to my joy and serenity—without realizing it, I had actually found my inner white wolf and had been feeding it in order to heal myself! But it had been my inner black wolf that had shown me the way, and all I had to do in order to truly heal was to befriend both wolves equally. I'll share more about this a little later.

My Introduction to Shadow

My "Transcendent Black Wolf" has indeed taught me many wonderful things, things that most people don't like to talk about very much, but things which I believe absolutely need to be addressed.

In my experience, the emergence of my black wolf from that dark tunnel was a metaphorical representation of my own growing awareness of the darker parts of myself, parts which I had long ago cast aside or hidden away because I had believed that they were unacceptable, inappropriate, or just plain bad or wrong. And yet, this wolf did not have dark, hateful eyes. Instead, his eyes were bright, clear, loving, and—surprising, in retrospect—innocent. This wolf had chosen to come out of hiding so that I could get to know him—that is, to know all the parts of *myself* that I had disowned earlier in my life.

While I was oddly attracted to the prospect of digging into my own darkness, I had a lot of fear at the same time. I was terrified by the idea of opening up the locked boxes I had created within myself and letting anything out. I was terribly worried that anyone who witnessed these parts of me would come to hate me and see me as evil. I thought they would want to cast me out so that I would have to live alone for the rest of my life. The idea of being rejected, abandoned, and unloved was so frightening to me that I very nearly turned and ran. But then, as I thought about it, I realized that, because of the way I had become a slave to my own anger over all those years, I was already pretty alone anyway. People were already avoiding me, my relationships were already damaged, how much worse would it get if I didn't do anything? So, I took the risk and started doing the work to look into those dark places and find out the truth about myself. And guess what happened? People did not run screaming into the hills to get away from me. Instead, they actually resonated with what I shared about my own darkness and began to draw closer to me. In a pretty short time, my fear about looking at my dark side diminished, and I actually began to see it all as a wonderful adventure in self-knowing. Today, I'm always curious about what new aspect of myself I might uncover when I get out my flashlight and start looking in the shadows.

What is Shadow?

As children, all of us grow up in the influential presence of adults—most commonly our parents, but also guardians, teachers, religious leaders, government officials, and so on. We often see these adults as "gods", people who have control over our lives, our behaviors, and our destinies. Some of these adults deliver wounds to us—consciously or not, maliciously or not, deliberately or not— and the intensity of those wounds influences how we show up in the world going forward.

Depending on the depth, painfulness and recurring nature of a wound, as a child, you may come to the conclusion that it is dangerous for you to engage in a certain behavior or to reveal a certain aspect of yourself. You may have been punished or ridiculed or laughed at or abused in some way each time you did so. You may have a natural and normal desire to reveal this part of yourself, but since you have learned that to expose it is either dangerous or wrong, you may have further decided that there is something wrong with you, that you are broken. As a result of the shame that begins to grow within you, you spend a good part of your life hiding and disowning this aspect of yourself. You learn to divert its natural energy by engaging in other behaviors that do not result in punishment or abuse—and which you conclude must be "okay" or "appropriate"; you do your best to shut down the unwanted behavior or to hide the disowned part of yourself. In many ways, your strategy works very well; you keep yourself safe by avoiding the punishment or humiliation, and this is a very smart thing to do—at least at first. But as you grow older, you find that, in spite of keeping this disowned part of yourself protected and hidden away, you still experience forms of abuse or punishment anyway that might be different but feel very familiar. Not only that, but because the part you've hidden away is a natural part of you, it seems to have a life of its own, and it finds ways to sneak out into the open. You find yourself being tripped up by this aspect of yourself and that it often happens "by accident", without your conscious awareness.

It doesn't take much for a parent or guardian to inflict a permanent wound on a child that leads to shadow behavior. More often than not, such wounds are delivered by parents who really love their children and want the very best for them; the motivation behind the delivery of the wound is usually to help the child learn how to behave in "acceptable" ways in society.

Recently, I was at a restaurant and there was a young Japanese boy playing with a ball in the aisle way; his mother and grandmother were sitting at a table close-by watching him and smiling at him. It was pretty clear that the boy, who was probably not more than 3 years old, was having a lot of fun with his ball, exploring the way it bounced and moved. He giggled and laughed and talked out loud. Mom and Grandma both smiled lovingly at him and seemed to be very encouraging and supportive. The rest of the patrons of the restaurant seemed to be either oblivious, tolerant, or accepting, but I didn't notice any irritation at all. When the boy's excitement about what he was doing elevated to the point where he let out a very high-pitched squeal of delight, his mother quickly responded—quite loudly—"Shhh. Stop that! You shouldn't do that."

Well, the boy did stop, and I noticed quite a surprised look on his face, with an expression that seemed to say, *"What's wrong? What did I do, Mommy?"* He seemed to recover quite quickly, however, and continued playing. Then, after a minute or two, he let out another two shrieks of delight, and his mother again shushed him quite loudly with similar words. This time, the boy did settle down, but I noticed that he seemed to be a little deflated. Now, I could tell that the mother really loved her son, but my suspicion is that she was more concerned about how the boy's behavior might be impacting the patrons in the restaurant; she might even have been worried about how people might perceive her as a parent.

Could such an isolated incident, delivered by a mother who clearly loves her son, result in a wound that could lead to future shadow behavior in the boy? Mothers are powerful influences over their sons, and the young boy undoubtedly loves his mom as much as she loves him, so there is a natural tendency in the boy to do his best to please his mom. The incident I witnessed had an impact on the boy (probably inducing some fear), and the energy of his mom's words rippled through his body and into his cells. Even if this is the only time it ever happens, the boy will remember the fearful feeling and will probably want to protect himself from experiencing that again. Nobody knows for sure what the ultimate impact of this one scenario might be, but this incident, coupled with other incidents of a similar nature over the course of the boy's childhood and adolescence (not to mention a possible decline in his mother's patience), will lead to an accumulation of wounding energy that will influence his decisions about himself as he grows into adulthood. He will keep certain parts of himself hidden from view and will show only those parts of himself that he believes others want to see; he will thus tend to show up inauthentically, because he is afraid of how people will perceive and judge him.

The situation I've described here is pretty typical, and most people experience things like this many, many times during their formative years. Every one of us can relate to the experience of being told what to do or how to behave, of being effectively controlled by someone else who was bigger or stronger. Most of us have lived through insults from adults in our lives, some of us repeatedly, some of us incessantly. No matter what our situation might be, we all have a natural tendency to want to please others in our lives—especially our guardians—so when these sorts of situations show up in our lives, we look for strategies and coping mechanisms that help us to short-circuit them or avoid them altogether. And in doing so, we disown parts of ourselves and allow only the "acceptable" aspects to show through.

A disowned aspect of the grown adult is what we call a *shadow*. While the idea of shadow has surely been with us for a very long time—perhaps even thousands of years—the notion was formalized in psychology by the work of Carl Jung, among others. Jung described the shadow as a region of the unconscious mind consisting of repressed parts of yourself that you judge to be weaknesses, shortcomings, or undesirable instincts. The more you are unaware of hiding these characteristics, the greater the *density* of your shadow—i.e. the more intensely it plays out in your life.

DEFINITION OF SHADOW

The Jungian view suggests that "shadow" may refer to any unconscious aspect of the personality which the conscious ego does not acknowledge or identify in itself. Because people generally tend to reject or disown their least desirable aspects, shadow tends to be perceived as negative, but as I've mentioned already, we can easily hide things we like about ourselves too. Carl Jung himself went even further than this. In his view, the entire unconscious—that is, everything of which a person is not fully aware—constitutes "shadow".

The more work I've done on my shadow, and the more I've helped others to uncover and heal their shadows, the clearer I've become about what shadow really is. As a result of my work, I've come to define shadow as follows:

> A shadow is any
> ***part, aspect, characteristic or behavior***
> that you
> ***disown, disavow, deny, hide or repress***
> because you believe it is
> ***unacceptable, inappropriate, bad or wrong.***

This definition allows for the possibility that you may be at least partially aware of your shadow—hence the use of the words *disown, disavow, deny,* and *hide*. However, most of the disowning is done unconsciously; hence the use of the word *repress*. It is important also to notice that the shadow may be any part of yourself. While it is true that we all tend to avoid showing those parts of ourselves that we don't like very much, it is also true that we sometimes hide our beauty and magnificence as well, because we've been taught that to show our light is considered self-centered or egotistical behavior.

In *A Little Book on the Human Shadow*, Robert Bly discusses the Jungian idea of shadow at some length, and uses the metaphor of a circle to help illustrate it. Bly describes our infant state as a *360-degree personality*; as infants, we are born expressing the full breadth and depth of our human nature, without editing or censoring. However, as we grow up, we learn that certain slices of our 360-degree pie are in some way unacceptable to the people around us. And since we are naturally so loving

Figure 20—Hiding from One's Shadow

and wanting to please those around us, we learn to hide those slices—the ones that got us hurt. Unfortunately, because our shadows seem to show up when we least want them to, there is no doubt that we are still carrying those aspects of ourselves around. It is almost as if we have tossed those undesirable qualities into a bag which we sling over our shoulders—and which we've been dragging around behind us ever since.

IT'S NOT ALL BAD

Shadow does not always represent something "bad". How often do you notice a trait in someone that you really admire? Who do you look up to? Who are your idols? We often project our *gold* onto others because these people represent the qualities we have disavowed in ourselves out of a false sense of modesty. The fact that we do this may result from similar wounds.

For example, in an attempt to control her young daughter's behavior, a mother might say (or yell) to her "settle down", or "don't be so rambunctious", or "you're always getting in the way with your toys", or any of a myriad of other messages that translate in the girl's young mind to something along the lines of *"Mommy's angry with me. There must be something wrong with me."* If this kind of message is conveyed frequently enough, it won't be long before the girl simply stops showing this aspect of herself, even though it really corresponds to a magnificent, joyful, playful and creative side.

GIFTS GET LOST IN SHADOW

In the physical world, we learn that shadow only exists in the presence of a source of light. When light shines on one object, the object prevents light from passing behind it, which causes a shadow to be cast over other objects that are in close proximity. This analogy of light and shadow is useful for describing some things that take place in the psychological world as well. When we want to hide something internally, we find for ourselves some kind of internal psychic shield that prevents the light from shining on it. This is usually in the form of a compensatory behavior that covers up or distracts attention from the characteristic that we don't want others to see.

Unfortunately, a shield erected to block the light from an undesirable aspect of ourselves can also block the light from other aspects of ourselves that we didn't really intend to protect. As a result, we often end up hiding really wonderful parts of ourselves along with the thing that we don't want people to see. The more we try to hide an unwanted aspect, the stronger (and usually bigger) our shield must be, and so the more we inadvertently prevent a desirable aspect from being seen.

If the unwanted aspect is the part that becomes shadow, then what becomes of the desired aspect? This aspect—the part of ourselves that brings great value to the world, but which we have accidentally hidden as a result of protecting ourselves from revealing an unwanted part—we call our *light* or our *gold*; it represents a kind of treasure that we are—to borrow a Biblical phrase—*hiding under a bushel*. What is even more interesting, and certainly something that we forget (if indeed we ever remembered it): the unwanted part itself may in fact have a lot of *gold* within it that we weren't able to see because we were hiding it so strenuously!

Peeking Into the Bag

From the perspective of Bly's metaphor, then, we can see that our shadows are all the parts of ourselves that we keep tucked away in an invisible *shadow bag* that we drag around behind us. These shadows are all those parts of ourselves that we have split off, disowned, or repressed—the parts of ourselves we are afraid to show—regardless of whether they are *positive* or *negative*.

But more than that, even as adults, it may seem both proper and useful to keep some of our shadows in the bag, at least as far as most of our interactions are concerned. However, we may at times find that the weight of the bag slows us down and prevents us from being who we really want to be. When this happens, it makes sense to open up the bag and take a closer look at some of the shadows inside. But because we have been hiding these parts for so long (and we might even have forgotten what we put in the bag), it might be scary or risky to look inside. Consequently, we might resist the idea of even opening the bag, let alone examining the contents.

One of the best ways to do this kind of *shadow* processing is to find a safe, supportive and non-judgmental place where you can look into the bag, inspect its contents, and see if there is something that needs to come back out. If you can find a *ritual container* (such as a shadow processing support group) in which it is safe to engage the energy of a shadow—head-on instead of sideways—without any real-world consequences, then you can *remember* and *recover* the beauty and gold that are intrinsic to that disowned part. Great healing can happen when you do this—at much less risk than you may have imagined—and a bonus is that, as you find ways to forgive yourself for hiding this part, you begin the process of healing and re-integrating that part into your whole self.

What the Shadow Wants

As I have shared before, I believe that

> **Every thought, word, action and feeling is motivated at its deepest level by a desire to give or receive love.**

This may be hard to accept when you look at the world and see all the pain and suffering that is going on as a result of dysfunctional behavior. I think the problem is that, as a result of physical, emotional and psychological wounding, people get distorted ideas about what love is. For example, if a young girl is subjected to sexual abuse from a father who professes to love her during the sexual episodes, she is almost surely going to be confused about what love really is, and it won't be unusual to hear that she will use sex later in life as a way of expressing her love for others. Or if a boy is regularly beaten by a parent who claims to be "doing it for your own good", he may come to believe that love is a force that is intended to shape unruly people into fine upstanding citizens. How sad for that same boy who grows up to become a raging alcoholic who beats his own kids in the distorted and twisted belief that he is somehow loving them.

One thing I have learned in my work is that every shadow—no matter how destructive or dysfunctional it appears—seems to have a positive underlying intent. Psychological research suggests that there are at least four core states that we all gravitate towards:

1. **Being**—characterized by words like *presence, fullness, wholeness,* and *sovereignty.*

2. **Serenity**—characterized by words like *inner peace, calmness, contentedness,* and *safety.*

3. **Love**—characterized by words like *freedom, acceptance, honesty,* and *unconditional love.*

4. **Oneness**—characterized by words like *inclusion, belonging, family,* and *relationship.*

Each of us tend to favor these over all other states; that is, most of what we do in the world is motivated by a desire to move into or stay in one of these states.

The motivation of any given shadow is no different—which should be no surprise, since your shadow is just a part of you that you've put into hiding! Each shadow has its own preferred core state, and that is fairly easy to determine just by doing a simple *in-depth interview* process with the shadow part directly;

inevitably, the shadow will report one of the core states as its motivation. In other words, the shadow is always seeking to connect to its preferred core state; the problem is that the shadow engages in dysfunctional activities in order to achieve it!

The lesson here is that we should not judge our shadows too harshly; they are just doing what is natural—even if the behavior appears to contradict that—in order to connect to a core state. The shadow is actually trying to get something good for us, and this is because of the much deeper motivation to give or receive love.

SPOTTING SHADOWS

Almost all shadows are unconscious, which means that we are mostly unaware of them—at least until we've done the work necessary to track them down. And tracking them down is hard, until you learn special techniques like the ones I'm going to teach you here.

In the world of quantum physics, scientists are often trying to isolate and observe sub-atomic particles. But since the particles may have never been "seen", they can be very hard to find. However, as any good scientist will tell you, we can always tell where a sub-atomic particle has been, and by looking at the right signs, we can recognize some of its behaviors. So what quantum physicists do is to figure out what the behavior is, and then they look for evidence of that behavior. The evidence they find strengthens their understanding of the particle, which eventually leads to experimental techniques that reveal the particle for everyone to see.

Shadow spotting is very similar! First we identify behaviors that we attribute to a shadow, then we come up with ways to understand and track that behavior so that we can eventually get the shadow to reveal itself.

SHADOW MARKERS

Over the years, I have learned many techniques to identify shadows, all of which have to do with recognizing tell-tale behaviors, thinking patterns and reactions. I have identified six categories of *shadow indicators*, which I have classified into a simple taxonomy.

These indicators are organized with the more obvious ones at the top of the list, becoming ever more subtle as you move toward the bottom of the list. You can also think of a ranking based on the degree of difficulty in recognizing the indicator: obvious ones are easier to spot; subtle ones are harder to spot.

When any of these indicators is present, there is a pretty high likelihood that there is a shadow lurking right around the corner.

1. Acting Out

No matter how old you are or how much inner work you've done, I'll bet you've found yourself acting out in a childish way from time-to-time. When the conditions are right, and you've been treated in a way that you think is unfair or unjust or mean, perhaps you indulged in a temper tantrum or an uncontrolled rage. Or maybe instead you slipped into thoughts of helplessness or self-pity or worthlessness, and found yourself sulking or whining. You may have lashed out at others nearby—either physically or verbally—or perhaps you simply withdrew. In extreme cases, you may have done real damage to yourself, to someone else, or to someone's property.

If you think about your mindset when you are acting out, there is a good chance you are having thoughts like *"Look what you've made me do now!"* or *"If you weren't such a <fill in the blank>, this wouldn't be happening!"* or *"I'm taking my bat'n'ball and going home!"* Essentially, as the emotional energy flows through you, you end up rationalizing your behavior by trying to make others responsible for it. This leads you to see yourself as a victim in the interaction, and as a result, you find yourself wanting to lash out and hurt them.

It's easy to recognize a childish behavior when it is happening. But once you get caught up in it, you may find it hard to disengage. This is because your ego-mind is actually the part that is running the show, and it keeps you engaged by feeding your inner dialog with all kinds of justifications and rationalizations that keep you going. It can be so hard to stop the acting out process, in fact, that you may find yourself just riding it out until the energy has dissipated, after which your only real option is to clean up whatever mess you might have created.

2. Triggers and Emotional Charges

Generally speaking, acting out will rarely occur unless there is a stimulus present that somehow triggers a strong emotional response. In other words, something happens or someone does something that "pushes your buttons". When the trigger is fired, you may react, and usually with pretty strong emotion. Usually anger shows up, but sometimes fear or sadness can be the dominant emotion. You may find yourself wanting to "get even" or make the other person "wrong"; you may even feel an inclination toward violence.

When an emotional charge appears in your body, your perspective changes and it's difficult to remain objective about the situation. Strong emotion brings your attention to whatever is happening, usually at the expense of other things that might also be important. When you are charged up with strong emotion, there's a good chance that you will see the situation as risky or dangerous, either to yourself or to someone you care about. Your ego-mind may start up one of its justification tape loops—and probably will, if you are not careful! When this happens, you may find yourself on the road toward lashing out, and your charge may become a full-blown excuse for acting out.

3. Judgments and Projections

Who doesn't have judgments, right? Of course—we all do. And let's be clear here that not all judgments are bad. There are plenty of things that happen in our lives every day that require us to make judgments about situations. And sometimes, having accurate judgments about people can be very necessary as well. But even when there is no real need for judgments, we still have them!

I'm talking specifically about how we tend to draw conclusions or create interpretations about people because of their appearance (including race, gender, body type, etc.), their behavior, their attitudes, their beliefs or opinions, their chosen profession, their food or exercise choices, their communication style, their parenting skills, or pretty much anything else! There is really no end to the things we can judge people about.

Judgments of this type are explicit manifestations of inner projection—that is, when we judge something we see in someone else, it's usually because of something very similar that we recognize within ourselves and have chosen to disown or hide. We'll talk more about projection a little later, but the point I want to make here is that our judgments are gateways to our projections—which in turn are wonderful beacons leading us to awareness of our shadows.

4. Compensatory Behaviors

A compensatory behavior is a behavior we learn—usually when we are quite young—in order to defuse or offset the pain in a message we have heard from others or a belief we have taken on about ourselves. Here are a few examples to clarify what I mean:

- You repeatedly hear a message like *"You never get it right"*. As a result, you develop a "perfectionist" habit, because you want to be right all the time.

- You don't succeed at a few things in your life, and come to believe *"I'm a failure"*. To compensate, you become a "con artist" in order to create the appearance of success.

- Your family's communication style seems to be a lot of talk and very little listening, so you start to believe that *"Nobody ever hears me!"* You compensate by raising your voice louder and louder until you become recognized as a "shouter" or a "loud-mouth".

- One of your parents leaves, and you decide it was your fault, and this leads you to believe that *"Everyone leaves me because I'm unlovable"*. So, you cope with this by looking for as many ways as possible to be nice— even to the point of violating your own boundaries—so that you won't be left alone again.

Everybody hears painful messages from time to time—some of us much more frequently than others—and, as a result, we may take on beliefs about ourselves and about our lives similar to those described above. However, the way we compensate for these usually unconscious beliefs varies from person to person, depending on far more variables than we can ever hope to count. So, for example, if you happen to be someone who fell into the "I'm a failure" camp, you might compensate by simply accepting a mediocre life and allowing yourself to stay small. Or, you might become the person to leave a relationship first so that you don't have to suffer the pain of being left alone again.

When we are young, we have very unsophisticated reasoning abilities, so we come to these compensatory behaviors in somewhat random ways. We may actually try a few different ideas, but as soon as we try something that seems to have a desired effect, we tend to continue using that strategy. Thus, a compensatory behavior may actually serve a useful purpose when we first adopt it, because it appears to keep us safe and secure. Unfortunately, as we grow older, we continue to engage in these strategies and we don't even remember how they came into being. They become a part of us, and we engage them unconsciously—even well into our adult lives.

5. Ego-Defenses

When we are faced with stressful—or worse, traumatic—situations, our ego-mind goes on high alert and looks for ways to keep us safe. As a result, we may find ourselves engaging in defense mechanisms in order to cope with those

...

situations, and the coping strategies we use have all kinds of different flavors. Psychologists today recognize many different ego-defense strategies ranging from subtle to gross, conscious to unconscious, and all with varying degrees of effectiveness.

Sometimes, as I suggested earlier, a defense mechanism can initially be engaged quite consciously, and found to be effective in the specific circumstance in which it was used. However, what can happen is that if a similar situation shows up at a later date, we'll tend to fall back on that same defense mechanism. If the situation repeats itself enough times, eventually we may find ourselves responding automatically—and unconsciously—with the same defense mechanism, even if it loses effectiveness over time. Thus, even though some defense mechanisms may start out from conscious choice, often they all end up disappearing into our subconscious—so we don't even realize we're engaging in them anymore.

Here are a few of the more common ego-defense strategies…perhaps you recognize some of them:

Mechanism	Meaning	Catch-Phrase
Denial	Arguing against something by stating it doesn't exist.	This is not happening.
Dissociation	Temporarily modifying one's personal identity or character to avoid emotional distress.	I don't remember what happened.
Projection	Attributing unacceptable thoughts, feelings and motives to another person.	It's happening to you, not me.
Conversion	Expressing a conflict as a physical symptom.	I shut down when it's happening.
Minimization	Mentally reducing the impact of an event in order to rationalize its occurrence.	It happened, but it wasn't so bad.
Repression	Unconsciously pushing the memory as deep as possible into the subconscious so as to reduce pain.	It didn't happen at all.

An important thing to understand and remember about defense mechanisms is that they serve to protect us from emotional pain. However, that doesn't really make the pain go away; rather, the pain is just covered over and hidden away. The resurfacing of that pain can happen pretty much any time, but most of us get pretty good at continuing to stuff it and hide it until many years after the original event. Eventually, however, we may find that this pain—which we erroneously believed was gone—starts to come out in ways that we never expected, potentially causing damage to ourselves or others around us.

In my own experience, my primary defense mechanisms were denial, repression and projection, and as I shared earlier, I was pretty successful at holding things in until I was in my late 30s. My pattern continued until I realized that my anger and resentment were leaking out and harming people around me. The pain inside was trying to find its way out, while I was busy fighting to keep it locked in! I am blessed to have awakened to this, because it helped me find my way to doing the personal healing work that I needed to do—in a safe and nurturing environment.

6. Rigid Beliefs

Everyone has beliefs. Some of them are based in fact; some of them are based in fancy. Regardless of where a belief comes from, it serves a purpose in our lives—or at least it did when it came into being. But if you think about it for a moment, a belief is really nothing more than a well-established repetitive thinking pattern. And as I mentioned before, such patterns can be like ruts in a well-traveled road, making it very hard to change lanes.

Another problem with beliefs—something that most people don't really consider—is that they immediately imply some form of limitation. That is, if you believe "X", then you tend to resist or reject the possibility of "not X". For example, if you are a strong believer in gun rights, you will probably resist any perspective that talks about gun control. Or, if you believe that "god is on our side", then you will probably reject the idea that "god might actually be on the side of the enemy". This is not to make anybody wrong for what they might believe, by the way; it's just about pointing out how polarizing a belief can be.

Remember, beliefs are one of the ego-mind's innumerable "safety nets". When you declare a belief in something (consciously or unconsciously), your ego-mind latches onto it and looks for evidence everywhere that justifies your continuing acceptance of it. If someone shows up with a different or opposing belief, then your ego-mind will now leap to your defense and protect you from "being wrong".

By the way, you can't change an old belief simply by attempting to create a new one; you must own and deconstruct the old belief first. This means becoming aware of your beliefs and understanding the energy behind holding onto them. Whenever I find myself feeling strongly about something—to the point that I am feeling strong resistance to a different point of view—I look to the underlying belief I have and I simply ask myself: "Is this a belief that I want to keep, or is it something that is due for revision?" Another thing I find helpful is to just check in with myself and ask "What does it mean about me that I have this belief? What might it mean if I did a complete 180 and believed the exact opposite?"

Using the Tools

Initially, as you begin to use these tools for spotting your own shadows, you'll probably find yourself examining some of the more obvious symptoms first. But with practice, you'll soon find yourself looking at some of the more subtle signs. Regardless of where you find yourself in this process, remember always to be gentle and compassionate with yourself. And as you become more adept at forgiving yourself, see if you can strengthen your curiosity and your sense of wonder and adventure. After all, you may be in the process of uncovering parts of yourself that hold some great secret super-powers that you didn't even know you had!

A DEEPER LOOK AT PROJECTION

One of the interesting—and quite revealing—aspects of *shadow* is its unavoidable tendency to appear magically in the behaviors and characteristics of other people. You've undoubtedly experienced this for yourself.

For example, perhaps because of some humiliation you experienced when you were young, when your parent or guardian demanded that you stop being "so full of yourself", you decided that you would simply stop showing up that way. You decided that you didn't like the feeling of humiliation, so you chose to hide this aspect of yourself, and you adopted what you believed to be a "humble" attitude. At a later time in your life—perhaps even after you had long forgotten about that decision—you learned to call your disowned characteristic "arrogance". And then, even later perhaps, you may have begun noticing how other people in your life seemed quite "arrogant" at times. In effect, you started to see the aspect of yourself that you had been trying to so hard to hide revealing itself in the behaviors and attributes of other people. You may even have developed a catalog in your mind of certain facial expressions that were enough to trigger the judgment of "arrogance" within you.

This phenomenon—experiencing in others the kinds of things that we have hidden or repressed within ourselves—is known in psychology as *projection*.

Psychology generally sees projection as a kind of defense mechanism: in order to avoid the pain of acknowledging a "bad thing" within ourselves, we deny or repress it within ourselves, and then unconsciously witness it in other people.

But in my view, projection is not necessarily a negative or undesirable phenomenon; in fact, I see projection as a very valuable personal growth tool—which is why I'm choosing to devote a whole section to the topic. As I see it, there are actually three forms of projection: shared experience, empathy, and judgment/shadow.

1. Shared Experience

Consider any experience that you've ever had in your life, from the typical or mundane (driving a car, cooking on the barbecue, or eating a piece of apple pie) to the more exotic (climbing a mountain, bungee jumping, singing your first solo in front of 500 people). If at any time after you have had this experience you happen to witness someone else doing any one of these things, you immediately begin to relate what you are seeing back to your own earlier experience. As the other person does whatever s/he is doing, you connect to the sensations, thoughts and emotions that you were experiencing when you were doing the same thing. In other words, you project your own internal experience onto the other person.

2. Empathy

But what if you witness someone involved in an experience that doesn't correlate closely with one of your own? Well, this is where empathy comes into play. As you watch what is going on for the other person, you tend to have thoughts, emotions and sensations of your own. And because that person's experience is foreign to you, you begin to imagine or interpret what is going on for him/her, based on the most similar experience you can recall from your own life. In a sense, you project your interpretation and imagination onto the other person.

3. Judgment/Shadow

This last form of projection—and probably the most insidious—is the one that psychology seems to focus on: where you find yourself judging someone else because of a perceived characteristic, aspect or behavior that you have disowned or rejected within yourself. I gave the example a moment ago about trying hard to hide "arrogance" and then seeing it showing up in others—and then judging it or even condemning it in them.

But as I mentioned before, judgment and shadow are not always associated with "bad" or "negative" things. For example, consider someone you know who seems to be very comfortable owning his or her gifts and sharing them with the world. While you might consider this at first to be "arrogant" or "not humble enough", there may be a part of you that wishes you could show up with as much confidence and self-love. You may in fact feel quite inspired by the other person, and secretly look for ways to bring yourself more fully into the world— while of course still keeping that "arrogant" part under control!

Everything is Projection

Everything that happens around us in the "real world" is communicated to us through our five physical senses and through our emotions. When something stimulates an emotion or one of our senses, this triggers a whole chain of events that results in some kind of realization within our brain. All of this processing occurs 100 percent internally, at such a rapid rate that we aren't even aware that it is happening.

As an example, suppose that Jill sees Joe playing blackjack in a casino and Joe suddenly slams his hand down on the table and his cards go flying all over the place. Light energy travels very quickly into Jill's eyes and interacts with the rods and cones there. Almost instantly, these interactions are translated into electrical and chemical signals which register in Jill's brain, where an image is formed. The image, of course, keeps changing as more and more light energy arrives in her eyes. At the same time that her eyes are being stimulated, Jill's ears are picking up sound waves caused by numerous events occurring all around her, many of which she may not be seeing. Similarly, her nose may be smelling the colognes or perfumes that people are wearing or the foods or drinks that are being served. Her skin may be feeling the coolness of the air around her, or the brushing of a person passing by. At the outset, before Joe's outburst, Jill may be experiencing no particular emotion, but at the moment when Joe's hand strikes the table, she may find herself engulfed by a feeling of fear or maybe even anger. This emotional energy causes the release of chemicals in her body that strongly enhance the entire experience and prepare her for some kind of action.

Notice that Jill's entire experience in this scenario occurs internally, as innumerable high-speed interactions in her body cause the transmission of chemical and electrical signals along millions of nerves and synapses. It is her experience and hers alone. (And, as brain scientists now believe, her experience would have been "identical" even if the entire sequence of events involving Joe had occurred only in her imagination!) Ironically, in spite of the fact that the experience occurs internally, Jill imagines almost everything to have taken place "over there", outside of herself! Jill projects the experience outwardly, to the blackjack table, to Joe, to the food and drinks, to the people passing by, to the cold air around her, and so on.

Projection is something that all of us do all the time—mostly unconsciously. The fact that we project outwardly doesn't mean that our experiences aren't real or that what we are projecting isn't true. However, it is easy for us to forget about this phenomenon and, as a result, to put the responsibility for our experience onto those people, events and circumstances that we see outside of ourselves. In other words, it becomes pretty easy for us to "blame the world" for our experience!

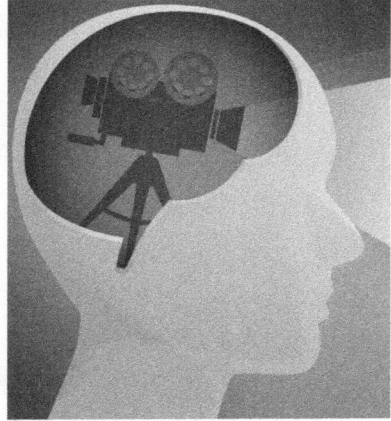

Figure 21—We are "Projection Machines"

Who's Right?

Let's consider another example.

Suppose Bob overhears Vicki speaking glowingly about her own strengths or capabilities. He might conclude that she is "arrogant". Bob can only come to this conclusion because of his own experience with arrogance—whether he happened to see the behavior before from someone else in his life, or (more likely) whether he has engaged in "arrogant" behavior himself in the past. Either way, he is projecting his own experience onto Vicki and using the term "arrogant" as a way to describe it. Bill, on the other hand, might see the same behavior that Bob sees and conclude something quite different. Depending on his life experience, Bill might see Vicki as "centered and grounded" because she is able to speak positively about herself. Bob might see Vicki's behavior as "negative" while Bill might see it as "positive". Which one of them is "right"?

And what about Vicki herself? Vicki, the person who had been doing the talking in the first place, might be really terrified of speaking about herself in

— 195 —

that manner; she might even describe her own behavior as "flaky and unsettled". Not only that, but if she happens to notice Bob and Bill watching her as she's talking, she might conclude from facial expressions or body language that Bob was being "judgmental and arrogant", while Bill was being "compassionate". Which of these interpretations is "right"?

Each of the people in this example interaction projected his or her own interpretation onto each of the other players in the scenario, and probably unconsciously. Each one of them, participating in the same interaction, came to a different conclusion. Who was "right"? In a very real sense, *all of them were "right"*! Because they were all just doing their best to describe a projected form of their own experience, how could any of them ever be considered "wrong"?

An Unconscious Process

Because of the fact that we are constantly projecting our internal experiences into the external world, we always face the risk of expressing something that doesn't align with someone else's experience. As a result, we end up in situations where other people disagree with us. A big problem with projection is that we usually don't realize (or, more accurately, *remember*) that we're doing it. We engage in the process more or less unconsciously. Consequently, we end up assuming that our personal experience of a situation is the *only* experience of that situation, and we find ourselves surprised or even hurt when someone else takes an opposing view of it.

In effect, our natural tendency to project can lead us into situations where disagreements or conflicts can arise, and the way to overcome these problems is to raise awareness of the fact that we are projecting in the first place, and to actively take ownership of those projections.

The Value of Projection

The main value in projections is that they often reflect the very aspect of ourselves that we don't want others to see. For this reason, they are a powerful source of information about ourselves, and they give us an opportunity to really get to know ourselves more deeply. However, because of the incredible energy we put into hiding the disowned aspects of ourselves, we tend to have a very strong resistance to accepting that everything we criticize in others has an equivalence within ourselves. Thus, it is very difficult for us to begin the process of owning our projections.

When you first start to integrate this awareness, you may find it painful to acknowledge that everything you hate, everything you loathe and can't stand, everything you have ever judged negatively is, at some level, in some form, a part of your own totality. When you realize that the process of projection is itself an unconscious defense against seeing yourself clearly, you can appreciate how difficult it is to recognize your projections and claim as your own the qualities or traits in others that triggered your reaction. Most of us would rather not acknowledge that we carry within ourselves the very things we judge as wrong in others.

Let your projections, therefore, lead you onto a path of recognizing every aspect, attribute, characteristic or behavior that you find so hard to accept in others. Typically these recognitions will show up as judgments in your mind. Let them raise a few simple questions in your mind:

- In what ways do I bring this very same behavior into the world?
- What is the deeper belief that keeps me from owning this aspect or behavior as my own?
- Where did this belief come from, and what pain have I been trying to avoid by disowning it?
- How can I heal that pain so as to increase my compassion and reduce my judgment?
- What can I do to deconstruct that old belief and choose something new that fully empowers me to embrace all of myself?

Projection Points to Shadow

If you want to know about a particular shadow in yourself, you can begin by looking at judgments you have about other people. Since a judgment is just a form of projection (possibly unspoken), this can be a strong indicator of something in yourself that you have tried very hard to hide, repress or deny—that is, a shadow. As we've already discussed at length, when you hide, repress, or deny a trait in yourself, you tend to be very aware of that trait in other people. This means that you are most aware of those traits in others which reflect your own shadows.

If the judgment itself is not enough of an indicator, then look next to your reactions. When someone does something or shows up in a way you don't like, notice how your body feels, what thoughts are you having, and what emotions might be moving in you. Your reaction is a clear indication of a trigger-mechanism, which very likely corresponds to a shadow within you. The more powerful the reaction, the more powerful the shadow that somehow resonates with the behavior you are experiencing in that other person.

Shadow Progression

Contrary to what some people might believe, shadows don't just materialize in isolation. Virtually every shadow I've ever encountered in myself or in a client had a history of its own. Usually the progression goes something like this:

1. You do something as a youngster that is perfectly natural for you, but that the adults in your world assert is "wrong" or "unacceptable". These adults may even ridicule or punish you for your behavior, causing you emotional pain.

2. You want to please those adults, and you want to avoid the emotional pain, so you look for ways to avoid the behavior that they don't like, even though you don't necessarily understand why it's "wrong" or "unacceptable" in the first place. In the process, you come up with a coping strategy that seems to work most of the time.

3. As you become more adept at implementing your strategy, you take on the adults' perspective and begin to believe that this behavior is "wrong" or "unacceptable" for *everyone*—not just for yourself. So, you become progressively more judgmental about anyone else who engages in that behavior.

4. As time passes, the memory of your original behavior fades away, to the point where you might have pushed it completely out of your mind. But the prevailing belief that you have taken on about that behavior persists, and it affects your other behaviors.

5. Every once in a while you might find yourself "accidentally" showing up in the way that you think is so "wrong" and "unacceptable", and you may wonder why on earth you ever did such a thing. You may see this as "not like me at all", and you probably hope that no-one else noticed—but usually, the "slip" has consequences of its own.

6. In time you may find that, even though your coping strategy served its purpose when you were younger, it seems to have lost its effectiveness today. You may actually experience the emotional pain you've been trying so hard to avoid—even though you are no longer engaging in the behavior that led to that pain in the first place.

No matter how hard you try to keep a lid on them, your shadows may leak out in ways that seems beyond your control. For example, you may promise yourself that you're going to spend more time with your family, when you actually spend more time at work. You may find yourself jumping into a questionable relationship, when you know that this person isn't right for you. You may ignore your own rules about eating, smoking or drinking. When you find yourself repeating a pattern of behavior involuntarily, that is a clear sign that your shadow is running the show.

A GIFT IN EVERY SHADOW

When you get to the place of uncovering a shadow, you will invariably find at least one wonderful gift within it. In truth, there was nothing "wrong" or "unacceptable" about you in the first place. Yes, it may be true that the adults in your life didn't like what you were doing or that they were irritated in some way. It may even be true that your behavior had an undesirable consequence, but that doesn't make it inherently "wrong" or "unacceptable".

Remember what I said earlier?

> **Every thought, word, action and feeling is motivated at its deepest level by a desire to give or receive love.**

As you uncover a shadow—along with the underlying belief that brought it into being—ask yourself the simple question: *In what ways have I been trying to give or receive love with that behavior?*

Each answer that comes up will almost always point to some "good" thing that your shadow's been trying to do for you for years—even (or especially) when it showed up "by accident" or "beyond your control". This is a time for celebration! Why? Because now you can channel the energy of your shadow into something that accomplishes that "good" thing in a more constructive and empowering way. That is, if you want to, you can re-purpose your shadow to serve you rather than getting in your way.

BACK TO THE TWO WOLVES

In my experience, my Black Wolf—representing the shadow parts of myself that I had essentially abandoned—turned out to be my greatest teacher. Once I was able to overcome my fear of going into the dark, I was able to see all kinds of amazing aspects of myself, aspects that would have died in the darkness otherwise.

In the metaphor of the story, if I had chosen only to feed the white wolf, it's quite possible that the black one would have been lurking everywhere, growing more and more hungry, desperate to stay alive. Eventually, he would have found his moment—perhaps a time when I wasn't paying attention—and he would have jumped out and attacked the white wolf in order to get the nourishment and love he craved.

But because I chose instead to acknowledge him and befriend him, I learned to understand him more fully, and he taught me that his qualities of tenacity, courage, and strategic thinking have an important place in my life too. I learned that the black wolf and the white wolf belong side-by-side, as equals, and that one isn't better than the other—in fact, it has become clear to me that one of them can't exist without the other.

I invite you to uncover, embrace, heal and integrate all of your shadows too… so that your Two Wolves can learn to co-exist in total harmony.

Chapter Summary—Shadow

Whatever we refuse to recognize about ourselves has a way of rearing its head and making itself known when we least expect it.—Debbie Ford

One does not become enlightened by imagining figures of light, but by making the darkness conscious.—Carl Gustav Jung

I embrace my shadow self. Shadows give depth and dimension to my life. I believe in embracing my duality, in learning to let darkness and light peacefully coexist as illumination.—Jaeda DeWalt

Highlights

1. Premature positivity is the process of applying positive thinking and affirmations before you have done the work necessary to uncover and correct limiting beliefs and disempowering thought patterns. This requires you to bring a light into your darkness.

2. A shadow is any part, aspect, characteristic or behavior that you disown, disavow, deny, hide or repress because you believe it is unacceptable, inappropriate, bad or wrong.

3. Shadow usually emerges from a coping strategy that appears out of a desire to avoid pain or humiliation associated with a particular behavior.

4. Putting an unwanted characteristic or behavior into the background often results in desirable things being hidden away as well; "gifts" get lost in the shadow.

5. Shadow parts almost always abide by the principle that *every thought, word, action and feeling is motivated at its deepest level by a desire to give or receive love.*

6. Shadows are usually trying to produce a core state of BEING, SERENITY, LOVE, or ONENESS.

7. Spotting shadows is similar to detecting sub-atomic particles: you can't always recognize them until after you have seen their behaviors.

8. There are at least six classes of shadow indicators, in increasing order of subtlety: acting out, triggers and emotional charges, judgments and projections, compensatory behaviors, ego-defenses, rigid beliefs. You can use these indicators to help you recognize and uncover your own shadows.

9. Projection is the process of mentally imagining something from your

own life happening in the context of someone else's life.

10. There are at least three types of projection: shared experience, empathy, judgment/shadow.

11. Ultimately, every expression of a personal experience is a form of projection—that is, bringing an internal experience outward into the world.

12. Projection is largely an unconscious process. By raising your awareness and owning your projections, you can deepen your understanding of yourself, and uncover your shadows.

13. When you are trying to identify and recognize a shadow, projection is one of the most powerful tools available because it helps you to determine where to look.

14. Shadows rarely arise spontaneously; they usually go through a progression that can take years to complete.

15. Every shadow—no matter how inappropriate or unacceptable it may seem—contains a gift; recognizing and embracing that gift allows you to channel the shadow's energy in a constructive functional way.

THE SHADOW KEY

Every shadow is a part of yourself that you have disowned or hidden—and usually for a reason that made a lot of sense when the situation first happened. However, the shadow is very much like a child that is just seeking some love and attention—which is why it sometimes shows up when you least expect it, and certainly at the most inconvenient times! Ironically, the more energy you put into trying to keep your shadow hidden away, the more that shadow tends to show up when you don't want it to.

Counter-intuitively, the best way to pacify your shadow is to embrace it with as much unconditional love and forgiveness as you can muster. If you can do this—essentially by bringing the tenderness of an unconditionally loving parent to a distressed child—you can create virtually instant healing within yourself. And this will lead to an amazing transformation within you that you might never have thought possible.

Remember, your shadow actually represents a big part of who you really are, and there is a great gift in bringing *all of you* into the world. Remember the words of this affirmation:

I am thrilled to embrace and integrate all of my shadows, and grateful for the powerful treasures they bring into my life.

CHAPTER 9: RELATIONSHIP

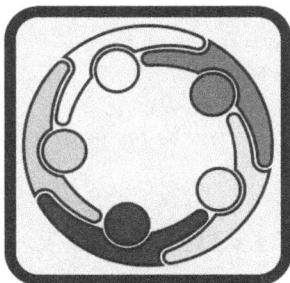

ENGAGE RELATIONSHIPS MINDFULLY AND PASSIONATELY

be one

i want to dive into your ocean
to swim and be swum
swept by your currents
moved by your swells
tossed and turned and embraced
by your unbroken and unbreakable waters
marveling at the endless mysteries of your depths
sharing space with the infinite lifeforms of you

i want to soar in your sky
swooping through your atmosphere
around and through your clouds
feeling your presence all around me
relishing your storms
and your winds
and your quiet sighs
and your silences
inhaling and ingesting the delightful sweet aromas of you

i want to dance in all your dimensions
back and forth across the veil
here and there where only souls reside
hither and yon beyond simple heartbeats
experiencing all of who i am
in the lovely dichotomies of all of who you are

i want to sit

here-now
face-to-face
heart-to-heart

in the earthnexus where sky and ocean forever meet
at the horizon of our love

i want to
be you be me be one

ONENESS VS INDIVIDUALITY

Earlier, I shared with you my story about *OMnitude*, and explained how each and every one of us is an important and unique expression of *All-That-Is*. At the same time, because we are all energetically connected to the same *Source*, we are in effect inextricably connected to each other. This is an interesting dichotomy and one which can create confusion for us in our physical domain—at least until we embrace and understand it.

But now, suppose you had to go through life and you had no way of fully experiencing yourself as who you really are. If that were the case, your experience would not be included in the *OMnitude Library*, and you'd have little if any sense of life fulfillment. Thankfully, when *OMnitude* decided to subdivide itself into sovereign individuations empowered to create and experience their own life journey, a beautiful and amazing thing simultaneously came into being: *relationship*. In the transition from oneness to individuality, *OMnitude* made it possible for all of us to relate with everyone and everything in our world, and the real gift here is that *every* relationship provides us with an opportunity to experience one or more aspects of ourselves as deeply as we choose to. But I didn't always understand this...

MY UNCONSCIOUS RELATIONSHIP DYNAMIC

Because I made the childhood decision to take on the belief that virtually everyone else in the world knew me better than I knew myself, I approached almost all of my relationships unconsciously—in the sense that I relied on the other parties in my relationships to inform my understanding of who and what I was. And by extension, I also counted on them to tell me what I wanted and needed. A side-effect of this way of thinking was that I tended to defer to others, acting in ways that I believed (or hoped) would make them happy. I lived according to this dysfunctional internal dynamic for much of my life, and I didn't recognize how ingrained it was until I was almost four years into my second marriage.

In 2004, I was attending a powerful workshop called "Healing the Mother Wound", during which I finally became fully aware of my "deferential people-pleaser" pattern. In fact, it was at this workshop that I realized to my chagrin that I had entered my second marriage not because I wanted to be married, but because I wanted to make my partner happy. This realization stunned me and even horrified me because it meant that I had married my wife under false pretenses. In reality, there is nothing wrong with wanting to make someone else happy; however, if the desire to make someone else happy is motivated by an unconscious desire to get something for yourself, that is not a healthy situation; on the contrary, it is clearly a *shadow* behavior. And that is precisely the situation I found myself in.

After that workshop, I went home with a new awareness, not to mention a pretty large dilemma: how do I clean this up with my wife? Do I continue to stay in a marriage that was based on an unconscious lie or do I tell my wife the truth? Since I was on a path of growth and I knew that I wanted to elevate myself out of my unconscious behaviors, I came to the decision that I could not in good conscience withhold this information from her. So, I took the risk to tell her the truth, knowing that it was something that she would almost certainly not like to hear. Well, it did cause her a significant amount of pain, and it put a strain on our relationship as you might well imagine. Indeed, my wife had difficulty imagining that I could build a relationship on one lie without engaging in other lies as well, and so—as part of her own *shadow* behavior—she began questioning a lot of my subsequent decisions. By the end of 2006, we were divorced.

IT WAS NO FAILURE!

It would be easy to dismiss that relationship as a failure. However, there were many wonderful and amazing things that came about as a result of it. For one thing, my ex-wife—a gifted and very empathetic psychotherapist—was one of my greatest supporters and cheerleaders as far as my personal growth was concerned. If not for her, I may never have been exposed to all the workshops, seminars, and programs that have done so much to help me. But that's not all! I've also been able to look back on earlier relationships with a whole new perspective that has helped me to see and understand with ever increasing clarity who and what I am today, and how I got to where I am now.

Since my second divorce, I have continued doing even more work on myself, and I've now come to a place in my life where I do my best to choose the truth every time. Today, I'd much rather speak the truth to everyone all the time than risk partial or incomplete truths—even in the name of making someone else's life easier or happier. That's because I've come to realize that other people's happiness is not my responsibility. My responsibility, as I see it now, is to show up honestly, openly, vulnerably and authentically to the maximum extent possible, and to allow others to do the same. I believe that the more all parties in a relationship adopt this way of thinking and being, the greater the degree of success of the relationship.

EVERY RELATIONSHIP MATTERS

Sometimes I hear people say to me, "I'm so glad I'm out of that relationship. In fact, I wish I'd never entered it." Maybe you've said words like this as well; I know I've certainly felt this way at times in my life. And let's be fair here: some relationships can be very unpleasant, painful even.

But one thing I've come to realize is that every relationship I've ever been in has helped me to learn something about myself—even if I could not appreciate the learning at the time it was happening. The unique path I followed in my life—and that includes all the relationships I've participated in so far—led me to where I am now. In fact, it's quite possible that I might never have gotten to where I am today if not for the things that have happened in my life.

I sometimes wonder what my life might have been like if I had never had any relationships at all. Think about that for a minute. What would happen if there was no such thing as a relationship? It's hard to imagine such a scenario, for sure. For me, I imagine that it would have to be some kind of situation in which I were completely and utterly alone, with no ability to interact with people or animals or any form of life at all. I can only imagine how lonely that would be, not so much because I would miss my connections with others, but more because I would not be able to get any reflective feedback of any kind from my environment. As a result, I would almost certainly lose my sense of self pretty quickly, and perhaps I'd even forget the whole concept of self altogether. I think that it would only be a matter of relatively short time before I went completely mad!

This little thought experiment has helped me to develop a powerful appreciation for *every* relationship in my life—including my relationships to inanimate objects. Why? Because every interaction I have with the world around me allows me to express and experience myself more fully. When I am interacting with another human, I get to experience myself one way. When I interact with a dog or a cat, I get to experience myself another way. When I bounce a basketball on the ground and then toss it into the basket, I get to experience myself yet another way. Every interaction allows me to experience a different aspect of myself. Thus, all my relationships are equally important to me, because they all contribute to my overall experience of myself.

Remember *OMnitude*'s Dilemma…the problem of knowing oneself as all that is, but not being able to experience oneself in that way? Well, that is exactly the dilemma we'd all find ourselves in if there were no people, animals, or things for us to interact with. We would not be able to "relate" to anything—and that would prevent us from experiencing the truth of who we really are.

Perhaps you've never thought of relationships in quite this way before. But that's how I see them all now. For me, every relationship is a kind of *sacred space* because it provides me an opportunity to show up and to be experienced in the way I am showing up. Then the participants in my relationship can respond to me and share their feedback…and this helps me to see myself even more clearly.

All relationships are important—even the ones that may seem to happen completely by accident…for after all, there really are no accidents. There are just situations, events, conditions and circumstances that appear in our lives because of the attractive power of our thoughts, words, actions and emotions— all of which, ultimately, are expressions of who we are. Thus, *who we are* is the attractive force that brings into our world everything we need in order to *experience* what our souls already know about us. And all the people, animals and things that show up in our lives provide us with endless opportunities to *relate*—which, in turn, broadens and deepens our experience of ourselves.

MOVING INTO CONSCIOUS RELATIONSHIP

As I just mentioned a moment ago, I entered most of the relationships in my earlier life without any real sense of intention. I believed that most things were just random events—*fate*, if you will—that appeared in my life. I hadn't yet developed the spiritual awareness to realize how much of this was my own creation, so I was living in the illusion that life was just something that happened *to* me. Because of my ego-mind's belief that I was separate from everyone and everything else, I didn't really recognize or appreciate the true value of my relationships, and so I entered into most of them completely unconsciously. It wasn't until I was well into my own awakening process that I began to see relationships for what they really were. And once I began to appreciate the power and value of relationships, I began to see how important it was for me to engage all of them as consciously as possible.

For me, entering into relationships consciously and intentionally means a number of things:

- Knowing that I have the power to create exactly the kind of relationship I want in order to accelerate my growth and awakening.

- Recognizing that the other party (or parties) in the relationship have their own needs, desires and objectives, and that they are choosing me to help them in their own spiritual growth.

- Remembering that we are all soul-mates in the true sense of the word, and that we are all inextricably connected to one another.

- Appreciating that no relationship exists independently of other things in life; everything is connected and inter-related.

- Welcoming, accepting and embracing the experience and feedback of the other party (or parties) in the relationship, and allowing that feedback to deepen my understanding and knowing of myself.

- Adopting and embracing an unshakable attitude of authenticity, honesty, and openness in all my interactions with everyone.

- Staying grounded in acceptance, compassion, forgiveness, gratitude and love in order to maximize the growth potential for both (or all) parties in the relationship.

This may initially seem like a tall order for any relationship, and it is indeed pretty likely that most of your relationships won't be quite this advanced—until they are! But what I've learned is that there is nothing more satisfying than sharing part of my journey with a spiritual partner—a soul-mate—who is also committed to his or her intentional growth. I've also found that, when I show up in a state of openness and vulnerability, my relationship partners invariably feel safer and more willing to reveal the deepest and most tender parts of themselves. When I share that kind of mutual openness with another person, I get to see and experience myself more deeply, and every such experience nurtures my continued growth into ever greater versions of myself.

EVERY RELATIONSHIP IS RIGHT NOW

In western culture, when we speak of "romantic" relationships, many of us are conditioned to believe that there is one person specifically for us, someone who will somehow "complete" us and make us whole. We have the idea that this person is meant for us, and that, if we are lucky enough to meet *The One*, then we have some kind of obligation to join with that person forever—until death do us part. To me, it seems like folly to subscribe to this belief system. Why? Because it suggests a number of disempowering subliminal messages:

1. You are not complete unto yourself.

2. If you don't meet the one person who will "complete" you, then you are doomed to live an unfulfilled life.

3. Anyone who is not "meant" for you is merely a distraction, and could impede or otherwise negatively impact your growth.

4. All "romantic" relationships involve only two people—and most often it is expected that they will be of different sexes—and any such relationship that is not "monogamous" is wrong or sinful.

5. You have to do everything in your power to make the relationship last as long as possible, and to leave such a relationship because it no longer serves you is "bad".

If you join a relationship consciously and intentionally, then you already know that you are complete unto yourself, and that you are merely seeking a way to experience your own completeness by sharing it with someone else. You can only do this when you are fully present; if you are dwelling in the past or worrying about the future, then you are not in a conscious space to be able to accept yourself or your partner unconditionally. If you are not able to bring yourself back into the here-and-now, then you are putting your ego-mind first, and the relationship will suffer. The more that you and your partner(s) are able to stay grounded in the present, the more success you will experience in the relationship. And if a relationship is healthy and successful, then it will last.

WHAT DEFINES HEALTH/SUCCESS IN RELATIONSHIP?

Each of us has our own ideas about what makes a relationship feel healthy or successful. There are, however, some common elements that I think most people would agree on. The more of these you experience for yourself in a relationship, the greater the likelihood that you will consider it to be healthy and/ or successful:

- You are treated as an equal partner—meaning that you get to be seen and heard just as much as everyone else.

- Your opinion and perspective are welcomed and respected—even if the other participants do not agree with you.

- You practice and enjoy empowered, honest, open, heart-centered communication with everyone in your relationship.

- You feel safe enough that you are able to share whatever is going on for you, knowing that you will be accepted and loved for who you are—no matter what.

- You find your relationship to be a powerful environment for learning skills that improve all aspects of your life.

- You experience your relationship partner(s) as open and vulnerable, which strengthens your sense of connection and intimacy.

- You find that everyone in the relationship is committed to resolving inevitable conflicts with love, respect, and mutual acceptance.

- You deepen your understanding and appreciation for who you really are.

While there may well be other characteristics you can think of that also belong on this list, most of us, I think, would jump at the opportunity to create and participate in a relationship that embodied all of these characteristics. But one thing seems certain: if we really want to, *all* of us have the power to work with our relationship partners to co-create these kinds of relationships.

Maximizing Relationship Success

It should not surprise you that the level of enjoyment in your life is directly proportional to the cumulative level of success in all your relationships. But as we all know and recognize, success in every relationship requires dedication and commitment on the part of all relationship participants. As I often tell my clients: *It takes work to make it work!*

But the work required to build a successful relationship need not be unpleasant drudgery. When you understand what it is you are trying to co-create with your relationship partners—and when you are all on the same page—then the work can actually be quite pleasant, especially as you begin to enjoy the fruits of your efforts.

If you want to make your relationships as successful as possible, start by remembering all the things that work best for you. What aspects of a relationship attract you? Which ones don't resonate for you at all? Consider the items I mentioned in the last section: which of those are you looking to experience in your relationships?

Not to sound trite about this, but it turns out that one of the most powerful ways to manifest what you want in your life is to create it for yourself. This may seem obvious, but it is something that people easily overlook. Once you have a good idea of what your ideal relationship looks like, you can begin asking yourself:

> *"How can I create this in my own life? What actions could I take to bring my ideal relationship into being?"*

When you ask yourself open-ended questions of this nature, you actually create a kind of knowledge vacuum that the Universe has no choice but to fill! Before you have even completely uttered the question, the Universe is already at work bringing you the answer, which may arrive in your awareness in unexpected ways. But even while you are waiting for the answer(s) to show up, there are things you can do that will accelerate the process for you:

1. Take all the things you have learned from the previous chapters and start bringing them consciously into every relationship you participate in.

2. Commit to showing up as authentically, honestly and openly as you can. When you show up in a genuine manner, you automatically inspire and empower the other participants to do the same.

3. Do your part to create a safe space for everyone to show up in the relationship.

4. Practice your first-person self-responsible communication skills as discussed in Chapter 2, and speak intentionally and truthfully all the time.

5. Develop your listening skills to the highest level possible so that you are always seeking empathetically to understand your relationship partners.

6. Stay connected to the truth of who you really are, and encourage all others to do the same.

AND SPEAKING OF LISTENING SKILLS...

I think it's fair to say that everyone appreciates being heard, because when we are heard then we know that others are more likely to experience us for who we really are. In my journey, I have learned that the best way to ensure that I get heard has been to develop and improve my skills in hearing others, for when I take the time to really hear someone else, that person is much more likely to be able to fully hear me. In other words, developing my listening skills has helped me both to hear others more fully, and also to improve the odds of being heard myself.

I've learned that there are five well-defined styles of listening, most of which I'm sure you've experienced—perhaps even on both sides of the equation!

Level 0: Ignoring or Non-Listening

This level occurs when you are so focused on yourself that you are unable or unwilling to pay any attention to someone who is trying to speak to you.

Level 1: Competitive Listening

At this level, you are actually paying *some* attention to what the other person is saying, but most of your energy is devoted to waiting for the first available opportunity to jump into the conversation and share your own perspective or opinion.

Level 2: Passive Listening

At this level, you are more focused on the other person, listening to what s/he has to say without necessarily offering any reflection. You may still find yourself relating the other person's share to what is going on in your own life, and this may lead you to see the situation as a "problem" that you need to "solve", so your responses may be geared toward "fixing" or "helping".

Level 3: Active Listening

At this level, you are able to release any attachment to your own personal issues and focus your entire attention on the other person. This level is characterized by a strong element of empathy, coupled with reflective or clarifying statements that confirm for the other person that you are actually hearing what is being said.

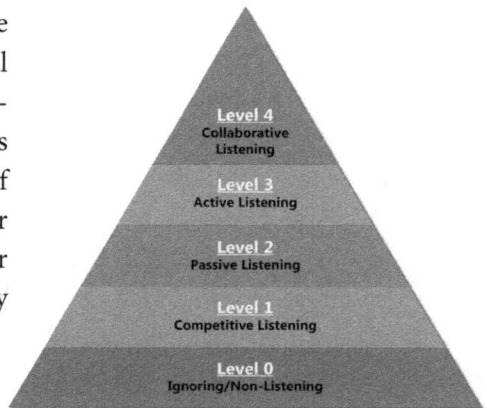

Level 4
Collaborative Listening

Level 3
Active Listening

Level 2
Passive Listening

Level 1
Competitive Listening

Level 0
Ignoring/Non-Listening

Figure 22—Listening Levels Pyramid

Level 4: Collaborative Listening

At this level, you are not only hearing and empathizing, you are also facilitating the other person to actually deepen his/her experience by asking authentically curious questions and paying attention to non-verbal cues such as body language, tone, and volume.

For Best Results...

If you can create a relationship environment in which everyone develops and practices their listening skills and becomes adept at Level 3 or Level 4 listening, you'll find that your relationships will magically become places where you really want to be. The more you and your relationship partners develop these skills, the more successful and healthy your relationships will feel.

SOME THINGS TO REMEMBER ABOUT LISTENING

1. The person speaking wants more than anything to be heard.
2. Unless specifically requested, the person speaking *does not* want you to:
   - Commiserate by going into a long explanation of a similar situation in your life;
   - Diagnose any kind of problem;
   - Try to "fix" something;
   - Evaluate or judge the situation or the speaker;
   - Offer advice about how to approach the situation;
   - Ask too many questions—especially if you just seem interested in the "gory details".
3. Unless you hear words to the contrary, then you can assume that the speaker *does* want you to:
   - Pay attention to what is being said;
   - Be fully present while s/he is speaking;
   - Reflect what you are hearing and ask for clarification if something isn't clear;
   - Empathize with him/her;
   - Remain in a non-judgmental place of love and acceptance, knowing that the speaker is sharing something vulnerable.
4. If the speaker is familiar with the *Collaborative Listening* level described above, then s/he will almost certainly be okay with you asking questions that help him/her to more deeply express and experience the situation. However, just remember to remain *authentically curious*—that is, ask

questions that help you deepen your understanding of what's going on for the speaker, and do your best to avoid looking for the "gory details".

SPIRITUAL PARTNERSHIP

Imagine joining with someone (or more than one person) for the primary purpose of accelerating and accentuating your spiritual development. Imagine a relationship in which everyone agrees that mutual spiritual evolution is the primary objective. Imagine a situation where the whole is greater than the sum of the parts, such that each member of the relationship evolves more quickly than s/he could do alone. In my mind, this is the ultimate form of a relationship, something that my heart yearns for, because such a relationship represents an opportunity for me to know and experience myself more fully, while encouraging and supporting my partner(s) to do the same.

Such relationships do exist—relationships in which the partners are enthusiastically committed to practicing unconditional love, empowered communication, and mutual support with and for each other. All it takes is for two (or more) people to come to consensus about what they want to create together.

The success of a spiritually conscious relationship depends on the willingness of members to recognize each other as unique but intimately connected individuations of the same Source—*OMnitude*. It is this awareness that enables participants to look beyond their differences and see the truth and beauty of their similarities, which in turn enables everyone to grow within a fertile field of nurturance and support.

Such a relationship requires a lot of maturity. In particular, each partner must possess a willingness to acknowledge the foibles and weaknesses of his/her own ego-mind and to do the inner work necessary to uncover shadows and overcome limiting beliefs. But this is where the beauty lies, because spiritual partners in a conscious relationship are presumably already interested in looking beyond the physical to where real "truth" resides.

We discussed earlier the concepts of shadow and projection. During that discussion, I pointed out that we can use the power of projection to understand and experience ourselves more fully. Since projections normally involve other people, it follows that they happen most frequently in the context of relationship. So, projection provides us a tool for seeing ourselves more clearly, and relationship provides us the space for using that tool. This is particularly true in a spiritual partnership, when both (all) partners are sufficiently aware that they can serve as non-judgmental "mirrors" for the other members of the relationship. Each of our "mirror" partners reflects to us what we may not be able (or willing) to acknowledge within ourselves. And it is this amazing reflection quality that makes our relationships so valuable. In a true spiritual partnership, you can safely use projection to understand and experience yourself more fully, and to embrace and integrate everything you learn about yourself.

CREATING A SPIRITUAL PARTNERSHIP

In my mind, Spiritual Partnership is an advanced form of relationship—perhaps even the highest expression of relationships of which we humans are currently capable—and it requires at least two people who are on a dedicated path of personal growth and who are open and receptive to the intimacy and connection that can lead to deeper self-awareness. In truth, you can view every relationship as a "spiritual partnership" in the sense that everyone who comes into your life is there to help you know yourself just a little bit more deeply than before. But when two people come together consciously for the purpose of creating a true Spiritual Partnership, a whole new paradigm comes into being, and both parties benefit immensely.

The creation of a Spiritual Partnership requires only one thing: **mutual commitment**. And to discover this mutual commitment, it helps to come to agreement with your partner(s) about what the relationship is going to look like. This means communicating with each other as openly and vulnerably as possible about all the things that each of you want to create for yourselves and for the relationship.

I believe if you start from a set of common guidelines, you will go a long way toward creating the relationship(s) of your dreams. Here is a commitment statement template that you can use with your partner(s) to help you get started.

We, _____ (names of all participants), believe that the primary objective of our Spiritual Partnership is to support each other on our individual paths of spiritual evolution. To this end, we commit to the following:

- We recognize and acknowledge that we are unique manifestations of the same Source (*OMnitude*) and that every aspect of our lives, our purposes, and our selves is equally important.
- We acknowledge our human existence as holistic beings and we support each other in bringing conscious nurturance, healing and love to our hearts, bodies, minds, and souls.

- We honor and respect each other in all interactions. In particular, we recognize and honor each other's declared boundaries, knowing that they can shift and move from one moment to the next.
- We dedicate ourselves to the highest form of truth and integrity. We communicate with each other openly, honestly, authentically, and vulnerably in all circumstances—especially when we are triggered or upset. We generously offer feedback from a place of unconditional love, without any attachment to how the other person chooses to use that feedback. We willingly and gratefully receive feedback, knowing that it is the honest truth of the other person, delivered with a desire to help us achieve our declared growth objectives.
- We recognize that fear and doubt may show up in our relationship from time to time; when it does, we pledge to uncover and heal the source of our fear and doubt so that we can return quickly to a field of compassion, forgiveness, and unconditional love.
- We seek to deepen and strengthen our spiritual connection with one another so that we can elevate and magnify our understanding and experience of ourselves. We recognize and share all of our projections so that we can experience each other fully as who we *really* are rather than who we *think* we are.
- We develop and share a regular practice of gratitude and appreciation for each other and for everything in our lives, knowing that our gratitude and appreciation ripple out and benefit the entire Universe.

I've tried to make this template generic and uncontroversial. However, you may find that some of the words or phrases don't quite resonate for you. Feel free to modify the text as you need in order to make it more personal to you—but remember that this template just represents the principles and guidelines that you and your partner(s) use in order to help you establish the parameters of your own Spiritual Partnership.

THE POWER OF WRITTEN AGREEMENTS

In 1890, an Australian/Irish politician named Bryan O'Loghlen was purported to have quipped: "A verbal agreement isn't worth the paper it's written on." Although this may have been intended as a tongue-in-cheek comment, I think there is wisdom in the statement, and I have come to the belief that an agreement doesn't really exist unless it is written down. This is because, without the benefit of hard-copy, all parties to the agreement may have different ideas or perspectives about what was actually intended, and as time passes, their memories of the original parameters of the agreement may diverge. Obviously, if all of these parameters are written down in an easily accessible place, then everyone can refresh their memories of the agreement and avoid conflicts later on.

The use of written agreements in business arrangements is pretty much mandatory these days, but interestingly, few people think about using this tool in the context of a relationship. I think this is actually a mistake that can lead to unnecessary pain and suffering.

The guidelines I outlined in the previous section are an excellent start for establishing a Spiritual Partnership with someone, but I think you can take this idea even further. I recommend that you discuss as many aspects of your relationship as possible, come to consensus about what works for you, and then write down your mutual understanding of each agreement.

What should you agree to? Well, that of course is up to you and your partner(s), but I would include everything that could potentially lead to conflicts down the road. For example, some people believe in the concept of "open" relationship—that it, the kind of relationship where individuals are free to interact in certain ways with other people who are not part of this relationship. In order to make the relationship safe and acceptable to both parties, it's important for them to come to agreement about what "open" really means to them, and this means looking at every perspective as honestly and authentically as possible.

I actually did this exercise with a recent relationship partner, and even though I found it uncomfortable talking with her about what was acceptable or unacceptable to me, what I discovered was that by having the conversation, I felt a great relief in clarifying my own boundaries and understanding the boundaries of my partner. And this led to a greater sense of freedom within the relationship, as well as with other people outside of that relationship.

Take the time with your Spiritual Partner to write down everything that you feel is important, and let the resulting written agreement free you both from pain resulting from potential misunderstandings. And remember: this agreement is a living document—that is, you should review the agreement together on a regular basis (at least semi-annually) and make sure that everything in the agreement still makes sense. When you do that, it is easy to make adjustments so that you both have the same understandings and expectations.

When a Relationship Ends

In every relationship, situations show up which bring us face-to-face with conditions, circumstances, beliefs and shadows that may trigger discomfort, pain, or upset within us. How we and our partners choose to deal with those situations impacts the success of our relationship.

If it turns out that either partner in the relationship is not willing or able to address such situations maturely and consciously, then it may be that the relationship in its current form is no longer viable. If that happens, then the participants in the relationship have two obvious options:

1. Review the agreements that form the backbone of the relationship. This means examining each agreement to determine its relevance, making revisions if necessary until everyone is able to reach consensus, and then re-committing to the new agreements.

2. Terminate the relationship altogether.

In truth, no relationship ever really ends—not in the spiritual sense. Because we are all intimately and irrevocably connected to one other, we are always "in relationship" with everyone all the time. If you were to look at this from a high enough level, you might visualize each relationship as follows:

The journeys of any two people appear to be like rivers flowing from two different directions, converging to a point where they are merged for a while, and then diverging again further down the line. The length of time that the two paths stay merged varies from one relationship to the next. Some relationships will be merged for relatively short periods of time; some of them will be merged for a very long time indeed.

The thing to appreciate is that the time together is a blessing for everyone because it contributes to an overall experience of life—while in the relationship, each party deepens his or her experience of him or herself.

With all of this in mind, even in the face of some pain arising out of a termination, participants can do themselves a great favor by separating from each other as consciously and lovingly as possible. If separation occurs from a place of mutual understanding without shame or blame, and both (all) parties are able to see each other with the same unconditional love and acceptance they experienced while together, then it can actually be an empowering and invigorating experience—helping them to stay connected always to the truth of who they really are.

Chapter Summary—Relationship

The meeting of two personalities is like the contact of two chemical substances: if there is any reaction, both are transformed.—C.G. Jung

You never lose by loving. You always lose by holding back.— **Barbara De Angelis**

Relationship is the most important experience of our lives. Without it, we are nothing.—Neale Donald Walsh

Highlights

1. The *OMnitude* story helps us to understand the difference between One-ness and Individuality; relationship provides us with a powerful mechanism for integrating these two concepts in a real-world experience.

2. Many of us enter our early relationships more or less unconsciously, without necessarily knowing what we are doing. Even so, each relationship still provides us with experiences to help us know ourselves more deeply. Therefore, no relationship should ever be thought of as a failure.

3. With experience and growth, we become more conscious and aware, and we bring our new learnings into subsequent relationships; over time we enter new relationships more and more intentionally.

4. Success in relationship depends on:
   - mutual acceptance and respect;
   - open-hearted communication;
   - vulnerable sharing of perspectives and opinions;
   - approaching conflicts as opportunities for growth; and
   - deepening self-understanding.

5. To maximize success in any relationship, start by committing to do your own inner work as long as necessary. Keep learning and practicing the skills that have been described in other chapters of this book.

6. There are five styles of listening:
   - Level 0—ignoring or non-listening;
   - Level 1—competitive listening;
   - Level 2—passive listening;
   - Level 3—active listening; and
   - Level 4—collaborative listening.

7. Become skilled at level 3 and above and you will supercharge all of your relationships.

8. The person speaking wants mainly to be heard, so avoid side-tracking, diagnosing, evaluating, judging, fixing, or offering advice.

9. Spiritual Partnership is a very elevated form of relationship in which two (or more) complete, whole beings come together for the express purpose of supporting each other in their spiritual development.

10. Spiritual Partnerships require maturity, awareness, intention, and unconditional mutual acceptance in order to succeed.

11. Spiritual Partnership begins with a clear understanding of what each party wants to create. A written statement of mutually acceptable guidelines helps all parties to be on the same page with the objectives and parameters of the relationship.

12. Spiritual Partnerships are more likely to succeed if they are supported by clear, well-articulated agreements that are reviewed and revised periodically.

13. Any relationship may come to an end at any time. Even though there may be pain in the termination of the relationship, all parties can benefit if everyone maintains respect, compassion and unconditional love.

THE RELATIONSHIP KEY

Relationship is the most powerful tool available in the Human Experience toolkit. A relationship serves to provide you with a full expression and experience of who you really are, because each other party in your relationship is like a "mirror", reflecting aspects of yourself that you might not otherwise be able to see.

Learn to see every relationship in your life—with a person, an animal, or an inanimate object—as a gift, no matter how pleasant or unpleasant it may be while you are in it. Remember, every person, situation, condition, and circumstance that shows up in your life arrives at exactly the right time to help you understand and experience something that expands your awareness of who you really are. And things that appear repeatedly continue to do so until you no longer need them in your life.

Help yourself to remember the power of relationship with the following affirmation:

I am a willing and active participant in my relationships with everyone everywhere, and I gratefully cherish these sacred partnerships for the mutual growth and self-expression they provide.

CHAPTER 10: FLOW

STAY PRESENT WITH EVERY MOMENT OF LIFE

FLOWNOWHERE

now, i am not as you remember me
but now i am, not as you remember me

pictures of motion
energy electrifying
the essence of body
emotion
flowing flowing through
body passages
ricocheting like water coursing
unstoppable
finding ways
around all obstacles
moving like god

motion of pictures
images traveling across
the canvas of mind
geometric patterns of pure thought
speeding along
channels of heaven
blurring-sharpening
angling sideways
through halls
of superconscious memory
where they wait to be remembered

i (am) not of your body
i (am not) of your body
i am beyond your body

i (am) not in your mind
i (am not) in your mind
i am out of your mind

where you must be if you want to be with me

we flow
like water   like electricity   like love
through around within without
endlessly continuously
in this moment
in every moment
all   now   here
we flow

let the pictures of motion propel you   let the motion of pictures carry you
          along the edges of sedate   like a cork
                    hushed fields   on the river
    through passages of memory   through passages of memory
             into your heart: into your soul:
          follow the motion   follow the pictures

                to be present in flow
                  is to be with me
                    no(w)here

    transcending yourself   traversing yourself
       you see pictures   you see the motion
   of the motion of pictures   of pictures of motion
spinning across your universe   wrapping around you
     like wheels of time   like a sacred shawl of eternity

         tiles promenade recursively in space
      frolicking in the delightful weightlessness of now
   arranging and rearranging beautiful kaleidoscopic tessellations
   (much so like the endless merging & diverging of flowing spirits)

Here is where i am
   where
body is (not) mind is (not) relative is (no more)

           Flow is inside and outside
              within and without
      and at the same time all momentplaces in between

               Now is the essence of me
             and everyone and everything
                and nothing and nowhere

           flownowhere

      here i am, not as you remember me
      but here, i am not as you remember me

        F L O W N O W H E R E

PRESENCE IS THE KEY

If you reflect on what we've discussed thus far, you will no doubt notice that the one ingredient common to every topic has been *presence*. This is not to say that past or future are not important; certainly, they have their place. But the truth is that we cannot change or fix the past, and we cannot really prepare for or create a future that we cannot see in advance. The only thing we have control over—if indeed we have any control at all—is what shows up in the current moment… in the *present*.

Probably the fastest way to become present is to raise our awareness—that is, to become aware of our situation, our circumstances, what is happening around us, and what is happening within us. The more focus and attention we place into what is, the more attuned and aware and *present* we become. As I mentioned earlier, awareness is your *Base Camp*, and you can get there quite easily by asking yourself powerful, open-ended **check-in** questions.

Start with questions about whatever is happening around you:

- Where am I and what am I doing?
- What is going on around me?
- Am I by myself or am I with other people?

Very quickly after raising awareness about your circumstances or surroundings, you'll find yourself naturally progressing to internal awareness, and you can easily begin asking yourself questions to deepen your awareness of how you are showing up:

- What emotions am I feeling right now?
- What thoughts am I thinking about this situation?
- How am I interpreting what I am experiencing right now?
- What kinds of conclusions, stories, and judgments am I creating in my mind?
- How do I imagine myself in relationship to my model of the world?
- How am I behaving in the current moment, and how do I feel about that?
- What changes am I noticing in the world or in myself?

You can come up with plenty of other questions that will also help in increasing your awareness, but I want you to notice something very specific about each of the example questions I've listed here:

> **Every question is framed in the *present* tense.**

This is very important. As long as you ask yourself questions in the present tense, your answers will be returned to you in the present tense. This cannot help but bring you into the present! And the more present you are, the more aware you are; the more aware you are, the more present you are. In fact, it might just be said that:

> **Awareness ↔ Presence**

To me, this "equation" says simply that, while awareness and presence are not exactly the same thing, one of them leads to the other and vice versa. That is, if you focus on raising awareness, you become more present; if you focus on becoming more present, you raise your awareness. It is a beautiful and powerful symbiosis that you can employ to great advantage in every area of your life.

Flow = Presence in Action

When you bring presence into your activities for extended periods of time, you create a psychological space in which all of your focus is on what is happening in each moment. If the focus is intense and intentional enough, you will be less distracted by the thoughts of your ego-mind. Indeed, you will find the ego-mind tending to fall away altogether, putting you into a state that many people refer to as "in the zone" or "in the groove". In effect, your intentional focus creates a whole stream of moments in which you are in a heightened state of presence—and you get to ride this stream, just as if you were flowing on a river.

This may sound a little abstract, and you may not get it quite yet, but I can assure you that you've had experiences of flow in your life.

Remember a Peak Experience

If you have difficulty remembering what it's like to be in a state of flow, then think instead to a time in your life when you had a peak experience. A peak experience is any experience that brings you into a heightened state of full presence and flow because you are so focused on what is happening right here, right now that there is no space left for your mind to dwell on the pains of the past or the worries of the future. Even though you are intensely focused on the activity or task you are engaged in, you aren't really concerned about what you are doing or having—instead, you find yourself in a motivational and inspirational space in which you are simply "being". When you are in this space, there is a good chance that you are feeling a lot of joy, gratitude and trust—although you may not notice those feelings until after the experience is over.

Let me give you an example of what I mean by a peak experience.

My First Afterburner Takeoff in a Voodoo

I was sitting on the button of the runway, waiting for the tower controller to clear me for takeoff. I was in the cockpit of a CF-101 Voodoo air defense fighter aircraft. My hand was poised on the throttle, and my feet were cramping from holding the brakes so tight.

"Breathe, McLeod!" My instructor chuckled from the back seat. "It's just another takeoff."

Easy for him to say, I thought. *He's done this hundreds of times.* Today would be my very first Voodoo takeoff with the after-burners engaged.

The Voodoo was a very powerful airplane. It had two Pratt & Whitney J-57 engines, each of which was capable of delivering about 12,000 pounds of thrust without afterburners. When the afterburners were engaged, that number increased almost 50% to 17,000 pounds. This meant that a fully loaded airplane could go from a dead stop on the runway to nearly 50,000 feet in altitude in just over a minute. Believe me, that's power! Well, it certainly was for a young man in his early twenties just about to do his first afterburner takeoff.

I was in the third week of my Voodoo training. For the first two weeks, all of my takeoffs had been done in what we called "military power"—that is, full engine power without afterburner. I remember that even my first "military power" takeoff had been exhilarating. Yet, in only two weeks, I had gotten used to the flow of pushing up the throttle, releasing the brakes, accelerating gently but quickly down the runway, rotating the nose, feeling the airplane lift off the ground, raising the landing gear, zooming upward, and enjoying the rush of making this beast conform to my every will!

Taking off in "military power" was somewhat analogous to restraining a thoroughbred race horse that just wants to stretch out and put everything it's got into charging ahead of all the other horses. Today was going to be different; today was the day that I'd be loosening the reins and giving my steed permission to bolt out of the starting gate at a full gallop.

"Relax, McLeod, you're hyperventilating!" My instructor's voice was simultaneously commanding and reassuring. He was right: I was pretty tense with anticipation. I had never experienced this before, so I had no real idea what to expect. All the talk from other pilots who had preceded me helped me to understand intellectually what I was about to experience, but nothing could prepare me for what actually happened.

I heard a click in my headset, then the controller's voice: "Bobcat 25, cleared for takeoff. Winds light out of the southwest. Give 'em hell!"

I took a deep breath. "25, Roger". I'm not sure if I said it or whispered it; I felt like a kid on the edge of a cliff contemplating what seemed like a 100-foot jump into the water below.

I relied on my training and started out pretty much in mental autopilot. I smoothly pushed the throttles up and watched the instruments to make sure the engines were spooling properly. Gauges and dials looked good, no warning lights, so I released the brakes. As I started rolling, I slid the throttles to the left to activate the burners. That's when all hell broke loose.

BOOM! BOOM!

An afterburner is basically just a glorified fire hose that pumps massive amounts of JP-4 jet fuel into the engine's hot exhaust stream at the rate of approximately 25 gallons per second. That fuel initially explodes, but then it just burns steadily, and greatly magnifies the push of the engines on the airframe. From the outside, it looks like a long beautiful yellow-orange flame projecting from the back of the airplane; from the inside, it seems to turn the airplane into a mini-rocket.

As is typical for the Voodoo, the afterburners did not ignite simultaneously, and to my untrained body it felt as if I had been slammed from behind by a huge Mack truck. Twice! First on the left side, which gave me the sensation that the plane was veering to the right, then, maybe a half-second later,

Figure 23—Voodoo during Afterburner Takeoff

on the right side, which made me think we were veering to the left. In reality, of course, the plane just continued its normal trajectory down the runway, but it was accelerating so rapidly now that I didn't even have time to react.

Before I knew it, I was airborne, and I just barely managed to get the gear and flaps up before we reached the 250 knot over-speed limit. I kept pulling back on the control stick to get us climbing out, and before I had taken two or three breaths, I was already above 5,000 feet with the nose at about 80 degrees of pitch when I finally heard my instructor yelling at me to come out of afterburner.

Oh, yeah, those things! I thought, and I felt my left hand move the throttles to the right. As I did that, everything seemed to go quiet, and it felt to me as if the airplane simply stopped in mid-flight. It turned out, however, that that was just a sensation that I was experiencing. The engines continued purring nicely at "military power", but my acceleration diminished and I actually started slowing down. So I pulled the nose down and around and finally leveled off at about 7,000 feet, brought my speed back to 350 knots and finally took a real deep breath.

"Another death gratefully averted!" I heard from the back seat, and I just laughed out loud. I was so energized and excited; I remember to this day having the biggest grin on my face. I'm sure I looked pretty stupid with that grin; thank god I had an oxygen mask on to hide it!

PRESENCE AND FLOW

This *peak experience* story is a very good example of flow—of *being in the groove*, of *being in the zone*. I tapped into some aspect of myself that dealt with every aspect of the situation moment by moment, and I had no thoughts or concerns about not being able to do what I was supposed to do. I was one with the Universe, and everything in the experience was perfect.

As I tell my story here, I take the time to reflect on things that were happening for me during that event, and I even throw in some relevant explanations here and there. But I'm sure you can imagine that during the actual experience, I was completely present to everything that was going on in the moment. I wasn't dwelling on what had happened to me yesterday or last week or last year. I wasn't thinking about any of the current issues in my life. I wasn't worried about any of the things that I knew were coming up in the near future. All of that stuff was completely out of my awareness as I stayed focused on what was taking place "right here, right now". And in that place of presence and flow, I was simply "being", with no attachment, no judgment, and no story.

I love this story, and I love the way I feel when I re-live it and share it with people. My "peak experience" story helps me to reconnect with what it feels like to be in that place of total presence and flow. The story also brings me back to what it means to just "Be", which of course means that it allows me to remember who and what I really am.

We all have peak experiences in our lives. If you take the time to remember such an experience, then you can use the memory of that experience to help you reconnect to the flow and presence that makes life so much more enjoyable and fulfilling. This is true regardless of your current life circumstances.

But how can you be in "presence" and "flow" at the same time? Isn't that contradictory? Or paradoxical? Or at least oxymoronic?

For me, "presence" just refers to the part of getting myself into the here and now. In other words, even though I may be very actively doing something and my attention and intention may be very strongly focused, I'm not necessarily "thinking" in the traditional sense. Sure, my brain is still working and my subconscious thoughts are still driving all my automatic functions such as breath and heartbeat and digestion. But my mind is so focused that I'm not aware of any thoughts other than those that keep my attention on what is happening in the present moment.

This is a rare and beautiful experience, something that I completely cherish. I am sometimes able to achieve this state relatively briefly by meditating, but I haven't yet developed my meditation skill to the point where I achieve the same feeling as a full-on peak experience that gets me into full presence.

"Flow", on the other hand, describes for me the sensation of moving with pure intention. It has the flavor of being guided along a path to some unknown destination, along a trajectory that only reveals itself instant by instant. In this space of flow, I feel nothing but trust, and I have a deep knowing that no matter where the flow takes me, I am totally safe. The experience of "flow" is a sacred and magnificent connection to what I call *Ultimate Source*—that place from which pure Love, Wisdom, Healing and Truth originate; that place that resides at the core of *OMnitude*.

POSITIVE VS NEGATIVE EXPERIENCES

When I first began doing personal growth work, I had a real hard time remembering events that I considered to be "peak experiences", mainly because I erroneously associated the word "peak" with "positive"! I assumed that a "peak experience" had to have a positive outcome. This was a big mistake in my understanding, and it took a pretty powerful—and ostensibly "negative" (at least outwardly)—event to change my perspective.

Have you ever had the experience of nodding off to sleep while you're driving your car? I've had that experience many times in my life, but every time it happened, I always felt a jolt of adrenaline that jerked me awake.

But that all changed on August 11, 2013.

I was on the freeway, driving a beautiful red Hyundai Sonata Hybrid that I had purchased less than a year earlier—it had less than 6,000 miles on the odometer! I was in cruise control, doing about 65 miles an hour, enjoying the summer afternoon as I headed northbound on 280 toward my home in Belmont. I had the sun-roof open and I was listening to some very funky progressive music by a friend of mine.

The next thing I knew I was hearing a sound that I can only describe as *"SCREEEEEEEEEE"!* But it wasn't fingernails across a blackboard as I first thought. It was oak branches scraping both sides of my car. In that moment, I realized that I had not simply nodded off; I had completely dropped into a sleep that was so deep and sudden that I had no awareness that it was happening.

As I jerked into wakefulness, I remember very clearly thinking, *"Oh, shit!"* as it dawned on me that I was no longer on the road. But then, an amazing thing happened: I heard a very powerful and commanding voice yelling at me from just outside my head.

"RELAX!", boomed the voice. It seemed to surround me from the entire interior of the car.

Time didn't merely slow down for me; it seemed to come to a complete stop. And this gave me the opportunity to consider my options:

- Option 1—Take control of the vehicle and somehow drive myself to safety.
- Option 2—Obey the voice and ride it out.
- Option 3—Sorry! No option 3!

The voice, though loud and commanding, was filled with confidence, love, and compassion, so I opted to choose relaxation over reaction—which, it turned out, was easier than I thought because my body still hadn't had a chance to go into full fight-or-flight mode. Besides, my view out the windshield was completely blocked by branches and leaves, so option one wasn't really viable anyway!

I took a deep breath. I put my hands in my lap. I closed my eyes so that I wouldn't be distracted by things going on around me. I whispered, "Okay, I'm ready", and I just waited for the ride to finish.

When the car came to rest, neither of my doors would open, so I had no choice but to climb onto the seat and work my way out through the sunroof.

When I poked my head out, I was completely stunned by what I saw. There, about 30 feet back from the car stood two big oak trees that appeared to be about 4 or 5 feet apart. These were pretty hefty trees, each with a 12- to 16-inch cross-section at the base, and they stood there like two giant goal posts. On each tree, there was a white strip about 18 inches tall where the bark had been peeled away. Apparently, these two trees had served to squeeze the sides of my car and slow me down enough so that I was able to come to a stop.

But then I did a double take.

Those two white strips were about *3 to 4 feet off the ground!* In other words, my car had literally flown off the freeway with such precision—or perhaps I should say guidance—that it threaded its way between two trees that—with no thought or concern for their own well-being—quite literally saved my life.

I just stood there on my seat, looking at those two trees, heart in my throat, tears pouring down my face.

After a while, I noticed that my body was shivering intensely, as if I had stepped out into the freezing cold with no clothes on. I'm not sure how long I had been standing there, but I finally regained my composure. I grabbed all my stuff and climbed out the sunroof and walked out of the bush to a nearby road that ran parallel to the freeway.

Within minutes, a firetruck showed up on the scene; someone had also had the foresight to call a tow truck, which showed up a few minutes later. Although I was still shaking pretty intensely, the paramedics checked me out and determined that I was medically sound. I had no obvious injuries except a swollen knuckle on my left hand, but they strongly recommended that I get checked by a doctor as soon as possible.

I had my cellphone with me, so I called my friends Bob and Christine to come pick me up. Before they arrived, I managed to take a few pictures of the aftermath of my experience; as you can see, they are a little out of focus—because I simply could not stop myself from shaking!

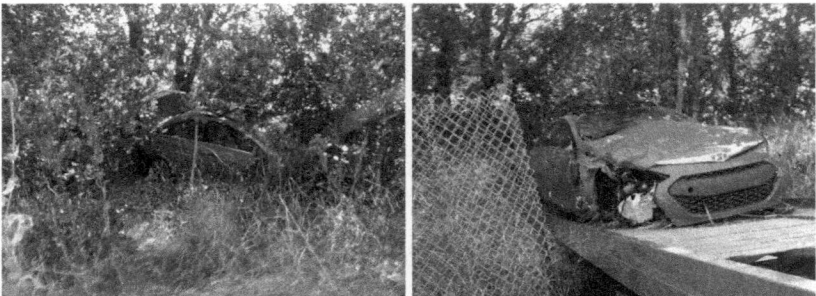

Figure 24—(L) After coming to rest; (R) Pulling the wreckage onto the tow truck

Why Was This a Peak Experience?

My car crash clearly wasn't a "positive" experience in the sense of being something that I'd *choose* to participate in. And yet, it was a situation that brought me into a state of full presence and flow. As soon as I committed myself to relaxing and riding it out, I was simply in the flow of the moment. I was not thinking about anything; I was simply "being".

Even after the car came to rest, I don't remember thinking anything at all. No thought of how lucky I was to have survived; no thoughts about what might happen to my kids. None of those kinds of thoughts showed up in my awareness until almost an hour later, when I was on the way to the emergency room with my friends.

Tapping Into Flow

I've shared two powerful examples of peak experiences in my life, one "positive" and one "negative". You may or may not relate to these experiences directly, but that is not really important. I'm just hoping that my experiences trigger memories of events from your own life. I'm hoping that you will be better able to remember times in your life when you felt completely unencumbered by fears or worries, when you felt fully present in the moment and were connected to a sense of flow.

You see, when you remember and perhaps relive a peak experience in your life, I believe that you also remember the deeper truth of who you really are, and you see your place in the world and in the Universe much more clearly. You get to feel and experience your most important and treasured values, and to bring them to the fore in your awareness. You get to bring what you remember from your peak experiences into your daily life, and therefore to live your life with a greater sense of purpose and fulfillment.

Helpful But Not Necessary

Peak experiences like I've described here are not the kinds of things that happen every day. Of course, depending on the kind of work you do, you may find yourself enjoying peak experiences more often than others do, but generally, I think our lives are pretty ordinary, not necessarily lending themselves to regular occurrences of peak experiences. Furthermore, as we become accustomed to the things that we do on a moment-by-moment basis, we become more autonomous about them, and so they may not seem like peak experiences once we get used to them.

Thankfully, you can connect to your own sensation of presence and flow in other ways; you don't actually need the peak experience to get there. Remember, the peak experience is just an example of being in flow. The key, as I mentioned before, is to become present—by raising your awareness about:

1. Who you really are.
2. What you are doing.
3. How you are showing up in the world.
4. How you are feeling about all of it.

This takes focus and intention. That is, no matter what activity you are involved in in any given moment, if you can maintain a maximum level of awareness in every instant while you are doing this activity, then you will bring yourself to a heightened ongoing state of presence. You will be in your own experience of flow.

A Scientific Perspective

In 1990, Hungarian psychologist Mihály Csíkszentmihályi published an excellent book called *Flow: The Psychology of Optimal Experience*. This book was not so much a recipe for how to achieve flow as it was a detailed explanation and discussion of many of the findings of his 30 years of scientific study about the subject. Csíkszentmihályi characterizes flow as

> **A state of concentration or complete absorption with an activity or situation.**

In describing their experiences of flow, people often resort to phrases like *being in the zone* or *being in the groove*, and individuals in Csíkszentmihályi's case studies frequently described themselves as vessels being carried by the current of a river or stream.

One of the key results of Csíkszentmihályi's research was an understanding of some of the component states for experiencing flow:

- **Intense, focused concentration.** All your attention is on the present moment, and any activity that is happening.

- **Merging of action and awareness.** The *I Am* and the *I Do* aspects of yourself seem to be one and the same.

- **Reduction or disappearance of self-consciousness.** Your ego-mind becomes less active, and may even retreat into total silence; all your worldly needs seem to vanish from awareness.

- **Clarity of goals.** You keep the intention of the experience in your awareness at all times.

- **Challenge-skill balance.** There is a match between the level of challenge in the activity and the level of skill you need to meet the challenge. This strengthens your belief in your potential to succeed.

- **Personal control.** You have a strong sense of personal control over the situation or activity.

- **Temporal distortion.** You lose track of time, or perhaps sense that time is slowing down or even stopping.

- **Autotelic experience.** Nothing else seems to matter; you find the experience intrinsically rewarding, in and of itself.

- **Feedback.** Your state of flow is enhanced and amplified when you receive immediate and unambiguous feedback.

Although any of these component states can—and often do—exist somewhat independently of each other, the flow state is more likely to be achieved when many of these component states occur simultaneously—the more the better!

Csíkszentmihályi's research formalizes the concept of flow in psychological terms. But it should be noted that this state has been recognized throughout history and across cultures. In Taoism, for example, there is a paradoxical concept called *wei wu wei*, which means "action without action" or "effortless doing"; both of these translations are perfectly aligned with the idea of flow. Similar teachings appear in Buddhist and Hindu texts as well, and even the Bible is rife with references to flow.

Scientifically, then, flow is considered to be an optimal state for enhancing creativity and enjoyment, and these in turn lead to a greater sense of fulfillment and satisfaction. And, as we've already found, flow can only exist in conjunction with a heightened state of presence and awareness. Therefore, in order to maximize enjoyment and fulfillment, it behooves us all to learn how to achieve a state of flow. Better yet if we can achieve this state intentionally and quickly, and keep ourselves there for longer and longer periods of time.

ACTIVE VS PASSIVE FLOW

Most of what Csíkszentmihályi and his fellow researchers study is what I call *active flow*—that is, flow that involves physical activity of some kind. It doesn't matter how strenuous the activity might be: for example, composing music is an activity; knitting a sweater is an activity—neither strenuous perhaps, but both very engaging for the people doing them.

But what if there is no physical activity involved? Can you still experience flow? I believe the answer is yes. As I see it, *passive flow* is exclusively a mental and spiritual activity, in which the power of imagination and visualization can induce the same state of flow that results from physical activity. One way to experience this—as I demonstrated earlier—is to let yourself become completely absorbed by the memory of a peak experience, and when in that imaginary space to tap into the way you are feeling as the memory fills you.

As science has demonstrated repeatedly, your brain cannot tell the difference between a "real" experience and a strongly "imagined" one. You can use this knowledge to imagine any situation or circumstance of your choice, and activate the visualization in such a way that it brings you into flow without your having to engage physical activity. For example, you might visualize a difficult challenge, imagine that the Universe has provided you with all the skills you need to complete that challenge, and then allow yourself to become fully immersed in the experience of this imagined scenario. As you feel yourself rising to the challenge and allowing all your imagined actions to be fully powered by the Universe in service to your imagined goal, you will quickly begin to experience the sense of timelessness and creativity and happiness that are the hallmarks of flow.

MOVING INTENTIONALLY INTO FLOW

Regardless of whether you choose the *active* or *passive* mode, you can enhance your experience of flow as follows:

Clarity of Purpose

Understand your reasons for doing what you are doing, and ensure that your objective is fully and unquestionably aligned with who you really are. Allow yourself to come up with one overarching statement that answers the question "Why?" It is the answer to this question that will keep you motivated—especially when unexpected challenges arise.

Intense Focus

Commit yourself fully to your chosen goal, and bring all of your attention and intention into completing the task in the way that only you can do it. Remember that you have all the skill—and more—to do what you have set out to do, so allow yourself to bring all of your abilities and talents to bear.

Authentic Power

Call upon the ever-present power of the Universe to flow through you and guide you to the completion of your task. This power is inclusive and supportive, allowing you to interact with any and all other parties from a place of cooperation and collaboration. Encourage others to shine as much as possible in their own way, even as you shine as brightly as you can.

Gratitude and Appreciation

Remain aware of everything that is going on in and around you, and allow yourself to feel appreciation and gratitude for all of it. As you increase your sense of gratitude, you naturally release any attachments you may have, and this in turn helps you open yourself to an even greater flow. Enjoy and appreciate the freedom, love, joy and fulfillment that increasingly shows up and flows through you.

MEDITATION

Meditation has been with us for thousands of years and has shown up in many cultures as a way to promote relaxation, build internal energy or life force, and develop desirable qualities such as compassion, love, patience, generosity, and forgiveness. Meditation was first introduced into Western culture in the late 1950s, when Maharishi Mahesh Yogi began teaching Transcendental Meditation to students in the US. Since that time, meditation has become more commonplace, even to the point of being almost "mainstream".

Meditation has been analyzed, dissected and probed through hundreds—perhaps even thousands—of academic studies, and the results are convincingly consistent. There is no longer any question about the wide-ranging benefits that practitioners can receive through a simple practice that takes only minutes per day and doesn't cost anything at all. For example, meditation can do all of the following and lots more:

- Reduce blood pressure and decrease the risk of heart attack and stroke;
- Reduce stress, fear, loneliness and depression;
- Enhance self-esteem and self-acceptance;

- Improve cognitive skills, creative thinking, and problem solving;
- Improve concentration and focus (leading to more flow!)
- Slow down aging and improve longevity;
- Strengthen all the major organs of the body, notably the heart and the brain.

At its core, meditation has but one essential goal: to quiet the mind and become totally present in the here and now. In effect, the objective is to get to a waking state of total relaxation that allows for thoughts to disappear. Many of the meditation techniques I've experienced employ the concept of focus as a way to bring attention away from the thoughts of the mind toward something immediate and easily recognized. For example, many meditation techniques favor a concentrated focus on the breath—noticing everything that happens in the body as the breath goes in and out. Why the breath? Simple, because every breath you take is happening right here, right now—and that is where you want to bring your attention and awareness, to the here and now.

When people hear the word meditation, they often think immediately of sitting in a particular pose, perhaps with their hands arranged in a specific way, with their eyes closed, reciting a mantra, or focusing on the breath. And while this is certainly a wonderful way to meditate, it is not the only way.

Remember, the key objective of meditation is to become fully present by quieting the mind. You do not have to be seated or arranged in a special pose in order to do this. In fact, you can be very active, actually doing something quite physical, and still be in a meditative state. For example, I find that I can easily get into a meditative state when I am doing something like washing the dishes or shoveling snow off my sidewalk. I also find walking and running and doing yoga exercise to be extremely meditative.

The point I'm trying to make here is that meditation helps to get you into a flow state, because you become present for an extended period of time. And presence—being right here, right now—is where true freedom resides.

GENERAL BENEFITS OF PRESENCE AND FLOW

There are many benefits that you can experience from a regular practice of presence and flow. Some of them have been mentioned in earlier paragraphs. Here are a few explicit benefits that you can experience if you adopt some of the principles mentioned in this chapter:

1. Stress Reduction

When you are focused intentionally on whatever is happening in the present moment, your pain from the past and your worries about the future seem to disappear from your awareness. In a sense, you create for yourself a complete trust in who you are right now and how you are showing up, and the complete absence of things to worry about opens up huge space for you to enjoy what is right now. This results in a great reduction in stress that helps to relax you by keeping your blood pressure down, normalizing your breathing and heart-rate, and reducing the amount of cortisol in your system. All of this, in turn, allows for an increase in oxytocin and DHEA *(Dehydroepiandrosterone)* in your system, both of which contribute to improved health and a greater sense of satisfaction and fulfillment.

2. Faith and Trust in the Universe

When you are flowing in the present moment, you are not concerned about past or future, and therefore, you have a sense of everything being perfect right now. It isn't that anything about your life situation has actually changed, it's just that your perspective has changed. And because everything appears to be perfect right now, there is no reason to believe that it won't continue to be perfect in the next moment, or the moment after that. In other words, you learn that you have the power to move into presence and flow whenever you want to, and that the Universe will provide you with whatever you need when you get there.

I know in my own life I've come to realize that, regardless of the obstacles, problems, challenges, or pains I have faced in the past, I am right here, right now. That is, so far I have always been able to find a way over, under, around or through every obstacle that has ever shown up in my life. If that were not true, I simply wouldn't be where I am now! So, the beauty of this for me is to know that, when the next obstacle shows up, I'll do whatever I think is appropriate to find my way over, under, around or through that one too—and I have no reason to believe that the Universe will not support me in that endeavor.

3. Heightened Creativity

When you approach any activity in the state of presence and flow, all of your attention is focused on the activity at hand, and because you are not burdened with troublesome thoughts about the past or the future, your mind is much clearer. Therefore, you can more easily find elegant and creative solutions to virtually any problem that shows up while you're engaged in that activity. And with heightened creativity comes a greater sense of satisfaction in whatever you are doing, adding even more to your enjoyment.

4. Improved Relationships

When you are interacting with someone, your ability to listen and truly hear what the other person is saying is greatly enhanced when you are fully present. That is because in your state of flow, your attention is on the present moment and what is happening right now, which means that you are less likely to be distracted by thoughts or interpretations or judgments about what the other person is saying or doing. As you get better at being present with people, you will quickly be seen as someone who knows how to listen—and as we've already discussed, one thing that almost everyone wants is to be seen, heard, and experienced for who they really are.

5. Authenticity, Honesty, Openness

Because you are fully present and in a state of flow, you have no concern for what others may think of you or how they may judge you. This eliminates any perceived need you may have to hide behind false *personas* and show up in anything less than an authentic way. As a result, you are empowered to open your heart so that you can show up vulnerably and honestly with people. And this improves your relationships even more!

6. Gratitude and Appreciation

When pains of the past and worries of the future fade into the background and you are totally present to what is happening right now, you see the world as a perfect, exciting, wondrous place that seems to be designed specifically for your benefit. It is easy to be grateful for such a place—a place that provides you with so many different opportunities for self-reflection, self-definition, self-declaration, and self-expression. And gratitude for what is right now helps you to become grateful for what has been in the past and what might be in the future—because all of it is part of your own creation anyway, designed to help you have a full and complete life experience.

And More...

There are many other benefits that I could name here, and maybe you can identify a few of your own. But one thing seems clear to me: the more I work toward staying in presence and flow, the more I feel myself connecting to that wonderful state in my childhood when I felt a powerful sense of curiosity, innocence, wonder and adventure about everything.

This is the state of *Sacred Flow* that I described at the beginning of this book, a state in which life seems easy and enjoyable; a state in which even the most mundane activities seem to take on special meaning and purpose.

Life Mastery is all about reconnecting to presence and flow as often as possible, for as long as possible. This is not an easy thing to accomplish, and in fact it may not even be a realistic objective. However, as many teachers remind us, the journey is far more important than the destination anyway. So, I invite you to give yourself permission to flow through your own life—with intention, clarity, and peace!

CHAPTER SUMMARY—FLOW

Those who flow as life flows know they need no other force. —
Lao Tzu

*As your faith is strengthened, you will find that there is no longer
the need to have a sense of control, that things will flow as they
will, and that you will flow with them, to your great delight and
benefit.—***Emmanual Teney**

*Synchronicity happens when you align with the flow of the
universe rather than insisting the universe flow your way. —*
Akemi G

HIGHLIGHTS

1. The one common thread throughout this book is presence. You can increase presence by increasing awareness; conversely, as you increase your awareness, your presence increases too.

2. Flow is "presence in action"—that is, staying present from moment to moment, no matter what activity you're involved in.

3. You can use the memory of a peak experience to bring you quickly into a flow state.

4. Peak experiences can be both "positive" and "negative". The essence of a peak experience is that it brings you into the present moment, regardless of how you might judge the outcome of the experience.

5. Tapping into flow helps you to remember (and experience) the deeper truth of who you really are—without story or judgment. It also increases your awareness of your most important values and helps you to bring them more actively into your life.

6. Csíkszentmihályi's 30-year study of flow revealed several key components: concentration; merging of action and awareness; reduction of self-consciousness; clarity of goals; challenge-skill balance; personal control; temporal distortion; *autotelic* experience; and feedback. As you activate more and more of these components, you increase your experience of flow.

7. Active flow involves physical activity; passive flow allows you to achieve the same experience through the power of your imagination.

8. If you want to move intentionally into flow, you can enhance your experience through clarity of purpose, intense focus, authentic power, and gratitude and appreciation.

9. Meditation can help you to move into a state of flow. This does not require you to adopt any particular posture or mantra; rather, all you need to do is find a technique that helps you to become totally present, whether you are sitting still or doing something active.

10. There are many benefits of flow: stress reduction; faith and trust in the Universe; heightened creativity; improved relationships; authenticity, honesty and openness; gratitude and appreciation.

THE FLOW KEY

Flow is the ultimate state of the whole Universe—everything is moving or vibrating; everything exists in the here and now. Past and future are ultimately just constructions of the mind; true reality only exists in the present. As you deepen your practice of connecting to presence and flow, you deepen your understanding and experience of yourself—as well as your understanding and experience of the whole Universe! Use the following affirmation to help you develop an ongoing practice of flow:

I am in a continual state of flow, present and fully alive in every moment, and I welcome every opportunity for self-expression with unconditional love and deep gratitude.

EPILOGUE

THE FIRST LOOP IS COMPLETE

Only one who devotes himself to a cause with his whole strength and soul can be a true master. For this reason, mastery demands all of a person.—Albert Einstein

To know yourself as the Being underneath the thinker, the stillness underneath the mental noise, the love and joy underneath the pain, is freedom, salvation, enlightenment.— Eckhart Tolle

---

CONGRATULATIONS!

Wow! It's been an amazing journey so far hasn't it? Just look how far you have come, and notice how you feel about arriving at this rest-stop. I bet if you remember back to when we first started this journey together, you'll have a pretty clear memory of yourself at that time. The journey may have taken you a few days or a few weeks or even longer—it wasn't meant to be a race, after all, and you traveled at your own pace—but if you compare what you know about yourself now to that mental image of yourself from when you started, I'm guessing you'll already notice and feel some shifts within yourself...

- Perhaps you have a better sense of who you really are.
- Perhaps you find yourself connecting more readily to your compassion and forgiveness.
- Perhaps you are excited and energized by a new sense of Purpose in your life.
- Perhaps you touched a shadow part that you haven't thought about for years, and discovered a way to integrate that into your life.
- Perhaps you have some new ideas about how to boost and improve one or more of your relationships.
- Perhaps your appreciation for presence and flow has been enhanced and you want to bring more of that into your life.

Any one of those things—or possibly some, many or even *all* of them—may be happening for you. Or maybe you simply find yourself opening to a greater awareness of your intimate and unbreakable connection with everyone and everything in the Universe.

No matter what your personal experience, I can guarantee that you are not the same person you were when you started this journey. And guess what? Now that you've initiated and expanded this process of intentional personal growth for yourself, you are welcome—indeed, encouraged—to continue the process and see what additional gifts and wonders you will uncover during your next cycle.

The Life Mastery Manifesto

As a way of reminding you of where we've been together, I offer you the following *manifesto* that you can use to guide and empower yourself as you continue on your journey.

My Commitment to Mastery

I am a sacred, sovereign being, empowered unconditionally to live my life to the fullest, and blessed with all the skills and attributes necessary to fulfill my own chosen destiny.

I choose consciously and intentionally to master all aspects of myself and my life, and to bring full awareness to everything I think, say, do and feel.

I commit to adopting, honoring and practicing the *Ten Principal Affirmations of Life Mastery*:

ACCEPTANCE	I am an open channel of unconditional love, and I continuously nurture my ability to release judgments and attachments in order to accept everything—including myself—as perfect, complete and whole in the current moment.
IDENTITY	I am a magnificent, divine, boundless spiritual being of light and love, sharing in the wondrous experience of the human adventure, and I remember this truth in every moment.
CHOICE	I am blessed with unlimited freedom to make all my choices consciously and intentionally, and I courageously take full responsibility for the results that they create.
COMPASSION	I am authentically compassionate towards everyone, and I seek always to offer my support from a tender place of loving empowerment.
FORGIVENESS	I am blessed, healed, and supported by the loving power of forgiveness, which reminds me always about who I am, and empowers me to love and forgive everyone for everything.

PURPOSE	I am empowered and motivated by a sacred spiritual purpose that guides, informs and inspires every aspect of my life.
INTEGRITY	I am a joyful and inspirational model of integrity, and I lovingly align all my thoughts, words, actions and emotions with my spiritual purpose.
SHADOW	I am thrilled to embrace and integrate all of my shadows, and grateful for the powerful treasures they bring into my life.
RELATIONSHIP	I am a willing and active participant in my relationships with everyone everywhere, and I gratefully cherish these sacred partnerships for the mutual growth and self-expression they provide.
FLOW	I am in a continual state of flow, present and fully alive in every moment, and I welcome every opportunity for self-expression with unconditional love and deep gratitude.

YOUR ANGEL NATURE

And now, *Maestro*, before we part ways, I'd like to share one more piece of information that I believe is true about you. Brace yourself…it's pretty awesome!

The word "angel" comes from the Greek word that means "messenger"—that is, someone with a message to deliver. And since angels are often associated with "good news", we often think of them as "messengers of love."

Well, I'm here to tell you that you are such a being!

It's true. You are a perfect creation of Love, a perfect expression of *All-That-Is*. You can argue with that, if you wish—and no doubt your ego-mind will happily oblige you with all kinds of rationalizations to disbelieve it—but it is the ultimate truth of who you are. And, like all other beings of the Human persuasion, you are motivated at the very deepest levels of your essence to give and/or receive love. That is, because you are a perfect creation of Love, you seek to channel your essence and share it with all other life forms. All of your thoughts, words, actions and feelings are motivated by the force of your essence—by the force of Love—and thus, you operate from an incredibly deep desire to share this Love.

Even your so-called "bad behaviors", when closely examined, reveal this unavoidable desire. You can love in any way you choose—functionally or otherwise—but Love is what you must express, because Love is what you are.

But, see here, my dear friend: since you *are* Love, then you *are* the message! Your Human nature is the form that you have taken to deliver and share that message; your Human nature is the messenger. But the true you that exists beyond the physical form—the *you* that we have spent many chapters getting to know more intimately—is the message! And everything your physical nature does in its limited form is to find ways of expressing and sharing that message.

You see, you *are* an angel—you *are* a messenger of love!

RESISTANCE IS FUTILE

I remember when I was first presented with the idea that I was an angel. Naturally, I scoffed at it! I resisted it; I fought it; I declared it blasphemy. But the idea, once offered, would not leave me. Why? Because it resonated within me at a very deep level. Even though my ego-mind did everything in its power to rid me of this crazy thought, there was something inside me that sang out with the truth of it.

As I worked with this idea and became more comfortable with it, I realized that much of my resistance was tied to old beliefs that had to do with the religious teachings I had been given as a child. And as I uncovered those old beliefs, I came to realize just how limiting and unhelpful they were—even though they may have been very well intentioned, and even though they provided support and comfort to me at the time when they came into my awareness. And then, as I released one by one all of those old beliefs, I began to see and appreciate the truth of the "angel story" that had come more recently to my awareness. I was able to embrace my own "inner angel" and I was immediately able to see the angel in everyone else.

Your experience may be different, but I encourage you to consider the possibility that what I'm telling you is a deep truth about yourself—something that, up to now perhaps, you have not been able to see for yourself.

As you deepen your connection with your "inner angel", I believe you will automatically and instantly begin to see and experience your own mastery and enlightenment.

LIFE MASTERY IS A PROCESS

People often talk as if enlightenment is a state of being, something that you can achieve, a stage in life that you can reach. I don't think this is the case at all. I've seen plenty of so-called "enlightened masters" falter on their journey.

The thing that I believe really distinguishes a *Life Master* from a *Life Dabbler* is what happens after he or she falters. Does a new awareness emerge from the event? Is there something to learn, and is the person open to learning it? Does the event bring the person back to a remembering of who she or he really is?

The *Life Master* will always accept the event for what it is (even if this acceptance follows a period of resistance), appreciate the gifts that it bears, embrace the truth that it contains, and take the deeper awareness into the next steps of his or her journey. The *Life Master* understands that mistakes happen, and sees each mistake as another opportunity for intentional growth. In this way, the *Life Master* unconditionally loves every aspect of life—even those aspects which to the ego-mind may seem to cause pain or suffering.

If you allow yourself to succumb to the seductive belief that you have achieved Enlightenment or *Life Mastery*, then you are allowing your ego-mind to run the show in your life, and you can expect a powerful life lesson to turn up right around the next corner. As my mom would sometimes say to me with a gleam in her eye, "You'll get your comeuppance soon enough, young man!"

This is not to make you wrong! The ego-mind likes to engage in comparisons and find itself superior to other ego-minds—this is just a part of being human. So, when it happens to you, take a breath and forgive yourself, and then laugh! Laugh with abandon at all your foibles, for each one is a powerful pointer to a gift that resides within you. And each mistake you make is just a reminder that you are on a journey toward *Life Mastery*, a journey toward Enlightenment. It is a process, not a destination.

The reality is, you are already as enlightened as you need to be…for the moment. You have all the wisdom, love and truth you need right now to provide you with everything you need to move to the next level of your evolution.

Let this knowing inform and empower every choice you make for your life as you continue to move forward. Let the truth of who you really are—as opposed to who your ego-mind *thinks* you are—guide you in your ongoing adventure!

A FINAL POEM

I'd like to leave you with a poem to acknowledge and celebrate the next greatest version of yourself that you bring into the world. Knowing what you know now, you are empowered to manifest this evolution from a place of total awareness, acceptance, and choice.

I look forward to witnessing your amazing creation, *Maestro*! May you always be pleased with it!

Arrival

I am arriving here in my incredible magnificent wonder and curiosity,
with a smile full of love and appreciation for what is all around me.

I am arriving with questions
and humming with my own truth and my own answers,
totally open to hearing yours.

I am arriving here with music and poetry pulsing through me
like little droplets of god
and when I see
    the truth in you,
    the beauty in you,
    the perfection in you,
my eyes simply melt into the laughter and joy
contained in this pudgy and huggable body.

I am arriving here fresh from the river,
    wet with love,
    dripping with sweetness,
    full of the dance,
wanting to stand on my feet and stand on my head at the same time.

I am arriving here full of anticipation
    for the adventures that await,
    for the bangs and bruises,
    for the kisses and hugs,
    for the wounding and healing
that create the experience of all that is.

I am arriving here alone,
knowing that I will share infinitely many precious moments with
you and you and you and you...

How blessed I am
that you are all here
waiting for me!

Much love and many blessings to you on your continuing Journey!

David McLeod

Meridian, Idaho

June 1, 2019

What's Next?

Now that you have reached the end of this book—and I truly hope you have gotten much value from it—you might be wondering what's next for you. Maybe you are quite excited about the shifts you have already experienced within you, and you are wondering how you can build on what you have learned. Of course, you can go through this book as many times as you like, and I'm sure you will get more and more out of it on each pass. But if you are like me, you may want some other resources in order to deepen your experience even more. Well, I've got good news! I have several additional offerings that you can access if you choose, and each of them will provide you with a different approach to deepening your experience with *Life Mastery*.

Life Mastery Way

This entire book has been transformed into a really amazing multi-media course that you can take at your own pace. The material has been organized into a powerful journey through a magical and transformative land where you visit different *Waypoints* and learn the lessons provided there. In each new location, you will have access to audio visualizations, video trainings, and easy-to-read text.

Find out more at https://LifeMasteryWay.com

Life Mastery Music

If you enjoy meditation and you are looking for powerful trance-meditation music with embedded brainwave entrainment technology to help you deepen your relaxation while simultaneously sharpening your focus, you will love what I have created for you: holistic rhythmic music to warm the heart, move the body, quiet the mind, and activate the soul.

Find out more at https://LifeMasteryMusic.com

Life Mastery Affirmations

I have worked with affirmations for years and I know how powerful they can be if they are used correctly. As I learned more and more about affirmations, I studied what works and what doesn't and I have now created a state-of-the-art program that brings together audio, video, and journaling as a way to make the experience as deep and powerful as possible. But that's not all! I also make use of brainwave entrainment techniques as well as subliminal message to deepen your experience even more.

Find out more at https://LifeMasteryAffirmations.com

Life Mastery TV

Twice a month, I offer live presentations on various aspects of *Life Mastery*, in a webinar format. I invite a guest onto the show to share his or her perspective, wisdom and expertise on the subject. All you have to do it sign up for a membership and you can watch every episode live, and also get access to the recordings. This is a real treasure-trove of material that is designed to help you become more and more adept at mastering your life.

Find out more at https://Life-Mastery-TV.com

Life Mastery Wisdom

If you would like to receive regular servings of inspiration and motivation to supercharge your life, then you'll want to check out my podcast.

Find out more at https://LifeMasteryWisdom.com

Your Life Mastery Coach

If you want even more support, coupled with a compassionate personal touch from a master coach and facilitator with many years of experience, then you might want to think about signing up for one of my coaching programs. I won't go into details about those here, but I will tell you that you can make an appointment for a free Discovery Session if you visit my website.

Find out more at https://YourLifeMasteryCoach.com

Recommended Reading

I have been touched and inspired by hundreds of amazing publications in the last 20 years or so. Many of them are still in my personal library, as I find myself drawn to them over and over for the wisdom they contain—or, to be more accurate (and consistent with the message in my own book), for the wisdom within myself that they help me to find! This list of books represents a subset of my collection, and I've chosen to include them here because I believe they are all relevant to the specific topics of *MagnifEssence* and *Life Mastery*. Enjoy!

Abadie, M. J. 1998. *Awaken to Your Spiritual Self.* Holbrook, MA : Adams Media, 1998.

Allen, Mary E. 2005. *The Power of Inner Choice: 12 Weeks to Living a Life You Love.* Fawnskin, CA : Personhood Press, 2005.

Andreas, Connirae and Andreas, Tamara. 1994. *Core Transformation: Reaching the Wellspring Within.* Moab, UT : Real People Press, 1994.

Arrien, Angeles. 1993. *The Four-Fold Way: Walking the Paths of the Warrior, Teacher, Healer and Visionary.* New York, NY : HarperCollins, 1993.

Bach, Richard. 1977. *Illusions: The Adventures of a Reluctant Messiah.* New York, NY : Delacorte, 1977.

Bach, Richard. 2013. *Illusions II: The Adventures of a Reluctant Student.* North Charleston, SC : CreateSpace Independent Publishing Platform, 2013.

Barry, Alyce. 2008. *Practically Shameless: How Shadow Work Helped Me Find My Voice, My Path, and My Inner Gold.* Longmont, CO : Practically Shameless Press, 2008.

Beck, Don and Cowan, Christopher C. 1996. *Spiral Dynamics: Mastering Values, Leadership, and Change: Exploring the New Science of Memetics.* Cambridge, MA : Blackwell Business, 1996.

Belitz, Charlene and Lundstrom, Meg. 1997. *The Power of Flow: Practical Ways to Transform Your Life with Meaningful Coincidence.* New York, NY : Harmony, 1997.

Bishop, Ross. 1998. *Healing the Shadow.* Santa Fe, NM : Blue Lotus, 1998.

Bishop, Ross. 2017. *About Life.* Santa Fe, NM : Blue Lotus Press, 2017.

Bly, Robert and Booth, William C. 1988. *A Little Book on the Human Shadow.*

San Francisco, CA : Harper & Row, 1988.

Bradshaw, John. 1988. *Healing the Shame that Binds You.* Deerfield Beach, FL : Health Communications, Inc., 1988.

Brezsny, Rob. 2005. *Pronoia Is the Antidote for Paranoia: How the Whole World Is Conspiring to Shower You with Blessings.* Berkeley, CA : Frog, 2005.

Brownell, Arlene and Bache-Wiig, Thomas. 2007. *Non-Adversarial Communication: Speaking and Listening from the Heart.* Boulder, CO : Velvet Spring, 2007.

Bryson, Kelly. 2002. *Don't Be Nice, Be Real: Balancing Passion for Self with Compassion for Others.* Santa Rosa, CA : Author's Publishing Cooperative, 2002.

Campbell, Joseph. 1972. *The Hero with a Thousand Faces.* Princeton, NJ : Princeton University Press, 1972.

Campbell, Susan M. 2001. *Getting Real.* Tiburon, CA : HJ Kramer, 2001.

Campbell, Susan M. 2005. *Saying What's Real: 7 Keys to Authentic Communication and Relationship Success.* Novato, CA : New World Library, 2005.

Carson, Richard David. 2003. *Taming Your Gremlin: A Surprisingly Simple Method for Getting out of Your Own Way.* New York, NY : Quill, 2003.

Chamine, Shirzad. 2012. *Positive Intelligence: Why Only 20% of Teams and Individuals Achieve Their True Potential and How You Can Achieve Yours.* Austin, TX : Greenleaf Book Group, 2012.

Chang, Richard Y. 2000. *The Passion Plan: A Step-by-step Guide to Discovering, Developing, and Living Your Passion.* San Francisco, CA : Jossey Bass, 2000.

Covey, Stephen R. 1989. *The 7 Habits of Highly Effective People: Powerful Lessons in Personal Change.* New York, NY : Simon & Schuster, 1989.

Csikszentmihalyi, Mihaly. 1990. *Flow: The Psychology of Optimal Experience.* New York, NY : Harper & Row, 1990.

Cushnir, Raphael. 2003. *Setting Your Heart on Fire: Seven Invitations to Liberate Your Life.* New York, NY : Broadway, 2003.

Dalconzo, Joseph Hu. 2008. *Self-Mastery: A Journey Home to Your...SELF!* New York, NY : Renaissance Publishing, 2008.

Dalconzo, Joseph Hu. 2018. *The Awakening: A Transformational Love Story.* Forked River, NJ : Holistic Learning Centers, Inc., 2018.

Deida, David. 2002. *Naked Buddhism: 39 Ways to Free Your Heart and Awaken to Now.* Austin, TX : Plexus, 2002.

Deida, David. 2004. *The Way of the Superior Man: A Spiritual Guide to Mastering the Challenges of Women, Work, and Sexual Desire.* Boulder, CO : Sounds True, 2004.

Dwoskin, Hale. 2003. *The Sedona Method: Your Key to Lasting Happiness, Success, Peace and Emotional Well-being.* Sedona, AZ : Sedona Press, 2003.

Epstein, Donald M. and Altman, Nathaniel. 1994. *The 12 Stages of Healing: A Network Approach to Wholeness.* San Rafael, CA : Amber-Allen Publishing, 1994.

Ford, Debbie. 1998. *The Dark Side of the Light Chasers: Reclaiming Your Power, Creativity, Brilliance, and Dreams.* New York, NY : Riverhead, 1998.

Ford, Debbie. 2002. *The Secret of the Shadow: The Power of Owning Your Whole Story.* San Francisco, CA : HarperSanFrancisco, 2002.

Ford, Debbie. 2003. *The Right Questions: Ten Essential Questions to Guide You to an Extraordinary Life.* San Francisco, CA : HarperSanFrancisco, 2003.

Foster, Ken D. 2009. *Ask and You Will Succeed: 1001 Ordinary Questions to Create Life-Changing Results.* Hoboken, NJ : Wiley, 2009.

Frost, Nina H., Ruge, Kenneth and Shoup, Richard. 2000. *Soul Mapping: An Imaginative Way to Self-Discovery.* New York, NY : Marlowe, 2000.

Garner, Alan. 1981. *Conversationally Speaking.* New York, NY : McGraw-Hill, 1981.

Gawain, Shakti and King, Laurel. 1986. *Living in the Light.* Mill Valley, CA : Whatever Publishing, 1986.

Gawain, Shakti. 1978. *Creative Visualization.* Berkeley, CA : Whatever Publishing, 1978.

Grabhorn, Lynn. 2000. *Excuse Me, Your Life Is Waiting: The Astonishing Power of Feelings.* Charlottesville, VA : Hampton Roads Publishing, 2000.

Hart, Martin and Alexander, Skye. 2011. *The Best Meditations on the Planet: 100 Techniques to Beat Stress, Improve Health, and Create Happiness—in Just Minutes per Day.* Beverly, MA : Fair Winds, 2011.

Heider, John. 1985. *The Tao of Leadership: Lao Tzu's Tao Te Ching Adapted for a New Age.* Atlanta, GA : Humanics New Age, 1985.

Hendricks, Gay and Hendricks, Kathlyn. 1990. *Conscious Loving: The Journey to Co-commitment.* New York, NY : Bantam, 1990.

Hubbard, Barbara Marx. 1998. *Conscious Evolution: Awakening the Power of Our Social Potential.* Novato, CA : New World Library, 1998.

Hunter, Erika M. 2004. *Little Book of Big Emotions: How Five Feelings Affect Everything You Do (and Don't Do).* Center City, MN : Hazelden, 2004.

Jeffers, Susan J. 1987. *Feel the Fear and Do It Anyway.* San Diego, CA : Harcourt Brace Jovanovich, 1987.

Jiwa, Azmina. 2018. *Freedom to Be Me.* Portsmouth, Hampshire, UK : Librotas Books, 2018.

Johnson, Robert A. 1986. *Inner Work: Using Dreams and Active Imagination for Personal Growth.* San Francisco, CA : Harper & Row, 1986.

Johnson, Robert A. 1991. *Owning Your Own Shadow: Understanding the Dark Side of the Psyche.* San Francisco, CA : HarperSanFrancisco, 1991.

Johnson, Robert A. 2008. *Inner Gold: Understanding Psychological Projection.* Kihei, HI : Koa Books, 2008.

Katie, Byron and Mitchell, Stephen. 2002. *Loving What Is: Four Questions That Can Change Your Life.* New York, NY : Harmony, 2002.

Kauth, Bill. 1992. *A Circle of Men: The Original Manual for Men's Support Groups.* New York, NY : St. Martin's Press, 1992.

Kirshenbaum, Mira. 2003. *The Emotional Energy Factor: The Secrets High-energy People Use to Beat Emotional Fatigue.* New York, NY : Delacorte, 2003.

Knight, J. Z. 2004. *Ramtha: The White Book.* Yelm, WA : JZK Publishing, 2004.

Lawley, James and Tompkins, Penny. 2000. *Metaphors in Mind: Transformation through Symbolic Modelling.* London, UK : Developing Co. Press, 2000.

Lazarus, Arnold A., Lazarus, Clifford N. and Fay, Allen. 1993. *Don't Believe It for a Minute!: Forty Toxic Ideas That Are Driving You Crazy.* San Luis Obispo, CA : Impact, 1993.

Lewis, Thomas, Amini, Fari and Lannon, Richard. 2000. *A General Theory of Love.* New York, NY : Random House, 2000.

Madson, Jennifer. 2014. *Head to Heart: Mindfulness Moments for Every Day.* San Francisco, CA : Conari Press, 2014.

Maxwell, John C. 2012. *The 15 Invaluable Laws of Growth: Live Them and Reach Your Potential*. New York, NY : Center Street, 2012.

McLeod, David D. 2012. *The Magic of 'I Am': Four Steps to Conscious Self-Creation*. San Francisco, CA : Messenger Minibooks, 2012.

McTaggart, Lynne. 2007. *The Intention Experiment: Using Your Thoughts to Change Your Life and the World*. New York, NY : Free Press, 2007.

McTaggart, Lynne. 2008. *The Field: The Quest for the Secret Force of the Universe*. New York, NY : Harper, 2008.

Melchizedek, Drunvalo. 2008. *Serpent of Light : The Movement of the Earth's Kundalini and the Rise of the Female Light*. San Francisco, CA : Weiser Books, 2008.

Miller, James E. 1998. *Effective Support Groups: How to Plan, Design, Facilitate, and Enjoy Them*. Fort Wayne, IN : Willowgreen Publishing, 1998.

Miller, John G. 2004. *QBQ! the Question behind the Question: Practicing Personal Accountability at Work and in Life*. New York, NY : G.P. Putnam's Sons, 2004.

O'Hanlon, Bill. 1999. *Do One Thing Different: And Other Uncommonly Simple Solutions to Life's Persistent Problems*. New York, NY : W. Morrow, 1999.

Om, Tomot. 2002. *Pro Evo: Pro Evolution—Guideline for an Age of Joy*. Chur, Switzerland : Asama AG, 2002.

Patterson, Kerry et al. 2012. *Crucial Conversations: Tools for Talking when Stakes are High*. New York, NY : McGraw Hill, 2012.

Patterson, Kerry et al. 2013. *Crucial Accountability: Tools for Resolving Violated Expectations, Broken Commitments, and Bad Behavior*. New York, NY : McGraw Hill, 2013.

Pachter, Barbara and Magee, Susan. 2000. *The Power of Positive Confrontation: The Skills You Need to Know to Handle Conflict at Work, Home, and in Life* . New York, NY : Marlowe, 2000.

Potter-Efron, Patricia and Potter-Efron, Ronald 1989. *Letting Go of Shame: Understanding How Shame Affects Your Life*. Center City, MN : Hazelden Publishing, 1989.

Potter-Efron, Patricia and Potter-Efron, Ronald 1999. *The Secret Message of Shame: Pathways to Hope and Healing*. Oakland, CA : New Harbinger Publications, 2011.

Polsky, Lawrence and Gerschel, Antoine. 2011. *Perfect Phrases for Conflict Resolution.* New York, NY : McGraw Hill, 2011.

Powers, Rhea and Bantle, Gawain. 1995. *Riding the Dragon: The Power of Committed Relationship.* Georgetown, MA : North Star Publications, 1995.

Psaris, Jett and Lyons, Marlena S. 2000. *Undefended Love.* Oakland, CA : New Harbinger Publications, 2000.

Rengel, Peter. 1995. *Living Life in Love: Integrating Western Psychology and Eastern Spirituality.* Larkspur, CA : Imagine Publications, 1995.

Richo, David. 1999. *Shadow Dance: Liberating the Power and Creativity of Your Dark Side.* Boston, MA : Shambhala, 1999.

Roberts, John Marshall. 2008. *Igniting Inspiration: A Persuasion Manual for Visionaries.* North Charleston, SC : BookSurge Publishing, 2008.

Robertson, Robin. 1992. *Beginner's Guide to Jungian Psychology.* York Beach, ME : Nicolas-Hays, 1992.

Rosenberg, Marshall B. 2003. Nonviolent Communication: A Language of Life. Encinitas, CA : PuddleDancer, 2003.

Rotermund, JoAnn. 2009. *The Forgiveness Habit: An Action Plan for Healing Ourselves and Our Planet.* Tomball, TX : Unumspiel Publishing, 2009.

Ruiz, don Miguel. 1997. *The Four Agreements: A Practical Guide to Personal Freedom.* San Rafael, CA : Amber-Allen Publishing, 1997.

Ruiz, don Miguel. 1999. *The Mastery of Love: A Practical Guide to the Art of Relationship.* San Rafael, CA : Amber-Allen Publishing, 1999.

Ruiz, Jr., Miguel. 2013. *The Five Levels of Attachment.* San Antonio, TX : Hierophant Publishing, 2013.

Ruiz, don Miguel and Mills, Janet. 2004. *The Voice of Knowledge: A Practical Guide to Inner Peace.* San Rafael, CA : Amber-Allen Publishing, 2004.

Satir, Virginia. 1978. *Your Many Faces.* Millbrae, CA : Celestial Arts, 1978.

Schreiber, Junie Moon. 2017. Loving the Whole Package. Carlsbad, CA : Crescendo Publishing, 2017.

Sheldrake, Rupert. 2009. *Morphic Resonance: The Nature of Formative Causation.* Rochester, VT : Park Street Press, 2009.

Sheldrake, Rupert. 2012. *Science Set Free: 10 Paths to New Discovery.* New York, NY : Deepak Chopra Books, 2012.

Small, Jacquelyn. 1991. *Awakening in Time: The Journey from Codependence to Co-Creation.* New York, NY : Bantam, 1991.

Small, Jacquelyn. 2005. *The Sacred Purpose of Being Human: A Journey through the 12 Principles of Wholeness.* Deerfield Beach, FL : Health Communications, 2005.

Stone, Hal and Stone, Sidra. 1989. *Embracing Our Selves: The Voice Dialog Manual.* Novato, CA : New World Library, 1989.

Steiner, Tej. 2006. *Heart Circles: How Sitting in Circle Can Transform Your World.* Phoenix, OR : Interactive Media Publishing, 2006.

Stephan, Naomi. 1994. *Fulfill Your Soul's Purpose: Ten Creative Paths to Your Life Mission.* Walpole, NH : Stillpoint Publishing, 1994.

Sullivan, Wendy and Rees, Judy. 2008. *Clean Language: Revealing Metaphors and Opening Minds.* Carmarthen, Wales : Crown House, 2008.

Talbot, Michael. 1991. *The Holographic Universe.* New York, NY : HarperCollins, 1991.

Tan, Chade-Meng. 2012. *Search inside Yourself: The Unexpected Path to Achieving Success, Happiness (and World Peace).* New York, NY : HarperOne, 2012.

Taylor, John Maxwell. 2006. *The Power of I Am: Creating a New World of Enlightened Personal Interaction.* Berkeley, CA : Frog, 2006.

Thondup, Tulku. 1996. *The Healing Power of Mind: Simple Meditation Exercises for Health, Well-Being, and Enlightenment.* Boston, MA : Shambhala, 1996.

Tolle, Eckhart. 1999. *The Power of Now: A Guide to Spiritual Enlightenment.* Novato, CA : New World Library, 1999.

Tolle, Eckhart. 2006. *A New Earth: Awakening to Your Life's Purpose.* New York, NY : Plume, 2006.

Tyme, Misty. 2017. *The Forgiveness Solution: A Step by Step Process to Let it Go.* Delray Beach, FL : Sacred Stories Publishing, 2017.

Von Franz, Marie-Louise. 1980. *Projection and Re-collection: Reflections of the Soul.* La Salle : Open Court, 1980.

Walsch, Neale Donald. 1996. *Conversations with God.* New York, NY : G.P. Putnam's Sons, 1996.

Walsch, Tara-Jenelle. 2015. *Soul Courage: Watch What Happens.* Ashland, OR : Rainbow Bridge, 2015.

Wilber, Ken. 2000. *Integral Psychology: Consciousness, Spirit, Psychology, Therapy.* Boston, MA : Shambhala, 2000.

Wilcock, David. 2011. *The Source Field Investigations: The Hidden Science and Lost Civilizations behind the 2012 Prophecies.* New York, NY : Dutton, 2011.

Wilcock, David. 2014. *The Synchronicity Key: The Hidden Intelligence Guiding the Universe and You.* New York, NY : Dutton, 2014.

Wilson, Robert Anton. 1990. *Quantum Psychology: How Brain Software Programs You and Your World.* Tempe, AZ : New Falcon, 1990.

Zander, Rosamund and Zander, Benjamin. 2000. *The Art of Possibility.* New York, NY : Penguin Group, 2000.

Zukav, Gary. 1979. *The Dancing Wu Li Masters: An Overview of the New Physics.* New York, NY : HarperCollins, 1979.

Zukav, Gary. 1990. *The Seat of the Soul.* New York, NY : Simon & Schuster, 1990.

Zukav, Gary and Francis, Linda. 2001. *The Heart of the Soul: Emotional Awareness.* New York, NY : Fireside, 2001.

Zweig, Connie and Abrams, Jeremiah. 1991. *Meeting the Shadow: The Hidden Power of the Dark Side of Human Nature.* Los Angeles, CA : J.P. Tarcher, 1991.

Zweig, Connie and Wolf, Steve. 1997. *Romancing the Shadow: Illuminating the Dark Side of the Soul.* New York, NY : Ballantine, 1997.

THE POEMS

All of the poems in this book were written by me during important phases of my life. None of them have ever been published before, so you are seeing them in a public forum for the first time. I chose these pieces because they seem to express my heart and soul in a way that is consistent with the chapters in which they appear. Here's the list again, with the dates I wrote them.

Title	Date Written	Where It Appears
Anchors	June 2004	Chapter 5: Forgiveness
Arrival	July 2008	Epilogue
be one	July 2011	Chapter 9: Relationship
Confession	June 2004	Chapter 7: Integrity
FLOWNOWHERE	November 2002	Chapter 10: Flow
i had a dream	April 2009	Preface
Love Just Smiled	August 2011	Chapter 4: Compassion
now is the time to know	November 2004	Chapter 6: Purpose
sad birds	September 2004	Chapter 8: Shadow
The Crystal Sphere	December 2009	Chapter 1: Acceptance
there are waves	March 2007	Chapter 2: Identity
to choose & declare	October 2003	Chapter 3: Choice

ABOUT DAVID MCLEOD

David McLeod is a writer, transformational speaker, life-mastery coach, spiritual counselor, and experiential facilitator who has been deeply involved in personal growth work since 1995. His principal focus has been to understand what it is that keeps people from fulfilling their potential—in relationships, in business, in personal health and fitness, in every aspect of their lives—and as a result has become a widely acknowledged expert in the area of psychic shadow. He has learned for himself—and continues to learn—the immense power of the shadow, and he generously shares his growing knowledge with others through his speaking, coaching, and training engagements. Ultimately, David's work is focused on encouraging and supporting men and women to re-integrate their disowned shadow aspects—through powerful processes that lead to core transformations—so that they can reclaim, embrace, and experience the full essence of who they really are.

In the course of working with women and men in group settings, David has developed many effective techniques and processes for empowering people to interact with one another authentically and compassionately.

A musician and poet who brings innovative creativity to all of his endeavors, David holds a Doctor of Philosophy (PhD) in Metaphysical Sciences and a Doctor of Divinity (DD) in Spiritual Counseling.

For more information, please visit:

https://YourLifeMasteryCoach.com

https://DavidDMcLeod.com

9 781943 625116